LAW IN MODERN SOCIETY

Toward a Criticism of Social Theory

Roberto Mangabeira Unger

 THE FREE PRESS
A Division of Macmillan Publishing Co., Inc.
NEW YORK

Collier Macmillan Publishers
LONDON

D1550411

The Free Press
A Division of Macmillan Publishing Co., Inc.
866 Third Avenue, New York, N.Y. 10022

First Free Press Paperback Edition 1977

Collier Macmillan Canada, Ltd.

Library of Congress Catalog Card Number: 74-27853

Printed in the United States of America

printing number
         7 8 9 10

Library of Congress Cataloging in Publication Data

Unger, Roberto Mangabeira.
   Law in modern society.

   Includes bibliographical references and index.
   1. Sociological jurisprudence. I. Title.
Law   340.1'15   74-27853
ISBN 0-02-932880-2 pbk.

LAW IN
MODERN
SOCIETY

NOTE

This study builds upon my *Knowledge and Politics* (Free Press, 1975). To make the present work intelligible to readers unfamiliar with *Knowledge and Politics,* it was necessary in some cases to restate ideas developed in the earlier book.

CONTENTS

CHAPTER 1. The Predicament of Social Theory   1

The "burden of the past" in social theory   1
Social theory and political philosophy   3
The unity and crisis of social theory   6
The problem of method   8
The problem of social order   23
The problem of modernity   37
Human nature and history   40
Law   43

CHAPTER 2. Law and the Forms of Society   47

The problem   47
Three concepts of law   48
The emergence of bureaucratic law   58
    The separation of state and society   58
    The disintegration of community   61
    The division of labor and social hierarchy   63
    The tension within bureaucratic law   64
The emergence of a legal order   66
    Group pluralism   66
    Natural law   76
    Liberal society and higher law   83

The Chinese case: a comparative analysis   86
   The hypothesis   86
   Custom and "feudalism" in early China   88
   The transformation period: from custom to
      bureaucratic law   96
   Confucianists and Legalists   105
Limits of the Chinese comparison: the experience
   of other civilizations   110
   The sacred laws of ancient India, Islam, and
      Israel   110
   The Graeco-Roman variant   120
Law as a response to the decline of order   127

CHAPTER 3. Law and Modernity   134

The perspective of modernization   134
The comparison of societies: a preliminary
   framework   137
   Elements   137
   Tribal society   140
   Liberal society   143
   Aristocratic society   147
   Social change   153
Law and European aristocratic society   155
   Between feudalism and liberalism   155
   Law in the *Ständestaat*   158
Liberal society and its law   166
   Consensus   166
   Hierarchy   170
   Law and the state   176
   Law, bureaucracy, and liberalism: a German
      example   181
The disintegration of the rule of law in postliberal
   society   192

Postliberal society 192
The welfare state and the decline of the rule
of law 193
The corporate state and the attack on public and
positive law 200
Formality, equity, and solidarity 203
The retreat from legality: the German story
continued 216
Beyond liberal society 220
The varieties of modernity 223
Comparing modern societies 223
Traditionalistic society 224
Revolutionary socialist society 231
The unity of modernism 234
Law beyond modern society: two possibilities 238

CHAPTER 4. The Predicament of Social Theory
Revisited 243

Revisiting social theory 243
The problem of method 245
The problem of social order 262
The problem of modernity 265
Social theory, metaphysics, and politics 266

Notes 269

Index 297

1

THE PREDICAMENT OF
SOCIAL THEORY

THE "BURDEN OF THE PAST" IN SOCIAL THEORY[1]

It is a commonplace that great men impose a burden upon those who come after them. When there has been remarkable achievement in politics, art, or thought, the generation that follows in its wake, and benefits from it, may suffer the paralyzing sense that nothing really important remains to be done. It may feel that the most brilliant opportunities have already been explored and turned to advantage. As a result, the successors seem faced with a dilemma: either they become mere caretakers of the monuments the great have left them, or, desirous of independence, but despairing of excellence, they drastically narrow their ambitions and set out to till, with technical proficiency, a small field.

In the history of speculative thought, this dilemma assumes a characteristic form. On one hand, the epigones may become exegetes of the classical texts even while they are guilt ridden by the loss of their autonomy. On the other hand, they may pretend that the preceding era belongs to some obscure prehistory of their science, in which it was still possible to work unhampered by distinctions among disciplines. They embrace specialization as an alternative that protects them from comparison with their forerunners at the cost of condemning them to a sort of permanent intellectual minority.

Both these responses to the problem of following an age of extraordinary accomplishments are failures of the mind and of the heart. They represent refusals to look straight into the face of greatness and to imitate, boldly and honestly, what one admires. Such cowardice exacts a high price, for it leads scholars to a secret disrespect of self, masked by a defensive skepticism about general speculation. In this situation, the only way people have to affirm their own identities is to quibble with details in their masters' work—to seek the glory of the Crab, which figures in the Zodiac because it bit the heel of Hercules.[2]

There are circumstances in which these attitudes may be harder or easier to avoid. Once a long period of time has passed since the age of greatness, it becomes simpler to stand on one's own feet. The thinkers under whose shadow one lives may be defined as classics. This act of defining the masterpieces of most immediate concern to one as classics may have a curiously liberating effect. For it means that one is already able to acknowledge and to emulate a past generation of theorists while retaining a sense of the uniqueness of his own situation and of the dignity of the tasks that remain to be carried out. Thus, he need no longer fear to confess that the unresolved problems in their work are his own problems, and he is free to enter into a partnership with them.

Everything that has been said in the preceding paragraphs about the relationship between greatness and posterity applies to our attitude toward the men who, in the latter half of the nineteenth century and in the first decades of the twentieth, created what has come to be known as social theory. One thinks especially of Marx, Durkheim, and Weber. Much of social thought since their time has been divided between commentary on their doctrines or specialization within the traditions they established. The further away these specialized fields move from the original ambitions of the founders, and the more they pretend to scientific independence, the less enlightening they seem to become.

Yet, from many sides, it appears increasingly true that we can begin to see Marx, Durkheim, and Weber as classics, and to view what they produced as a classical social theory in contrast to the long tradition of political philosophy that preceded it.

SOCIAL THEORY AND POLITICAL PHILOSOPHY

Social theory is the study of society whose characteristic features began to appear in the writings of Montesquieu, his contemporaries, and successors and which reached a sort of culmination in the works of Marx, Durkheim, and Weber. It first established its identity by contrast to the political thought of the ancients and the Schoolmen. Two features chiefly distinguish it from the earlier tradition: one has to do with its conception of its own aim and method; the other with a view of the relation between human nature and history. Both aspects are familiar enough, but their implications for the central issues of social thought remain misunderstood.

The political philosophy of the ancients was at once descriptive and prescriptive. This means much more than that it was interested in determining how society ought to be organized or that it tried to put its views of the individual and of society to practical use, for both things may be said of much modern social theory. It signifies that the method employed by the traditional theory was one to which the distinction between fact and value, description and evaluation, was largely, though not wholly, alien.

One who understood what individuals in society really were would also apprehend what they ought to be. At the heart of this doctrine lay a view of the relation between purpose and being and a corresponding vision of the laws that govern both nature and society. Every being strives to accomplish its inherent purpose or good, which is the more perfect realization of its own nature. In so doing, it also serves God's plan. Man's consciousness consists of the fact that he does not instinctively know his aim; he must discover it by thought. Consequently, he has the power to deviate from it.

The striving for fulfillment of purpose imparts to all phenomena a certain regularity that is perceived as obedience to law. Such laws, determinative of the good and established by God, show us both what things are like and what they ought to become. In this tradition of thought, there is little or no place for distinctions between (a) descriptive or explanatory laws about the interrelations of natural or social phenomena and (b) moral or political rules designed to determine how individuals should act.

The contrasts of fact and value, of science and moral judgment, and therefore also of law in the descriptive and the prescriptive sense are among the main themes in the tradition of social theory, as well as in the growth of the natural sciences. Many of the ambiguities that mark the writings of the creators of the tradition from Montesquieu onward are due to the fact that these thinkers had not yet cut the links that bound them to the older view.[3] Marx and Durkheim did not clearly distinguish between the emergent in history and the political good; among the classical theorists Weber alone accepted the distinction unequivocally.

This brings me to the second chief point of opposition

between ancient political thought and social theory: the view of the relationship between human nature and history. A major feature of the outlook against which the classic social theorists rebelled was the notion that there is a universal human nature, common to all men, regardless of their place in history. The best regime for the ancients is the one able to make the most of the better aspects of human nature and to suppress most effectively man's evil side.

One consequence of this approach was the tendency to treat history as a kind of backdrop to life that changes the circumstances of existence without modifying its basic problems. For these are firmly rooted in man's unchanging nature. Another result of the doctrine of a unitary, suprahistorical human essence was the disregard for the sets of values and understandings that may be peculiar to a type of social life and more or less widely shared by all who participate in it.[4] On one side, there are the universal characteristics of the human mind; on the other side, the beliefs and ends of individuals. Between the universal attributes of human knowledge and the mentalities of particular persons, there is no such thing as a social consciousness or a culture.

In opposition to the view I have just described, social theory is engaged in a quest for an understanding of the different forms that people's awareness of each other, of nature, and of themselves assume in each kind of social life. It is less interested in the psychology of individual minds or in the constitution of a universal human nature than in the historically unique systems of shared understandings and ideals that make up the culture of a society. Indeed, it is often willing to sacrifice the very notion of a unitary human nature to the sense of history.[5]

The historical conception of human nature and the emphasis on the difference between understanding and evaluation are intimately connected. To the moderns it came to seem that the ancients had created an illusory and useless body of learning, based on a view of man as he ought to be rather than as he is. The ancients were accused of shallowness because of their failure to take account of the demonic depths of human nature. The moderns were quick to become specialists in evil.

THE UNITY AND CRISIS OF SOCIAL THEORY

Two complementary theses are often voiced in contemporary thinking about the social sciences. The first is that our present-day studies of society, carried on in the specialized branches of social science, rest on a legacy of concepts, methods, theories, and tacit assumptions, handed down to us by the leading social theorists of the late nineteenth and the early twentieth century. This is what makes their work classic for us; our relationship to it is one of both dependence and departure. There is usually implicit in this view the stronger and less obvious thesis that the different strands within the classical heritage in fact make up a unified whole. As much as thinkers like Tocqueville, Marx, Durkheim, and Weber may differ from one another, their distinct approaches are said to overlap in ways which are more than trivial.[6]

The notion that we continue to be tied down to the framework in which classical social theory has placed the understanding of society is increasingly accompanied by a second perspective on the present condition of social thought. It is the idea that something very important is wrong with the classics and hence with their successors. Sometimes the conclusion is based on a conception that there are certain vital inadequacies in the methods of classical social theory. At other times, the objection goes to the subject matter: the kind of society the classical social theorists analyzed has changed; hence, their ideas will no longer do. In the more subtle and far-reaching criticisms, the two points are combined.[7]

Thus, it is said that our contemporary understanding of society is in a "crisis" and that the crisis is closely connected with a deep transformation in society itself, just as the creation of the classical theory was associated with the emergence of the modern liberal capitalist state. We can move out of this quandary only by recasting the conceptual and methodological apparatus of social theory in light of the problems that the emergent conditions of society press upon us. In the effort to devise theories that will account for the peculiar features of our own historical situation, we may deepen our understanding of what is universally true about man and society.

One can neither evaluate the preceding claims nor decide how to act upon them without analyzing them more carefully. Take first the issue of the unity of classical social theory. It is difficult to discover even the outline of a single doctrine in the writings of the classic social theorists. Indeed, once one goes beyond the basic traits that distinguish social theory from the Aristotelian tradition in political philosophy, one finds disagreement among the moderns on almost every decisive point. Nevertheless, despite this divergence of answers, there is a remarkable similarity in the questions asked. If classical social theory has a unity, it is the unity of a common predicament rather than that of a shared doctrine, an agenda of puzzles raised and left partly unresolved.

There are three main problems. First, there is the issue of method: How should we represent in thought and in language the relationship among social facts? Second, there is the question of social order: What holds society together? Whereas a theory of method is a view of how to arrange our ideas about society, a doctrine of social order offers an account of the arrangement of society itself. Its chief concern is the rules by which people organize their dealings with each other. Third, there is the problem of modernity: What distinguishes modern society, as it arose in Europe, from all other societies, and what is the relationship between its self-image and its reality, between what it appears to be and what it really is? The three questions are connected, though in an extraordinarily obscure and complex manner.

The break with ancient political philosophy decisively shaped each of these issues in ways that became clear only gradually. Whether they were dealing with explanation, social order, or modernity, the classic social theorists found themselves facing certain dilemmas from which they tried to escape through more comprehensive views. It was the fact of their being caught in the same maze that made these European social thinkers the exponents of an identifiable movement in the intellectual history of the West.

This hypothesis about the unity of classical social theory suggests a tentative view of that theory's crisis. The central issues of explanation, order, and modernity remain unsolved in important respects. And the difficulties that result from the failure to dispose of these matters are compounded by the transformation of modern society.

But it will turn out that these unanswered questions cannot in fact be answered by social theory as it was formulated by its makers. For a resolution of the problems of explanation, order, and modernity would require a redefinition of the very premises upon which social theory asserted its independence from Graeco-Christian philosophy: the contrast of understanding and evaluation and the denial of a suprahistorical human nature. To carry out its own program, social theory must destroy itself. Now let us follow this argument through by examining one by one the focal controversies of the sociological tradition.

THE PROBLEM OF METHOD

The way in which the social theorists approached the issue of method and in which we continue to deal with it was largely determined by the severely limited fund of basic schemes of explanation available to modern Western thought. In fact, one may say that all these procedures are variations on two pure types: logical analysis and causal explanation. Each provides an interpretation of what it means to account for something both in the sense of telling what it is like, which is description, and in the sense of establishing why it had to follow from something else, which is explanation in the strict sense. (Whenever I use "explanation" without qualification or contrast, I mean it to include both description and explanation in the narrower sense.)

Neither logic nor causality achieved its present meaning all at once. On the contrary, both have a long and tortuous history: they appeared at particular moments and they underwent a variety of changes. The alternative they present seems to tell us something deep about the human mind and its development. I shall begin by stating the logical and the causal schemata in their most simple abstract forms and then go on to indicate how social theory makes use of them and what obstacles it faces in doing so.

Both logical entailment and causal explanation describe relationships with the attributes of necessity, sequence, and objectivity. In each case, there is a statement if a, then b. In both, given a, b must follow. At least, b is made more probable. (Probability is in this sense a diluted necessity.) And in each, a is somehow prior to b; even in logical entailment it is not always true that "if a, then b" can be commuted into "if b, then a." Finally, whether b follows a, either logically or causally, is an objective fact about the world or a fact that can be assessed by reference to criteria so universal that all persons might be brought to acknowledge them.

The logical and the causal relationship differ in that the latter adds duration to sequence, whereas the former exhibits sequence alone. The joining of sequence and duration is called time. A causal explanation is always an account of the relationship among events in time. A logical analysis deals with the connection among concepts outside time.

Another distinction between the two sorts of accounts has to do with the universality or particularity of their terms. The logical relationship is always formal: it represents the universals it brings together as abstract forms whose content does not matter. Its animating spirit is the distinction between content and form. Causal explanation, by contrast, always begins as an effort to elucidate the relationship among particular events. Even as it moves toward ever higher levels of generality, its ultimate justification continues to be its power to explain the temporal sequence among particulars in experience.

The two differences between logical analysis and causal explanation are the reverse sides of each other. In the world of time, with which causal thinking deals, objects and events have substance. This means that they differ from one another as individual entities, although one must rely on theory to determine what counts as an individual entity. In the extratemporal realm, to which logical analysis addresses itself, one encounters only universal genera, classes, or concepts whose members have no individual differences. There are universals, but no particulars.

The great mystery of logical analysis is how and in what sense, given its formality, it could ever apply to the world. The paradox of causality has to do with the possibility of discrete causal judgments. Causal explanation requires the imputation of particular effects to particular causes. But the more complete and therefore accurate the account, the more do all past events seem responsible for any given occurrence in the present. The chain of causality extends uninterruptedly in every direction of space and time. Thus, there is a conflict between the needs for discreteness and completeness in causal understanding.[8]

The logical and the causal method serve as the starting points for two ways of dealing with the problem of explanation in social study. In some respects, classical social theory is an attempt to overcome the limitations of both modes of thought. One of its fatal weaknesses lies in its failure to accomplish this task.

The first type of social thought relies on the logical method. I shall call it rationalism. Perhaps neoclassical economics comes closest to exemplifying it. The rationalist strategy starts with the selection of a few general premises about human nature, chosen for the explanatory power of the conclusions they make possible rather than for their descriptive accuracy. From these postulates it draws a growing string of consequences by a continuous process of logical deduction and conceptual refinement, as well as by the introduction at many points along the way of certain empirical assumptions about nature and society. Rationalist social science aspires to become a system of propositions whose interdependencies are governed by precise logical notions of entailment, consistency, and contradiction.

The whole body of thought, save for the perplexing but inevitable introduction of empirical assumptions, disclaims any pretense to describe what actually happens in social life. It moves at the level of the hypothetical: its conclusions are descriptively true only to the extent its premises hold. By tightening or relaxing the strictness of the premises, by making them more or less complex and therefore more or less faithful to the social reality we want to apprehend, we are able to control the balance between simplicity of explanation and descriptive fidelity.[9]

The more we lean toward the former, the greater the danger that our inferences will fail to apply to any world in which we are actually interested. The more we tend to the latter, the higher the risk that our conjectures will degenerate into a series of propositions so qualified and complicated that we are just as well off with our commonsense impressions. Whether simplicity or faithfulness to fact is emphasized will depend on the particular purpose for which we choose between them.

The tradition of thought that has stood in starkest opposition to rationalism in its treatment of the problem of explanation usually goes under the name of historicism. Historicism is exemplified by the kind of historiography associated with the Romantic movement, just as rationalism is a creature of the Enlightenment. It accepts the relationship of cause and effect rather than that of logical entailment as its dominant scheme of thought. Its program is to discover what has actually happened and why; it is a procedure for description as well as for explanation.[10]

The historicist stands before a dilemma that is a counterpart to the dilemma faced by the rationalist and a particular form of the general paradox of causality. If he wants to maintain clear lines of causality, in which cause and effect are neatly matched in one-to-one sequences, he has to tear certain events out of the "seamless web" of history, in which everything seems to bear on everything else. But in so doing he willfully disfigures the truth of history, which it was his aim to establish. His causal hypotheses, like the rationalist's deductions, remain neat only insofar as they become simplifying distortions and thereby lose touch with the actual flow of particulars in historical experience. When the distortions generated by the search for causal understanding are used as tools for building general theories of society, they result in the appeal to providential "key factors" or to "ultimate causes," economic, political, or religious.

Suppose the historicist refuses to sacrifice complex historical truth on the altar of one-way causation. Like the rationalist who multiplies his empirical assumptions, he may begin to insist on the pervasiveness of circular causation. Having discovered that all things cause each other in social life, as in the world at large, he wants to find a way to represent this insight in what he says about society. Alas, his eagerness is self-defeating. The more causes he takes into account, the less he is able to distinguish discrete relationships of cause and effect. In the end, the very notion of causality flounders in ambiguity.

The attempt to come to terms with the preceding dilemma leads in historicism to a near abandonment of causal thinking itself. In the frantic effort to find a surrogate for causality, the great historians in the historicist tradition appealed to the metaphors of the organism and of the work of art as patterns on which to model their reconstructions of the unity of a society or of an age.[11] They claimed or assumed that the different elements of a historical situation are connected with each other in the same manner as the parts of an organism or of a work of art. Such a set of organic or aesthetic interdependencies defies the strictures of simple "mechanical" causality. But is it still causality, and, if not, what then?

Thus, rationalism and historicism end up placing the student of society in similar quandaries. In both cases, he is caught between an approach that seems precise but misleading and a view that leads back to reality only to dissolve along the way into vagueness. Consequently, one must choose between the more or less arbitrary isolation of premises or processes and the loss of clarity in method.

Another look suggests that the rationalist and the historicist position have a second disquieting trait in common. In their pure forms, they both describe necessary connections of entailment or causation. Thus, unless expanded to the point of confusion, they invite some sort of determinism and thereby falsify or dismiss the experienced open-endedness of social life and of history.

Once we grasp the situation brought about by the Hobson's choice of rationalism and historicism, it is easy to understand the implicit methodological program of classical social theory. The program has rarely been stated in a simple and direct fashion, yet it clarifies and brings together much that is otherwise unclear and disjointed in the work of the great social theorists and in the latter-day practice of social science.

The way to avoid the pitfalls of the rationalist and the historicist approach is to fashion a method that repudiates what the logical and the causal mode of explanation have in common despite their important divergence: the concern with sequence and the search for relationships of necessity. A redefinition of what it means to account for something, or to describe and explain it, is at stake.

Instead of sequential patterns connecting elements abstracted from their settings, we need a way to describe and to explain the connections through time among the different aspects of a social situation. Once again, the task is to reconcile our understanding of how and why events succeed one another with an acknowledgment of the interrelatedness of all the elements of a situation. Moreover, one wants to do justice to this interrelatedness in a way that is both simple and precise.

At the same time we must try to describe relationships among elements in a manner that escapes the implications of necessity. We want a mode of explanation that will show how the elements of a social situation "fit together," though some of them could be present without all the others. The nature of such a relationship of reciprocal possibility or adequacy remains to be elucidated. But we can already see that the issue of method bears directly on the metaphysical question of free will and determinism. The problem of determinism remains insoluble as long as every explanatory account of something must take the form of a proof that, given certain causes or premises, the effect or consequence must follow.

The urge to dispense with linear sequence and the importance of avoiding determinism do not exhaust the requirements of a satisfactory method in social theory. There is a third aspect of the problem of explanation, about which the rationalist and the historicist are both silent because of their commitment to objectivity. The sense individuals attribute to one another's acts is what gives their conduct its distinctly social or human meaning. To disregard this meaning is to neglect an integral part of the experience for which an account is to be given.

The relationship between people's self-understanding in everyday life and the theorist's description or explanation of behavior brings us up against a riddle every bit as vexing as the puzzles that spring directly from the rivalry of the rationalist and the historicist method. If we disregard the meanings an act has for its author and for the other members of the society to which he belongs, we run the risk of losing sight of what is peculiarly social in the conduct we are trying to understand. If, however, we insist on sticking close to the reflective understanding of the agent or his fellows, we are deprived of a standard by which to distinguish insight from illusion or to rise above the self-images of different ages and societies, through comparison. Thus, subjective and objective meaning must somehow both be taken into account.[12]

One of the sources of unity in classical social theory was the persistent effort, carried through under many different guises, to find a method that would accomplish the tasks I have enumerated. Such a discovery would have suddenly enlarged the range of our powers to comprehend society. Against this background, one can make sense of the varied attempts to forge a procedure that would account for a social or historical situation as a whole, in conformity with the requirements previous modes of thought had failed to satisfy. Thus, all the elements or aspects of the situation subject to explanation would be linked together in a way that would bring out their reciprocal, nonlinear interrelatedness. One-to-one statements of necessary connection would be eliminated. Finally, the interdependency among the elements of the situation would be represented so as to explain how the persons being studied viewed their situation. Yet this approach would not remain confined to the participants' own reflective understandings.

The quest for such a method is the common ground of a set of different but overlapping conceptions that have dominated methodological doctrine and practice in social theory. Among these conceptions are the "dialectic," the "ideal-type," and the "structure." Each has distinct meanings and is associated with a characteristic intellectual tradition. For my immediate purposes, however, their shared attributes are paramount. The dialectical method as developed by Marx, the ideal-type used by Weber, and contemporary "structuralism" are all would-be escapes from the unhappy dilemma of rationalism and historicism.

The elements joined together by the dialectic, the ideal-type, or the structure comprise a whole. They cannot be sorted out in a linear series in which *a* precedes *b* and *b, c,* without doing violence to the simultaneous and circular interconnectedness that this mode of explanation seeks to underline.

The parts of the dialectical, ideal-typical, or structural whole form a kind of unity, but not one in which each element necessitates, and is necessitated by, all the others. By virtue of what, then, do they hang together? This question brings us to the third feature of the family of methods to which I am calling attention. The unity of the parts within the whole is a unity of meaning: together, the parts make up a more general principle or conception of the individual, society, or nature. But what precisely is semantic unity?

Sometimes the unifying conception is attributed to the

persons being observed. Thus, for example, the orientations and beliefs that Weber places in his ideal-type of the Protestant Ethic make concrete a vision of man's place in the world entertained by the adherents to the ethic.[13] At other times, the common conception that underlies the unity of the parts is one held by the theorist rather than one acknowledged by the persons whose beliefs and conduct are being studied. According to a version of Marxist dialectics, for example, ideology, politics, and economy under capitalism are interconnected in a way whose true character may remain unknown to most of the members of capitalist society, including the capitalist class itself.[14] The weakness of these criteria of semantic unity is that they either make it impossible to formulate a comprehensive theory of society or they sacrifice the social aspect of understanding, its reference to the subjectivity of the agent.

Hence, a third kind of theory tries to unite the subjective and the objective approach to meaning and to remedy the defects of each. The unifying conception is attributed to universal tendencies or patterns in the "unconscious" of the observed. Thus, as in the dialectical method, one has a basis for judgments and comparisons that cut across societies and historical periods. Nevertheless, by postulating that the principles which join the elements of the whole are innate in the minds of the persons whose conduct we are trying to understand, we concede something to the notion that meaning is subjective. But we do so only at the cost of severing the link between the ideas of subjectivity and of consciousness. This is the path taken by all forms of contemporary social science that rely on the notion of unconscious "structures" in the mind (e.g., Chomsky's linguistics, Lévi-Strauss's anthropology, and Gestalt psychology).[15]

The distinctions among the dialectical, the ideal-typical, and the structural method become important with respect to the way in which one defines the relationship between what theory can teach us about people and how people conceive of themselves in everyday life, between theoretical explanation and reflective understanding. But these distinctions lose much of their significance when we consider the methods as a set of analogous responses to the conflict between rationalism and historicism. Viewed in this light, all the methods suffer from similar incurable flaws.

These deficiencies are responsible for some of the great unresolved issues of method in the study of society. One difficulty has to do with the relationship between causal explanation and dialectic, ideal-typical, or structural accounts. A still more basic obstacle is the fatal imprecision of the efforts to specify what the alternative to logic and causality is.

Every form of social thought must grapple with the need to describe how, and to explain why, certain events succeed each other in history. Insofar as one emphasizes the nonsequential interrelatedness of social phenomena, the basis for an understanding of historical sequence disappears. To explain history, we always seem compelled to return to the kinds of causal judgments we have been trying to avoid. Thus, we end up with two methods, one causal and the other not, whose relationship to each other is undefined.

In Marxist dialectics, this problem appears as an ambiguity in the very notion of a dialectical relationship. At times, this notion is used to describe a causal nexus, although one diluted into circular causation. Often, however, it becomes a device for the sort of noncausal account of ordered wholes mentioned earlier. Consequently, the dialectic lives in two worlds: one, causal-deterministic; the other, structural and antideterministic.

A more overt duplication of methods takes place in the works of the thinkers who use the ideal-typical and structuralist rather than the dialectical notions. Thus, for Weber the ideal-type is part of an apparatus of methods that also makes room for causal explanation. And for structuralists like Lévi-Strauss, the causal judgments of history (the "diachronic") have a place alongside, but separate from, structural analysis (the "synchronic").

Looking back, we can now grasp the basic methodological unity and limitations of social theory. Social theory seeks to find an alternative to logical and causal explanation. To this goal it sometimes adds the purpose of reconciling, in the interpretation of conduct, the standpoint of the agent with the perspective of the observer—subjective and objective meaning. The two goals are connected because if the appeal to unities of meaning is the way out of the dilemma of logic and causality, one has to establish the vantage point from which the semantic unity can be assessed. Neither an objective nor a subjective criterion seems enough to satisfy, by itself, the aims of social study.

Thus, there are three main methodological limitations to the tradition of classical social theory. First, no precise and detailed definition has yet been given of a noncausal, nonlogical method. Second, in part for this reason, the relationship of this third kind of account to causality remains unclear. Third, it must be shown how the claims of subjectivity and objectivity can both be respected in the understanding of human action.

To these one might add a fourth methodological issue which is less a failing distinctive to social theory than a difficulty running through the entire Western tradition of rational discourse. It is a problem at once more concrete and more abstract than the other three, though it is connected with them. The characteristic manifestation of this riddle in social study is the relationship of historiography to a systematic theory of society. Like the ancient political philosophers, the classic social theorists wanted to formulate a general view of social life. But, because of their commitment to descriptive understanding and to a historical conception of human nature, they expected their ideas to illuminate concrete situations. How can one devise a social theory that is both generalizing in its method and rich in its historical references?

The persistent inability of social theory to answer this question in a satisfactory manner led latter-day social science in two opposite directions. On the one hand, there were formal studies with little historical content. These tended to degenerate into classificatory schemes that often contributed little to the understanding of past and present experience. On the other hand, there were efforts to pursue in a historiographic fashion aspects of the broader issues studied by the classics. But such efforts, because of their narrower scope, frequently lost sight of the more basic concerns of social study. As a result, these ethnographic and historical investigations could offer an enormous increase of information, but no process by which this growth in the amount of factual knowledge could be transformed into an improvement in our methods or in our general ideas about social order. The heroic effort to synthesize systematic theory and historiography was, for the most part, abandoned.

To understand why the attempt had always been difficult to carry out, one must appreciate the basic metaphysical obstacle facing it. To formulate even the most modest general ideas about a sequence of particular events or a set of particular acts, the student of society must make two sorts of connections. He has to form a view of the way the events or acts are linked together. And he must order his theoretical propositions in a manner that itself obeys certain standards of coherence. The events, one might say, are ordered causally, whereas the concepts are arranged logically; the former belong to the phenomenal world of time, whereas the latter, in a sense, do not. (It should be remembered, however, that Aristotelian logic may be only one of many possible forms of conceptual coherence.)

Each time the theorist considers introducing a new proposition into his system, he has to determine both how it fits what he knows about the events and what logical relationships, of consistency or contradiction, coherence or incoherence, it has with other statements in his theoretical system. There is, however, no a priori reason to believe that the demands of causal fidelity can be reconciled with those of conceptual consistency, regardless of how the latter are defined. A proposition that seems true with respect to given historical events may nevertheless have false implications when its theoretical consequences are drawn out according to the rules of theory construction the student has adopted. Thus, the theorist may be forced to choose between restricting the generality of his theory and sacrificing its accuracy.

A similar puzzle may confront the natural sciences at crucial junctures of their development. Thus, it has been suggested that the kinds of mathematical language appropriate to the description of different parts of nature (e.g., subatomic particles and biological inheritance) may be ultimately incompatible.[16] In the social sciences, however, the problem is, as we shall soon see, much more serious.

The recurring conflict between generality and accuracy is a constant preoccupation for "social scientists" and historians alike. Its root is the tension between the concrete perception of particulars and the abstract knowledge of universals. To reason about the temporal world, in which things exist individually, is to draw general inferences about particular phenomena, whose particularity one disregards for certain purposes. Theoretical generalization advances through a flattening out of particularity.

This, however, presents a special problem for social study. Once we grant that people's views of what they are doing must somehow become a part of any specifically social understanding of their practices, we are no longer free to disregard the distinctions they make among events, situations, or persons.

It might be possible to formulate a unified physical account of social life that reduces all history to a few lawlike explanations. Still, the justification for what I have called social understanding would remain undiminished. Any such approach to society would treat the felt particularity of historical phenomena as important for its own sake. And it would have to recognize that the features that interest us most in a society, a person, or an event are often those that distinguish it from all others. The conflict between historiography and systematic theory is really just an aspect of the larger issue of universality and particularity in knowledge, and it cannot be overcome as long as rational discourse continues to mean a kind of thinking that abstracts from the particularity of things.

Perhaps the most sustained effort in the literature of social theory to resolve this conflict was Weber's doctrine and practice of the ideal-typical method. The type is a conceptual scheme designed to elucidate a unique historical situation, just as a work of representational art presents an image of a unique phenomenon. Yet the type is also designed to show how certain kinds of actions and beliefs tend to go together with other kinds. It thereby allows us to improve the quality of our general understanding of society. In a similar fashion, a great work of art may change one's entire vision of the world.

Nevertheless, one must still determine the level of abstraction or concreteness at which the elements of the type are to be described and connected. The need to do this threatens to reinstate the dilemma of universality and particularity, systematic theory and historiography, from which the typological method seemed to offer an escape. Moreover, the solution to the problem of types presupposes an answer to all the other basic methodological questions of social theory. If the tie among the components of a type is neither logical nor causal, what is its nature? What is its relationship to causal explanation? And should the unity of its parts be assessed according to the beliefs of the observer or of the people he observes?

THE PROBLEM OF SOCIAL ORDER

The problem of social order arises from a deep puzzlement one may experience about the very existence of society, just as the problem of method comes from wondering how to study social life. Can we discern beneath the changing forms of association something basic to the social bond? This is a riddle we confront before we reach the more concrete issue of the reasons for harmony and conflict in society.

Let no one mistake the question for a philosopher's pastime. Our theories of culture and social organization depend on the view we have of human conduct and of interpersonal relations. By rejecting the doctrine of a suprahistorical human nature, classical social theory abandoned the attempt to arrive at an understanding of conduct that might be prior to, and independent of, an account of social relations. But it did not thereby free itself of the need tò make assumptions about what it is in social relations that makes organized group life possible.

To begin with, such assumptions are indispensable as guides in empirical research. Furthermore, the wealth and ambiguity of the materials of social experience are such that an unequivocal proof of the truth of competing views of social order on the basis of observation alone seems unlikely in the foreseeable future. Lastly, each of the doctrines of social order to be discussed here has a more or less hidden moral component from which the doctrine can never be entirely separated. In every case there is an indissoluble reciprocal link between beliefs about what society is and beliefs about what it ought to be. No amount of factual inquiry seems sufficient to prove the truth of a general conception of social order.

The stage for the discussion of the problem of social order in classical social theory was set by a struggle between two traditions of thought. One of the traditions might be called the doctrine of instrumentalism or private interest, and the other the doctrine of legitimacy or consensus. Starting from very different backgrounds and concerns, most of the classic social theorists came to believe that the two modes of thought were inadequate, in the same way that they rejected both rationalism and historicism in their treatment of the problem of method.

My first task will be to define the two views of social order against which social theory reacted and to point out the defects of each. Then I shall indicate the lines along which an attempt was made to overcome their deficiencies by synthesizing the two traditions. My final purpose will be to show how once again the projected reconciliation failed in certain important respects and how this failure has helped determine the present responsibilities of social thought.

The doctrine of private interest is a conception of the basis of social order often identified with utilitarianism and classic political economy.[17] But it is also an important strand in many other intellectual traditions. It may be characterized by its attachment to a certain conception of the social bond and to a particular view of the nature of the rules on which organized social life depends.

It holds that men are governed by self-interest and guided by judgments about the most efficient means to achieve their privately chosen aims. The idea of self-interest may be enlarged to include an altruistic concern for the welfare of others as long as the ultimate basis of this choice is one's own will, even if what one wants is that others get what they want. Contrast this to a mode of thought in which the good for oneself or for others is quite independent of any individual's egoistic or altruistic desires. According to the private-interest theory, the ends of each individual are relatively independent from those of other individuals; even though they may have been more or less influenced by other persons' goals, they can be meaningfully treated as distinct. This theory places the immediate determinant of conduct within the individual rather than in the groups to which he belongs.

There is no logical relationship between an assertion of the primacy of individual purposes and the commitment to means-ends judgments as the dominant scheme of thought and behavior. One can conceive of an instrumentalism at the service of collective values. Nevertheless, there are two reasons to believe that the commonplace association of the ideas of private interest and instrumentalism has a rational basis, though one which falls far short of proving a necessary interdependence.

The first reason is that the broader the scope and the more detailed the content of the collective interests and the greater their authority to determine what an individual should do, the less of a role is left for personal efficiency judgments. The individual may more easily be able to reorder his own ends in the light of his knowledge of the means available to him than to influence the shared ends of the groups to which he belongs.

The second factor is that the notion of manipulation of nature, which exemplifies instrumentalism, may also suggest the idea of manipulating others. Both nature and others constitute the external world contrasted with the individual. Moreover, instrumentalism is often seen as the province of pure operational intelligence, and it may be easier to imagine a moral sense of the group than a collective intellect.

The doctrine of private interest acknowledges that the objectives of different individuals tend to conflict, either because they are desires for different things, e.g., arguments about the ends governmental power should serve, or because they are desires for the same things of which there are not enough, e.g., conflicts over scarce resources. The first category of antagonisms is usually resolved through democratic procedures, and the second, through the market.

Both political deliberation and economic exchange depend on the promulgation and enforcement of rules or laws. Without rules, the benefits of coordination in social life would never be reaped, and the existence of a social order, except perhaps as a product of the dictatorship of an individual or a group, would remain an impenetrable mystery. The doctrine of private interest has certain implications for what such a system of rules would have to be like. Together, these implications point toward what may be described as an instrumental view of rules.

Instrumental rules are treated by the individual as one more factor to be taken into account in his calculus of efficiencies.[18] This means that he will comply with the rules only to the extent that his own goals are better served by compliance than by disobedience. Consequently, the sanction becomes the crucial part of the rule. The fear of the sanction operates to internalize the requirements of social order in the individual's reasonings about the most effective means to attain personal ends.

Insofar as instrumental rules are made according to procedures that accord in the long run with everyone's self-interest, even when they violate that self-interest in particular instances, their claim to obedience need not rest on the mere terror by which they are imposed. This hope, which characterizes much of modern political philosophy, introduces a whole new world of complications I shall not discuss here. Instead, let me go on directly to deal with the weaknesses of the doctrine of private interest, failings that rightly led to its abandonment by social theory, though not by the still dominant tradition in economics.

The first and most fundamental objection to the logic of instrumentalism is its failure to explain how human conduct could ever have enough continuity over time and similarity among individuals to make either an organized society or a social science possible. To see the core of human action in the process by which individuals select means for the advancement of their individual goals is to assume that the ends of conduct are in some meaningful sense individual. The more these ends become immediate reflexes of natural or social circumstances, the less do we have reason to treat human action in terms of means and ends rather than of cause and effect. And the more features of an individual's situation are included in the category of ends to be attained or to be avoided, the fewer the aspects of that situation which can be treated as simply a matter of means. Nevertheless, as we emphasize the randomness of the ends of each person with respect to his natural and social circumstances and the diversity of the goals of different individuals, we also seem to undercut the basis for understanding what holds people together: what allows them to communicate with one another and to agree at least on the procedures for rulemaking. Thus, the instrumentalist doctrine breaks down at precisely the point at which our perplexity over order in society becomes most acute.

A second argument against the theory of private interest is that it has contradictory implications for one's view of the place of rules in society. These implications suggest that the premises from which they derive achieve a semblance of plausibility at the cost of a hidden incoherence. We have already seen how this view of social order produces an instrumental picture of rules. Yet, at the same time, it needs a noninstrumental notion of rules to plug up the holes in its descriptive account of human association. There are several reasons for this.

As long as the laws are obeyed only when the fear of punishment exceeds the hope of gain, there always remains the danger that in particular instances the expectation of profit may surpass the fear of loss. Whatever the drawbacks of such an outlook as a foundation for beliefs about what society ought to be like, there seems little doubt of its inadequacy as a description of how persons in fact conceive the constraints social rules impose on their relations to one another. It is a commonplace that they often prize and obey the systems of rules that govern their interaction even when every identifiable consideration of individual advantage counsels disobedience.

Moreover, the exercise of instrumental judgments presupposes a conception of the range of legitimate means. Unless there were noninstrumental limitations on the choice of means, anything might in principle be used as a means to any end. It would then become impossible to provide for well-defined entitlements of individuals and groups; hence, no stable social order could exist.

Finally, the expression and development of personality seem to demand that men live under rules or procedures that command their allegiance because of a rightness or goodness irreducible to individual desires or to a calculus of means and ends. It is perhaps an ineradicable feature of moral discourse to admit that certain things must be done and others avoided whether one likes their consequences or not. If extreme consequences cry out for a qualification of the standard, this may be because they highlight a deficiency in its initial formulation. Without such constraints on the scope of instrumental judgments, it would be impossible for individuals to treat one another as moral persons—as beings capable of distinguishing what they want to do from what they ought to do. Only by asking the latter question can they overthrow the tyranny of blind desire and establish a social order that will not be at the mercy of private interest.

The main thesis of the argument about the contradictory implications of the doctrine of instrumentalism for the theory of rules may be summarized in the following way. The greater one's reliance on private interest, privately defined, as a key to the explanation of conduct, the more acute the need to account for the possibility of social order by the existence of noninstrumental rules that ought to be obeyed, and in fact tend to be obeyed, independently of the individual's calculus of means and ends. Yet, at the same time, the theory seems to imply that all rules are instrumental. It provides no basis for exempting certain features of social life from the reach of efficiency judgments.

A third argument against the doctrine is overtly moral or political. Even when it takes altruism into account, the conception of social life embodied in the private interest theory seems to make no room for the values of solidarity. These values represent the worth that may attach to the practices, to the institutions, and to the very existence of group life regardless of their use to the individual will or to some combination of individual wills.

Now that the outlines of the instrumentalist view and of the grounds of opposition to it have been traced, we can go on to the second major conception of human conduct and society with which classical social theory had to come to terms: the theory of legitimacy or consensus. Once again, one may distinguish in it a general approach to human conduct and a particular view of rules. Some of its more extreme examples can be found in the organicist interpretations of society characteristic of the Romantic movement. Its link to the idealist tradition in philosophy will become apparent as my discussion moves forward.

Whereas the doctrine of private interest takes off from the individual and his ends, the theory of legitimacy starts with society or the group and its shared values and understandings.[19] These ideals and beliefs may vary as to the extension of agreement with them, as to their relative degree of abstraction or concreteness, as to the intensity of adherence to them, and as to their coherence. But despite variations in extension, concreteness, intensity, and coherence, the presence of commonly held moral and cognitive orientations is always what makes organized social life possible. Shared beliefs allow people to understand one another and to know what they ought to expect from each other. The basic scheme of human conduct is therefore the internalization of shared understandings and values, rather than the choice of efficient means to attain individually defined ends.

Notice that this account of conduct differs in two key respects from the one suggested by the opposing tradition of social thought. First, it rejects the assumption of the individuality of ends. Not only do shared values precede individual ends in time and in authority, but they are also incapable of being adequately understood as outcomes of a combination of individual ends. The second critical difference between the two doctrines of the nature of action is that the logic of legitimacy discounts and subverts the significance of the means-ends dichotomy. The shared standards and perceptions of the group color every aspect of an individual's situation with positive or negative values; there is nothing he can treat simply as a means to which no moral weight attaches. Thus, the very distinction between means and ends breaks down.

The consequences of this view of society and of conduct for our ideas about rules are far-reaching. Set against this background, rules become manifestations of the shared values of the group.[20] They perform subsidiary though indispensable tasks: to clarify the implications and the boundaries of these collective ends and to reassert them against would-be violators. But the broader the extension, the concreteness, the intensity, and the coherence of the consensus, the less necessary do rules become. It is their nature to survive in the crevices of consensus.

Hence, the main reason for which laws are obeyed is that the members of the group accept in belief and embody in conduct the values the laws express. One's allegiance to the rules derives from their capacity to give expression to the common purposes in which one participates rather than from the threats of harm with which their enforcement is guaranteed. Thus, the focus of interest shifts from the sanction to the standard of conduct prescribed by the rule.

Now let us review the objections that can be made to the doctrine of legitimacy and to its attendant conception of rules. These criticisms are the counterparts to those directed against the instrumentalist theory, for the two views of society neatly oppose and complement one another.

The first and fundamental drawback of the consensus doctrine is its inherent tendency to explain both too much and too little. It accounts for the possibility of a harmony of outlooks and ideals, but not for the existence of conflict. Within this framework of thought, conflict can never be more than a mark that something is missing. It must represent a falling away from the agreement upon which social order is based, a failure due to some limitation in the extension, the concreteness, the intensity, or the coherence of a society's shared values and understandings.

But why should we suppose that conflict is less intrinsic to the nature of social order than harmony? And what do we gain by appealing to the notion of shared beliefs and ideals unless we can determine the conditions under which consensus is destroyed and transformed by conflict? Without answers to these questions, the doctrine of legitimacy merely replaces one mystery with another.

The preceding doubts as to the validity of the theory of consensus are heightened when one turns to its implications for the understanding of rules. The tighter the agreement that binds individuals together and the greater its power to determine their conduct, the less of a role remains for rules. All rules can then do is to clarify the proper standards of conduct where the shared values of the group fall short in their concreteness or coherence and to ensure their enforcement when these values are deficient on the scales of extension and intensity.

But the paradox remains. Rules are said to be primarily expressions of common values, yet it is precisely some gap, weakness, or imprecision in the hold of these values that makes rules indispensable. Laws are the creatures of, and the antidotes to, conflict, which is the very aspect of social life the doctrine of legitimacy leaves unexplained. So the paradox of rules to which the consensus theory leads is just a more particular manifestation of this theory's inability to do justice to the precariousness of consensus in society and to explain how latent disagreement can break out into open defiance and struggle.

We are now in a position to understand the third criticism, for it is only a transposition of the two previous objections from a descriptive to a normative key. It accuses the doctrine of legitimacy of an ineradicable bias toward collectivism, a bias built into the descriptive outlook of the theory itself. By emphasizing the priority of the comprehension of social relations to the analysis of individual conduct and the overriding importance of the shared values of the group, the theory seems to undercut the basis for taking the separateness of persons seriously and to reject the claims of individual autonomy in favor of those of collective solidarity. Moreover, by suggesting that the evaluation of conduct does and must ultimately rest on consensus, it appears to sanctify whatever standards happen to prevail in a given collectivity. Strangely enough, the result is to repeat a defect previously detected in the instrumentalist doctrine: the denial of the moral point of view, a denial which consists of taking what men want to do for what they ought to do.

Nevertheless, it must be kept in mind that neither the collectivist nor the conservative conclusion follows necessarily from the factual premises of the doctrine. Even if they did, the moral criticism would remain hypothetical; its pertinence depends on the force of the arguments one can make in favor of the acknowledgment of the separateness of persons and of the worth of moral discourse. A discussion of these matters would lead us once again straight into metaphysics and morals, and I shall not pursue them further for the moment.

Let us now take stock. I have described in skeleton form the major features of the two views of society, of action, and of rules available to the classic social theorists when they set out to create a science of society. The discussion has suggested that both views suffer from equally serious, though opposite, defects. One might simply disregard the theories as implausible on their face were it not for the fact that the task of synthesizing them or moving beyond them remains.

From its very beginnings, the "scientific" study of society rebelled against the doctrine of private interest, represented by utilitarianism and utilitarian economics, and the theory of consensus, embodied in idealist, organicist, or Romantic collectivism. It proposed to bring together and thereby to correct and to deepen the partial insights provided by these traditions of thought. In this project, however, it was no more successful than in its related effort to escape the dilemma of rationalism and historicism.

It may be useful to reduce to its simplest elements the alleged alliance of the two modes of thinking about social order. The particular resolution I shall sketch and criticize is far from common to all classic social theorists, but it has played a major part in the tradition that runs from Weber to Parsons.[21]

Its first step is to grant that the existence and the internalization of shared values are indeed crucial to the possibility of a social order; this much is conceded to the doctrine of legitimacy. But to this concession it immediately adds that shared values are always more or less limited in their extension, concreteness, intensity, and coherence. The standards of behavior implied by the commonly held understandings and ideals must be made concrete and coherent enough to guide people in their dealings; hence the need for a set of explicit laws or rules. Moreover, the laws must be backed by a threat of force that can preserve their efficacy when the limits to the extension of their underlying values or to the intensity of the adherence these ends command are surpassed—and deviant conduct takes place.

If there existed a completely integrated system of common values of which all persons partook with equal intensity and which determined unequivocally the rights and wrongs of conduct, a set of formulated coercive rules would be unnecessary. But if no basis for cognitive and moral consensus existed, the making and applying of rules would be impossible, except under a dictatorial regime. Even then, the commands of the dictator would likely be ineffective. Thus, the consensus theory is said to provide an important but partial insight into the social order.

Whatever the relationship of enforceable laws to consensus, dominant values and public rules establish only the outer limits of permissible conduct. Within the area they mark off, there is room for the individual determination of ends and for the making of instrumental judgments. Thus, in the synthetic view I am outlining, the doctrine of instrumentalism reappears as the description of a mode of behavior and of choice that takes place where the force of social agreement stops.

As long as there are such limits to consensus, the need for the individual determination of the ends of conduct is inescapable. Furthermore, aspects of an individual's circumstances on which group values or individual standards have little bearing can be subjected to the calculus of means and ends. One will view these circumstances solely as means or obstacles to one's goals.

It is a corollary of the attempted reconciliation I describe to recognize the importance of instrumental rules, i.e., the norms that summarize a judgment of efficiency. Yet, at the same time, this view affirms that there exist rules that have more than a strictly instrumental sense because they are conceived and used as expressions of group values.

If one looks more closely, however, one may begin to wonder whether the desired fusion can really be carried through on anything resembling such a basis. The two conceptions of social order seem to be juxtaposed in a contradictory way rather than merged into a coherent picture capable of abolishing the distinctions between them. Moreover, the approach fails to explain the relative importance of the internalization of group values and of the calculus of means and ends to different forms of social life. Are we to understand that the synthetic view applies equally to every kind of society? Or should we believe that the degree and the character of consensus, on one side, and the area of free play left to efficiency judgments, on the other, depend on particular features of the way each form of social life is conceived and organized? If the latter, more plausible view is accepted, one must understand the decisive historical conditions for the applicability of each view of social order. Such an understanding may require theories we do not yet possess. Thus, the classical synthesis seems to be both incoherent and fatally incomplete.

The calculus of means and ends or of costs and benefits describes a state of consciousness that contrasts sharply with the one implied by an acquiescence in the legitimacy of shared values. The two could be merged only if they applied, in any given social situation, to clearly distinct aspects of life. But in fact, what is a means in one context becomes an end in another. What seems from one angle to be a problem of unrestricted individual choice appears from another as a question about how to interpret values we share with our fellows in the groups to which we belong.

The kind of harmonization of the doctrines of instrumentalism and of legitimacy sketched in the preceding pages perpetrates a confusion. It obscures the mechanisms by which the orientations and states of mind to which each of the two theories refers pass into their opposites. When Weber points to the distinction between "instrumental" and "value rationality,"[22] or when Pareto emphasizes the antithesis of "residues" and "derivatives,"[23] they are engaged in just the sort of reconciliation of which I have been speaking. But it is perhaps equally clear that they are giving us a classification when what we need is a theory.

The antagonism between the two interpretations of action and order is brought out into the open by the contradictory implications of instrumental and noninstrumental ways of viewing rules.[24] The instrumental rule tells you how to get something done if you want to do it. Such a rule must always remain hypothetical in a double sense. First, it applies only on the condition that one choose to accept the end of conduct, an end not itself prescribed by the maxim that suggests the shortest way to reach it. Second, even given the acceptance of the underlying goal, there is always the chance that in a particular instance one may be able to find a more effective way of reaching it than the one suggested by the norm.

Rules that accord with the requirements of the theory of legitimacy cannot be instrumental in either of these two senses. They demand from their addressees an adherence to the values to which they give expression. And, though to apply them it may be necessary to inquire into their underlying purposes, they are not to be simply set aside whenever the rule applier thinks he has discovered a better way to ensure the realization of the values for which they appear to stand.

The classical synthesis of the two conceptions of social order implies both an instrumental and a noninstrumental view of rules. Yet it fails to explain how the two views can ever be brought into harmony or to define the social conditions under which one of them becomes more appropriate, as a description or as an ideal, than the other.

The recognition of the need to go beyond the partial truths contained in the theories of private interest and consensus constitutes a bond of union among the great social theorists of the late nineteenth and the early twentieth century just as strong as their shared perception of the importance of avoiding both rationalism and historicism.

THE PROBLEM OF MODERNITY

The third issue to obsess the classic social theorists was the problem of modernity: What distinguished their own society, the modern European nation-state, from all other societies? What marked the experience of modernity and what was its place in world history? What was the relationship between modern society's view of itself, as expressed in the culture of its dominant groups, and that society's true nature? My present discussion of the problem of modernity will be very brief; there will be a better opportunity later to pursue it in greater detail.

For all the classic social theorists, the effort to state a comprehensive view of men and society was inseparable from an interest in understanding the condition and the prospects of their age. In this they simply repeated the eternal lesson that all deep thought begins and ends in the attempt to grasp whatever touches one most immediately.

This unanimity of concern was compatible with strong differences of approach. Some emphasized the structure of production as the basis for the identity of modern society. Others looked to the character of recurring social relations and the form of the division of labor. Still others laid the heaviest weight on the new vision of the world that had emerged in the course of post-Renaissance European history. Indeed, the very conception of "modernism" as a meaningful theoretical category might have been rejected by many classical theorists, as it has been attacked by a large number of their successors.[25]

The problem of formulating a conception of modernity nevertheless persists. It takes on a peculiar subtlety because of the relationship between ideology and actuality in modern life. The attitude of the classic social theorists toward this relationship was brought out by their reaction against a line of thought that, since the mid-seventeenth century, had already opposed the Aristotelian tradition in political philosophy. This was the social contract doctrine.

The social contract theorists from Hobbes to Rousseau and Kant had abandoned the belief in an objective knowledge of values. The traditional view of a continuity between the natural and the moral order was overthrown and replaced either by the reduction of the moral world to the natural one or by the idea of a complete separation between the two realms. At the same time, however, the social contract theorists continued to rely on the assumption of a suprahistorical human nature.[26] This curious halfway position between ancient political philosophy and modern social theory was embraced by utilitarianism and enshrined in English and Austrian political economy, which to this day are regarded in most parts of the world as the science of economics.

The proponents of the social contract doctrine viewed society as an association of individuals, with conflicting interests, and capable of being bound together by coercively enforceable rules and economic exchange. This doctrine foreshadowed a ruling ideology, and therein lies its chief interest for us as for the classic social theorists before us. Through the eyes of its dominant groups and of their intellectual spokesmen, modern society saw itself as a highly individualistic civilization in which order and freedom were guaranteed by law. Yet the ties of interdependence may never have been tighter than they became in modern Europe, and legal rules seemed to play but a minor role in shaping social life. What was one to make of this conflict between pretense and reality in the modern era?

One solution would be to take the ideology at its word as a description of what society actually was or could become. This was what the publicists of the liberal state proceeded to do. But another response was to reject the ideology altogether as a mere cover-up for a truth that was its opposite. This is the path suggested by some of the cruder interpretations of Marx.

For the most part, however, the classic social theorists tried to steer clear of these two positions. They wanted to transcribe the dialogue between consciousness and actuality in modern society and thereby to show how this society reveals itself in the very process of hiding itself.

It is easy to see how closely this program is connected with the problems of method and of social order and how it ties these two issues together. To relate appearance to reality in the modern age one must be able to reconcile subjective and objective meaning, which no strictly logical or causal method can do. And one must succeed in synthesizing the doctrine of private interest, which belongs chiefly to official ideology, with the theory of consensus, which mainly describes, in an idealized form, the social experience of subjection to groups and to their hierarchies or practices. This experience enters into conflict with the ideology it mysteriously breeds.

Thus, insofar as the social theorists failed to resolve the problems of method and order, they were also bound to stop short of complete success in their efforts to deal with the issue of modernity. This failure, as we shall later see, has been aggravated by two subsequent developments that have added new dimensions to the puzzle of modernism.

The first event is the change of modern Western society into a form of social life that in certain fundamental respects is different from the one the classic social theorists studied. What makes the changes fundamental from our point of view is that they have transformed the character and the direction of the dialectic between consciousness and actuality.

The second event is the proliferation of industrial societies that share many of the economic and technological attributes of Western society, but differ from it in their characteristic styles of consciousness and organization. Faced with this multiplication of modern societies, one is tempted to put aside the concept of the modern and to despair of arriving at general truths about seemingly unique events.

Both these trends complicate the attempt to define and to resolve the problem of modernity. Yet it will turn out that they also contribute to its solution.

HUMAN NATURE AND HISTORY

To complete the resolution of the problems of method, social order, and modernity, one ultimately needs a view of human nature.

Logic and causality fail as sufficient methods for social study because they refer to aspects of being with characteristics that differ from those of social phenomena. Logic addresses the order of ideas; causality, the order of events. (An idea may be taken as either an extratemporal concept, connected by relations of entailment and contradiction to other concepts, or as an event in somebody's mind, with causes and effects, like other events. Logic deals with ideas in the former sense only.) The logical analysis of ideas and the causal explanation of events share the traits of sequence, necessity, and objectivity thanks to common characteristics of the aspects of being they examine.

Everything a person says can be treated as an idea capable of logical analysis. Everything he does may also be subject to causal explanation. However, if rationalism and historicism fail as adequate tools of social study, this must be because human beings have yet a third dimension: consciousness. The realm of consciousness seems to overflow the boundaries of the orders of ideas and of events precisely because it involves a peculiar relationship between awareness and existence, between thinking and doing. This relationship does not allow itself to be grasped by a strictly sequential, necessary, and objective knowledge. An adequate appreciation of the third aspect of being and of the third method that corresponds to it depends on an understanding of man and of his place in the world.

The two conflicting images of order represented by the doctrines of private interest and of consensus rely, in the end, on different views of human conduct and of the relationship between the individual and the social side of personality. To determine the character of action in a way that connects individuality with sociability, one must know what man is like.

Upon closer inspection the problem of modernity turns into an issue about how to compare forms of social life: modern European society with its predecessors and the different kinds of modern society among themselves. But if what lends unity to a form of social life are analogies of meaning or style rather than logic or causality, we need well-defined criteria of comparison. Otherwise comparative study will be lost in arbitrary assertions of similarity or difference. Rigorous comparison becomes possible to the extent that we are able to conceive of a unitary human nature that underlies all forms of social life. Each society can then be viewed as the manifestation of certain aspects of humanity and compared, with the help of the general doctrine of human nature, to other societies.

The idea that a view of human nature is necessary to advance the program of social theory is a disturbing one. After all, social theory established its own identity by the very act of rejecting the notion of a unitary human nature above history. This rejection allowed modern thinkers to study people as they were rather than as they ought to be and to inquire into the particular way each society shapes conduct and consciousness. These achievements must not be given up. The real issue is whether one can extricate the ancient insight into the unity of human nature from the ancient illusion that humanity is unchanging throughout history. The task is to develop a doctrine that recognizes the unity of human nature in a more than trivial fashion while affirming that this nature changes in history and that it is reinvented and transformed by each new form of social life; indeed, by every individual.

Such a theory of human nature cannot readily limit itself to description. A general image of man that characterizes his circumstance in the world carries implications for what he can and should become. Conversely, the choice among possible views of humanity is likely to be itself influenced by moral and political perspectives that cannot be wholly justified by the view one chooses.

If this were to be the case, as I have argued in another

book,[27] the attempt to develop a theory of human nature would force us to cross the divide between understanding and evaluation and thereby to violate the other great stricture social theory laid down in its rebellion against ancient political philosophy. But how can we go beyond the fact-value distinction in the study of society without abandoning the characteristically modern ambition to understand men as they are?

Thus, we see that the problems of social theory cannot be resolved unless the truths of social theory are reconciled with those of the older political philosophy. The progress of thought requires that the two traditions be brought together in a more inclusive form of learning.

There is an alternative way to define the ultimate aim. The outlook of classic political philosophy did not entirely vanish with that philosophy's disappearance. It survives in the religious conception of the world, or in everyday moral and political thinking, which refuses to draw sharp distinctions between facts and values and relies on more or less explicit ideals of man and his good. How can we unite the truths contained in these religious and commonsense beliefs with the achievements of social theory?

LAW

In the next two chapters and thus for the greater length of this essay, I shall not deal head on with the questions raised in the preceding pages, nor shall I offer any comprehensive answer to them. In part, this is because I have attempted a general statement elsewhere. In part, it is out of a desire to show how the overarching issues can be cut down to more manageable proportions.

The problems of social theory will be approached by indirection, through a speculative study of the place of law in modern society.[28] Law seems a peculiarly fruitful subject of inquiry, for the effort to understand its significance takes us straight to the heart of each of the major unsolved puzzles of social theory.

First, law is involved in the problem of method. Once Aristotelianism in political thought was swept aside, it became necessary to describe and to explain social phenomena in terms different from the traditional ones of purpose and being. At the same time, however, it became clear that we do rely on prescriptive rules. These rules are not just facts devoid of moral significance to those who make, apply, and follow them, and give praise or blame according to them. To disregard this rule-guided aspect of existence would be to set aside the subjective meaning of behavior. One must therefore determine the relationship between the scientific search for factual regularities in society and the use of rules in everyday life. The elucidation of the link between the law that describes and the law that ordains becomes central to the theory of society.

Second, an inquiry into law bears closely on the problem of social order. The doctrines of private interest and of consensus include and depend upon conflicting views of rules. If we knew in which circumstances different kinds of law emerged, we might also be able to see the limits and uses of the two elementary views of order and to prepare the way for their synthesis.[29]

Third, the resolution of the problem of modernity requires us to discover the relationship between a dominant ideology that puts impersonal law at the center of society and a day-to-day experience for which such law stands at the periphery of social life.

Thus, an examination of law's place in modern society brings together the major concerns of social theory. Yet it also focuses them on topics that can be defined quite concretely.

The overall plan of this essay includes two long chapters, surrounded by two shorter ones: the present theoretical introduction and a final theoretical conclusion. In each of the two central chapters an aspect of the study of law in society is related to one of the main difficulties of social theory. Thus, Chapter Two deals with the varieties of law and with the conditions under which each of them arises. And it uses its subject matter as an occasion to address the issue of social order. Chapter Three discusses the significance and the transformation of the rule of law in modern society. But it examines this topic as part of the problem of modernity itself. Chapter Four reexamines the topics described in this introduction in light of what has been learned from the intervening study of law. It summarizes the implications of the argument for the problems of social order and modernity, and it develops the essay's methodological presuppositions.

Thus, the issue of method will be kept in the background until the end. A preliminary word may, however, be helpful to an understanding of my approach. I take seriously the need to work toward a reconciliation of generalizing theory and historiography. This need is inseparable from all the other unanswered methodological riddles of social theory. It is also deeply implicated in the question of social order, a large part of which is to distinguish our general ideas about the social bond from our particular views of the character of that bond in different kinds of societies. And it is directly relevant to the problem of modernity: the way we reinterpret our historical situation will, as always, limit, and be limited by, the way we think about society.

In grappling with the tension between systematic theory and historiography within my limited field of inquiry, I shall start off from the most successful procedure yet devised to resolve this tension—the typological method. The types of law and of society to which I shall refer will be situated at various levels of abstraction. Some will be simplified descriptions of a unique historical phenomenon, intended to permit analogies and contrasts. Others will be general categories meant to represent and to help explain recurring forms of law or of association. Still others will be hermeneutic devices, designed less to describe actual historical events than to serve as extreme cases or hypothetical possibilities that can be useful in explaining what did happen.

At the conclusion of the essay, there will be occasion to return to the dilemma of generalizing thought and historical understanding and to put it back in its true context: the predicament of social theory.

2

LAW AND THE FORMS OF SOCIETY

THE PROBLEM

This chapter deals with the problem of social order through discussion of the relationship between forms of law and of society. It has already been shown that both major doctrines of social order include a view of the nature and uses of rules. If each of these doctrines is most appropriate to a particular kind of society, one should also expect to find that the character of law changes from one form of social life to another. Each society reveals through its law the innermost secrets of the manner in which it holds men together. Moreover, the conflicts among kinds of law reflect different ways of ordering human groups.

The first step in clarifying the relationship between law and society is to distinguish the major sorts of law. For without such a classification we lack a language in which to describe the connections between species of law, on one side, and of society, on the other.

The next stage of my argument will be to suggest, in a speculative fashion, the historical conditions for the emergence of each of the main types of law. This analysis will indicate some relationships between culture and organization in different forms of social life, and it will lead up to the issue of how and why postfeudal Europe developed its unique kind of legal order. The answer to this question might contribute to an understanding of the peculiar identity of modern Western civilization. Moreover, it promises to shed light on the riddle of social order, since the modern rule of law ideal arises in a situation in which the mechanisms described by the theories of consensus and of private interest are strangely and precariously combined.

The discussion of the historical bases of modern Western law will be rendered more concrete and, to a limited extent, corroborated by a comparative treatment of law and political thought in ancient China. For the events that resulted in the Chinese imperial unification had much in common with those that produced the Western nation-states. Yet their legal consequences were very different. The significance of the Chinese comparison will be brought out through reference to civilizations whose legal experience stood somewhere between the ancient Chinese and the modern European.

The final part of the chapter will reexamine the problem of social order from the perspective of my view of the conditions and varieties of law.

THREE CONCEPTS OF LAW

The disciplines that have related the study of law to the problems of social theory have often been at loggerheads. Looked at more closely, however, many of their disputes turn on a pervasive confusion of terms, which ought to be dispelled at the outset. Thus, some schools of thought see law as a universal phenomenon, common to all societies.[1] They are therefore unable to attach any meaning to the notion that law might appear or disappear. An opposite tendency restricts the concept of law to a particular kind of modern legal system.[2] From this standpoint, it is impossible to use the comparative study of the place of law in a wide range of societies as an occasion to investigate more general issues of social theory. We need a conceptual apparatus that will allow us to distinguish the sense in which law is indeed a universal phenomenon from the ways in which it is distinctive to certain kinds of society.

In the broadest sense, law is simply any recurring mode of interaction among individuals and groups, together with the more or less explicit acknowledgment by these groups and individuals that such patterns of interaction produce reciprocal expectations of conduct that ought to be satisfied. I shall call this customary or interactional law.[3] There are two sides to the concept of law as interaction; each corresponds to an aspect of a traditional notion of custom.[4] One element is factual regularity in behavior. The other dimension is normative: the sentiment of obligation and entitlement, or the tendency to identify established forms of conduct with the idea of a right order in society and in the world at large.

For customary law, the issue of what in fact happens can never be kept clearly separate from the question of what ought to be done. There is a point at which deviations from the rule remake the rule itself. Thus, every act leads a double life: it constitutes conformity or disobedience to custom at the same time that it becomes part of the social process by which custom is defined. Therefore, the distinction between the choice of rules and the making of decisions under the rules, like the contrast between habit and duty, remains ill defined in the world of customary law.

Law as interaction is neither public nor positive. Its nonpublic quality means that it is common to the entire society rather than associated with a centralized government that stands apart from other social groups. It consists of the accepted practices on the basis of which all communication and exchange is carried on.

Custom also lacks the attribute of positiveness: it is made up of implicit standards of conduct rather than of formulated rules. These standards are tacit, though often highly precise, guidelines for how an individual of a certain rank ought to act toward one of different or similar rank in particular situations. Thus, for example, they determine what one should expect from one's kinsmen in a variety of circumstances and what they in turn may and will demand of him.

Customs are characteristically inarticulate rather than expressed. They apply to narrowly defined categories of persons and relationships rather than to very general classes. And they cannot be reduced to a set of rules; to codify them is to change them. It is precisely because custom is nonpositive that it is foreign to the distinctions between regularity and norm, or between the choice and the application of rules.[5]

Custom can be found in every form of social life, but there are situations in which its dominion is almost exclusive. The ethnographic description of savage societies has acquainted us with conditions in which law exists only as a set of largely tacit customs. In such circumstances, there are neither formulated general rules nor a separation of government from society that would make it possible to characterize certain rules as state law.

A second concept of law is that of bureaucratic or regulatory law. It is distinguished from custom by its public and positive character. Bureaucratic law consists of explicit rules established and enforced by an identifiable government. Wherever bureaucratic law appears, there exists a state to define more or less effectively the powers different groups may exercise over one another. This is not inconsistent with the recognition that from a broader perspective the power relations among these groups may determine what the government is like and what it can do.

Regulatory law is no universal characteristic of social life. It is limited to situations in which the division between state and society has been established and some standards of conduct have assumed the form of explicit prescriptions, prohibitions, or permissions, addressed to more or less general categories of persons and acts. With the advent of bureaucratic law, distinctions between habits and duties, or between rulemaking and the application of rules, become meaningful for the first time.

The reason for calling this type of law bureaucratic is that it belongs peculiarly to the province of centralized rulers and their specialized staffs. It is a law deliberately imposed by government rather than spontaneously produced by society. The concept of bureaucracy, however, is used in this definition only in the broadest sense to describe any state agency that makes or administers law.

Bureaucratic regulation is always accompanied by other kinds of law that may drastically limit its scope. This pattern may be clearly seen in the great empires of antiquity, perhaps the clearest examples before modern times of societies that produced a body of bureaucratic law. In these imperial states, governmental regulation was usually limited in two ways.[6] On one side, there was custom, which continued to govern much of everyday life. Customary standards might both influence and be influenced by state law, yet they kept their own identity and their own inertia. On the other side, there was a body of sacred law, often in the hands of an independent priesthood. This holy law was shaped by theological precepts over whose content the sovereign frequently had no direct authority.

Take, for example, the way Islamic law distinguished the

areas of custom, sovereign discretion, and sacred law. The sacred law or *shari'a* applied by the *kādīs* differed from the administrative discretion of the princes *(siyāsa).*[7] Similarly, the Hindu sacred law *(dharmaśāstra)* limited the prince's power to issue ordinances *(kṣatra).*[8] In a different way, the Roman *ius civile* acquired its own identity first by freeing itself from, and then by supplanting, the pontifical *fas.* And in the late empire, an ever larger gap appeared between strict law *(ius civile)* and administrative discretion (the emperor's *cognitio extraordinaria).*[9] These contrasts reflected conflicts among priestly bodies, governmental authorities, and merchant groups, but they were also connected with more general tendencies, to be discussed in the next section.

Custom and priestly law, on the one hand, and bureaucratic regulation, on the other, divided the social world into two halves: the first, more or less beyond the prince's command; the second, subject to his almost unlimited discretion. There were societies in which priestly law prevailed over bureaucratic rule, and at least one empire, the Chinese, in which no important body of sacred precepts ever eluded governmental control. In the West, a unique balance between divine law and princely discretion was to develop, with decisive consequences for the history of legal ideas and institutions.

There is a third and still narrower concept of law. We shall see that far from being common to all kinds of societies, it appeared and survives only under very special circumstances. It may be called the legal order or legal system. Law as legal order is committed to being general and autonomous as well as public and positive.

Autonomy has a substantive, an institutional, a methodological, and an occupational aspect. Law is autonomous in a substantive sense when the rules formulated and enforced by government cannot be persuasively analyzed as a mere restatement of any identifiable set of nonlegal beliefs or norms, be they economic, political, or religious. More specifically, an autonomous legal system does not codify a particular theology. As a body of profane rules, it stands apart from the precepts that govern man's relationship to God and from any single religion's view of social relations. Law is institutionally autonomous to the extent that its rules are applied by specialized institutions whose main task is adjudication. Thus, the distinction between state and society is complemented by a contrast within the state itself among legislation, administration, and adjudication. Law is autonomous at the methodological level when the ways in which these specialized institutions justify their acts differ from the kinds of justification used in other disciplines or practices. This means that legal reasoning has a method or style to differentiate it from scientific explanation and from moral, political, and economic discourse. Lastly, the legal order is characterized by occupational autonomy. A special group, the legal profession, defined by its activities, prerogatives, and training, manipulates the rules, staffs the legal institutions, and engages in the practice of legal argument.[10]

Substantive, institutional, methodological, and occupational autonomy are interdependent. Moreover, taken together, they give a special significance to the ideal of generality in lawmaking and of uniformity in the application of law. Bureaucratic law may consist either of rules with a wide scope or of commands addressed to situations narrowly defined in space and time. But a legal order differs from politics and administration precisely because of its attachment to the aims of generality in legislation and of uniformity in adjudication. The laws are expected to address broadly defined categories of individuals and acts and to be applied without personal or class favoritism. Whereas generality can never be more than a matter of expedience in bureaucratic law, it acquires special significance in the context of a legal system. For it is the generality of law that establishes the formal equality of the citizens and thereby shields them from the arbitrary tutelage of government. Administration must be separated from legislation to ensure generality; adjudication must be distinguished from administration to safeguard uniformity. These two contrasts represent the core of the rule of law ideal.[11] Through them, the legal system is supposed to become the balance wheel of social organization.

The legal order emerged with modern European liberal society. The distinction between politics or administration, on one side, and adjudication, on the other, became the cornerstone of constitutionalism and a guiding principle of political thought. In the liberal state, there is a separate body of legal norms, a system of specialized legal institutions, a well-defined tradition of legal doctrine, and a legal profession with its own relatively unique outlook, interests, and ideals. It is important to understand that a legal order operates against the backdrop of customary and bureaucratic law and that the differences among the types of law always remain fluid.

Thus, regulatory law persists in the liberal state in the form of policy decisions or administrative commands. These decisions or commands may be limited in scope by the legal order, but they are not themselves administered by specialized legal institutions or developed and applied within a framework of distinctively legal doctrine. On the contrary, the agencies responsible for making and applying them are part of the general administrative or political staff of the state, and the logic by which they are justified and criticized is drawn from the available fund of modes of political argument. We shall see later that the relationship between bureaucratic regulation and the legal order is a wonderfully revealing sign of social change.

Customary law persists in the patterns of interactional expectations and usages on which the legal order relies and

inadequate and misleading. Taken together, they compensate for each other's deficiencies.

Is there a feature of social consciousness that, without being common to all societies, provides an indispensable support for the conception of social life within which it makes sense to distinguish state from society? Perhaps this key belief is the notion that social relations are and ought to be an object of human will. Such a conception contrasts with the earlier and more universal idea of society as the expression of an order that men do not and ought not control. On the contrary, each person sees himself as a barely differentiated part of a larger natural and social whole, which has its own rhythms and requirements. Hence, the normative order must be intrinsic to the constitution of society rather than susceptible to fabrication and amendment.

The implications of the view of social life are far-reaching indeed; they explain many of the previously mentioned characteristics of interactional law. When people acknowledge that society has an intrinsic order that is good as well as enduring, it is impossible for them to distinguish meaningfully between understandings of what persons usually do in different social situations and views about what they ought to do. Moreover, because the normative order in the setting of interactional law is at once self-evident and tacit, it need never take the form of rules pronounced and enforced by a specialized set of institutions.

The divorce of state from society, however, presupposes a very different conception of the relationship between normative order and regularities of conduct. The state is defined precisely by its mastery over social relations. The signs and instruments of its preeminence are the public rules it lays down. Insofar as such rules palpably influence social practices, people may come to view these practices as artifacts of human will.

There are two important qualifications to the thesis of

the relationship between the state-society distinction and the idea of society as a creature of will. One qualification, which has already been mentioned, is that, though the state appears as a manipulator of social life in the short run, its character and activities may in a deeper and more distant sense be determined largely by power relationships among groups in the society. Indeed, this fact may be recognized in social consciousness without its destroying the conception that human will can impose its designs upon society. A second qualification is that the new world of governmental law ushered in by the separation of state and society tends to produce a division between a sphere of social life that is sacred and untouchable and one that is subordinated to the sovereign's interests.

The distinction between state and society and the development of rules with the attribute of publicity accompany a change in social organization as well as in social consciousness. This change is the development of the division of labor and the related ordering of society into ever more differentiated ranks (castes, estates, classes). Each rank is defined by a set of inherited positions of access to knowledge, power, and wealth.

The organization of society as a hierarchy of groups has direct implications for the contrast between state and society and for the emergence of public rules.[17] As soon as there is a well-differentiated set of social ranks with varying degrees of power over one another, group relationships are thrown into a permanent, though often latent, instability. The perpetuation of the existing social order and of the forces committed to it requires an agency that will keep the system of ranks intact. The more pervasive relationships of dependency and domination among groups become, the more imperative the need for a state.

Only an entity that somehow stands above the conflicting groups can both limit the powers of all the groups and pretend to the posture of impartiality, impersonality, or providential harmony which sanctions its claim to their allegiance. At the same time, the state must reinforce the relationships of domination and dependence, and the persons who man its agencies must necessarily come from particular ranks. All the basic conflicts that mark the history of the contrast of state and society derive in the end from the paradox implicit in this situation. The state, which is the child of the social hierarchy, must also be its ruler; it must be distinct from any one social group in the system of domination and dependence. Yet it has to draw its staff and its purposes from groups that are part of this system. Whenever either side of the paradox is forgotten, the true relationship between state and society is obscured.

Thus, the development of public rules and of the state-society dichotomy is connected with particular changes in the way society is organized and in individuals' conceptions of social life. The connection will be illustrated, though not proved, in a later section of the chapter by the examples I shall take from Chinese legal history.

The disintegration of community

Bureaucratic law is positive as well as public. The crucial condition for the emergence of positive law is what one might call the disintegration of community. It will be useful to resort once again to the complementary perspectives of social consciousness and social organization.

From the standpoint of consciousness, the disintegration of community means the development of a situation in which one feels increasingly able to question the rightness of accepted practices as well as to violate them. Only then do explicit and formulated rules become possible and necessary. Positive law remains superfluous as long as there is a closely held communion of reciprocal expectations, based on a shared view of right and wrong. In this setting the normative order will not surface as formulated rules; indeed, it may remain almost entirely below the threshold of explicit statement and conscious understanding.

The further one moves away from this hypothetical extreme of moral integration, the more acute the need for made standards to replace tacitly perceived and accepted custom. This process of articulation presupposes a diminution of the extent to which men may be counted on to act in set ways without overt guidance or agreement. On the one hand, they are no longer as sure of what ought and ought not to be done in particular situations of choice. For this reason, positive rules must be laid down to clarify what the disintegration of community has made dark and slippery. On the other hand, there is less of an unreflective allegiance to common moral understandings and, consequently, less of an internalized and self-executing assurance that people will remain faithful to these expectations. Hence, positive rules must on the whole be capable of coercive enforcement by the state. Both aspects of the process may be captured by the statement that the situation described by the consensus-oriented doctrine of social order must lose some of its overpowering hold for the passage from tacit particularistic standards to positive law to occur.[18]

The disintegration of community as a change in consciousness would remain incomprehensible unless one were able to identify its counterpart in the history of social organization. This counterpart is the same tendency toward increasing specialization and hierarchy that seems chiefly responsible for the separation of state from society. It is a trend that erodes the basis for an inclusive set of shared beliefs; once it has taken hold, it will be difficult for relationships among social ranks to rely upon the same community of perceptions and ideals that plays so large a part in the internal life of each of those ranks. If this hypothesis is correct, one should expect to find positive law within a society develop first and most vigorously in the area of intergroup relations and only later and less completely inside groups.

The division of labor and social hierarchy

The appearance of a state and the disintegration of community, which are the bases of bureaucratic law, both depend on a change in social organization. I have defined this change as a pronounced advance in the division of labor together with a broadening of the spectrum of stratification and a hardening of lines within it. The two aspects of the process are interwoven. The individual's place in the hierarchy ordinarily determines how he fits into the division of labor. Thus, the existence of well-defined hereditary social ranks provides automatic criteria for allocating jobs according to their prestige and power. Conversely, job specialization, and the improvements it makes possible in the production, preservation, and exchange of wealth, reinforces social stratification.

But what accounts for these two simultaneous and interdependent trends? One possible explanation focuses on the idea that a social hierarchy helps introduce and support the division of labor. Moreover, the specialization of tasks increases the efficiency of material production and, more generally, the capacity of all kinds of conduct to promote accepted social ends.[19]

An alternative hypothesis connects job specialization with a view of the moral development of mankind. By disrupting earlier forms of kinship-based community or by limiting their influence on social life, specialization and stratification make the individual more aware of his separateness from others.[20] To be sure, within his own social rank, each person may recognize the closeness of the ties of common understandings and values that bind him to the other members of his rank and make him a person similar to them. But, as specialization and stratification progress, men become increasingly able to acknowledge and to assert their apartness from those with jobs or rank positions different from their own.

Moreover, even in the most rigid and comprehensive social hierarchy, there is always some trace of a conflict between the logic of kinship and that of social stratification. Each person belongs to a kinship group that is at least partially distinct from his estate, caste, or class. Insofar as the individual can define his identity by reference to membership in several groups, he has a better chance of perceiving and developing the sense of individuality. His family position provides him with a means with which to begin distinguishing himself from the other members of his rank.

The two possible explanations I have suggested for the tendencies that underlie the movement toward bureaucratic law are complementary rather than inconsistent. Neither can be proved within the limits of this hypothetical argument, yet both are based upon elementary features of human existence. The first relies on the ideas that a system of specialized jobs serves the desire for wealth and power and that a hierarchy based on birth provides a simple way to establish and preserve such a system. The second hypothesis rests on the notion that no form of social life can permanently suppress either the quest for community or the longing for individual self-assertion.

The tension within bureaucratic law

Whatever the reasons for the social changes that explain the development of public and positive rules, bureaucratic law suffers an internal conflict that makes it unstable and leads to its transformation. We can infer from the implications of the state-society dichotomy that public law serves as the device with which the state manipulates social relations. Law becomes a tool of the power interests of the groups that control the state.

At the same time, however, the decline in the scope of men's unconscious perception and fidelity to common standards of conduct endangers the established form of social life. If the normative order is construed as a set of tools with which to satisfy the power interests of the rulers, it will lack any claim to allegiance save the terror by which it is imposed. Moreover, it will fail to satisfy the need of rulers and the governed alike to justify the structure of society by relating it to an image of social and cosmic order. The public and positive rules must therefore also be recognized as inherently authoritative, objective, or necessary rather than as made by the ruler according to his conceptions of what is good for himself or for society at large.

But how can the imperatives of instrumentalism and legitimacy both be satisfied by bureaucratic law? They run, as we have seen, in opposite directions. Insofar as the public and positive rules are regarded as mere devices of state policy, they may be freely replaced whenever the views and interests of the rulers change. If, on the contrary, the laws appear to embody some inherently right or necessary order, they will be treated by both the rulers and the ruled as standards that government cannot or should not disturb.

This dilemma explains why bureaucratic regulation is almost invariably accompanied by a body of religious precepts. The sacred law is viewed as an expression of the true and right order of things and placed beyond government's reach. It provides a framework of legitimacy for social arrangements. The bureaucratic law itself, without any higher support or constraint, is subordinated to the sovereign's view of his own convenience or of the welfare of his subjects. It responds to the promptings of instrumentalism.

I cited earlier the contrast of Koranic law to *siyāsa* and of the Hindu *dharmaśāstra* to the *kṣatra* as cases of the opposition of sacred and bureaucratic law. Another example might be the coexistence of Neo-Confucianist and Legalist influence on the organization, the ideology, and the law of the Chinese imperial state.

Enough has been said to suggest that the antagonism between the sacred and the discretionary element in law poses the problem of the choice between the legitimacy-oriented and the instrumentalist approach to social order. This issue, which at first seemed little more than a methodologist's puzzle, now reappears as a concrete political experience, strongly intimating conflict and change.

THE EMERGENCE OF A LEGAL ORDER

The legal order is a far rarer historical phenomenon than bureaucratic law. Indeed, it may be impossible to find a single telling example of it outside the modern Western liberal state. Other civilizations that at first seem to possess a legal system turn out, on closer inspection, not to have one. Two kinds of historical conditions give rise to the rule of law.

The first set of conditions describes an experience and a view of group relations. For a legal order to develop, there must be a situation in which no group occupies a permanently dominant position or is credited with an inherent right to govern. Such a relationship among groups might be called liberal society or, in the more graphic language of contemporary American political science, interest group pluralism. The second aspect of the historical background of a legal system is reliance on a "higher" universal or divine law as a standard by which to justify and to criticize the positive law of the state.

Group pluralism

What kinds of relationships among social groups and what sorts of perceptions of society are needed for a legal system to appear? These conditions of organization and consciousness must differ from the ones that account for the development of bureaucratic law.

The laws of imperial bureaucratic states like the ancient Chinese may have had certain features of universalism and specialization which made them superficially similar to the legal systems that emerged in postfeudal Europe.[21] It is also true that the degree of generality and autonomy characteristic of the actual operation of legal institutions in modern Western societies falls far short of what the prevailing political theories demand. Nevertheless, differences remain between bureaucratic law and legal order, as well as between the kinds of society that correspond to each of them. Though these distinctions may seem subtle at first, and more qualities of doctrine than features of practice, they color every aspect of social life.

The commands of the sovereign in systems of bureaucratic law often take the form of rules applicable to very general categories of persons and acts. But this will simply be a generality of political expedience, a way to get things done most effectively. It may and will be violated whenever the considerations of administrative efficiency that led to its adoption point the other way. In other words, there are no commitments to generality in lawmaking and to uniformity in adjudication that must be kept regardless of their consequences for the political interests of the rulers. Bureaucratic law may also have traces of substantive, methodological, institutional, or occupational autonomy. But these will be incidental, for they will arise from the tendency of institutions and of the groups that staff them to develop their own orientations rather than from basic features of the way society is organized and perceived.

There does, however, exist a form of social life, which may be called liberal society or group pluralism, whose very nature predisposes men to struggle for the rule of law ideal at the same time that it keeps them from fully achieving this ideal. In such a situation, legal generality and autonomy are no longer simply unintended consequences of the development of government; they are necessary concomitants of the effort to order society and to distribute power in a way that can be justified or at least widely tolerated. After sketching some general characteristics of liberal society, I shall advance a hypothesis about the particular way in which group pluralism contributed to the emergence of a legal order in modern Europe.

A liberal society is one in which there is a structure of group, and specifically of class, domination, a structure not sufficiently stable and comprehensive to win the spontaneous allegiance of its members. The social hierarchy is too volatile and uncertain, too open to changes of rank, and too vulnerable to political attack to be accepted as part of the natural order of things. Thus, paradoxically, the weaker the structure of domination becomes, the stronger the felt need to justify and to limit what remains of it.

Earlier I discussed the sense in which the rise of social stratification helps fracture the experience of community. It might therefore seem that any weakening of hierarchy would automatically increase the opportunities for consensus. But this is not so. A comprehensive system of ranks may not be able to sustain the same level of cohesion among the sentiments and perceptions of different individuals that characterizes a nonstratified society. But it also could not survive and operate unless it were identified with a preexisting moral order that gave it legitimacy. The less stable and precise the hierarchy becomes, the less it can count on being unthinkingly accepted as part of the way things are. Thus, the experience of having a hierarchy and then losing it seems more likely to aggravate than to diminish moral conflict.

The liberal type of social organization generates, and is

reinforced by, a style of consciousness whose substance is the image of society as an arena of conflicting subjective interests. The disintegration of a well-defined hierarchy and of the related sentiment of a natural moral order contributes to the view that in the final analysis values are a matter of arbitrary choice. The awareness of the fluidity of all social bonds encourages people to believe that all interests are ultimately individual interests and that the good of the group is simply an amalgam of the ends entertained by its individual members.

This way of organizing and perceiving society has revolutionary implications for law. Liberal society cannot resolve its problem of social order through the mere imposition of bureaucratic law; it is a form of life in which no one group is able to command for long the loyalty and the obedience of all other groups. Thus, it becomes important to devise a system of law whose content somehow accommodates antagonistic interests and whose procedures are such that most everyone might find it in his own interest to subscribe to them regardless of the ends he happens to seek.

Such a system will characteristically be expected to prevent any class of persons from imposing a dictatorship on all other classes. But beyond this most general objective, the system will constantly be pulled in two opposite directions. The more powerful segments of society will expect the legal order to preserve existing inequalities by selectively protecting private activity from governmental interference. The less advantaged classes may want to use the law as a means with which to circumscribe, and eventually to subvert, the influence of private as well as of government power.

One possible response to these competing demands is the creation of a legal order with the attributes of generality and autonomy. Rules and procedures that cut across distinctions of class and rank lay a claim to everyone's allegiance. They might be said to represent, over the long run, that universal interest which consists of the accommodation of all particular interests. The obligation of government to act under law seems to limit the capacity of officeholders to turn public power to private use or to employ it as a weapon of personal oppression. It reconciles a minimum of freedom and security with the existence of broad differences among individuals in their access to wealth, power, and knowledge. The interpretation of these laws by specialized institutions, manned by a relatively independent professional group, steeped in its own craft and techniques of argument, guarantees that the persons whose power the law is designed to restrain will not be the ones to determine, in the final instance, its meaning.

In the next chapter, I shall return to these themes in greater detail and elaborate further the theoretical analysis I have begun to sketch here. But for the moment my concern is a different one. The argument thus far has emphasized issues of legitimacy or justification instead of the actual struggle for power among social groups. It has shown why a legal order is necessary rather than how it comes into being. The way to correct these deficiencies is to focus on the particular form group pluralism assumed in postfeudal Europe. For this was the age in which the legal order first came into its own. The decisive event was the success of established aristocracies or of an emergent "third estate," composed of merchant and professional groups, in preserving or acquiring a measure of independence from the monarchs and their staffs. Were it not for this success, however limited and transitory, the rule of law ideal might never have won its preeminent place in the modern West.

The method I shall use to draw out the significance of this event for the development of legal systems will be the hypothetical reconstruction of interests. My aim is to establish what the predominant orientation of a group to a certain issue would be, given its structure and its beliefs: what it would have reason to hope for and to fear. Then I shall compare the results of the hypothetical inquiry with what in fact is known about the ways such groups dealt with the issue in various historical settings. This procedure represents one of the temporary bridges that may be thrown across the abyss which separates general theorizing about society from the understanding of particular occurrences.

If the rulers of a state are only a handful of individuals—a monarch and his family or advisers—they have an interest in the development of regulatory law. By means of public and positive rules, coercively enforced, they can hope to control the lives of vast numbers of persons throughout extended territories, and with considerable continuity over time. Most important, such laws can become tools for the organization of bureaucracies, setting out guidelines that ensure the execution of the sovereign's policies and providing for the internal arrangement of his staff.

But the ruler has no immediate or apparent interest in allowing himself or his servants to be bound by the constraints on government action implied in the rule of law ideal. He will want to treat generality in lawmaking and uniformity in adjudication as mere expedients of administrative efficiency, to be set aside whenever, on an enlightened view of long-term political advantages, they seem inconvenient. Similarly, the sovereign is likely to regard the rules he promulgates more as an imposition of his own policies than as a balancing of the beliefs and wants of different groups. He will be wary of tendencies on the part of his staff to assert their institutional autonomy from him and to employ methods of decision that threaten to limit the free play of his discretion.

Indeed, the bureaucracy itself, jealous of its own prerogatives, fights a war on two fronts: anxious to extend its control over the populace, it also wants to gain some independence from the prince. How can it be expected to show anything but hostility to the emergence of a legal order? The rule of law imposes constraints on the powers of administrators as well as on those of the prince. And a specialized legal profession is a bureaucracy in the wings; its very existence breaks up the bureaucracy's monopoly on government.

Thus, a hypothetical reconstruction of the interests of the rulers and their staffs fails to suggest any reason that might have led away from bureaucratic law toward the distinctive ideals of a legal order. This conclusion is consistent with the puzzling fact that the rule of law, unlike bureaucracies, is a rare phenomenon which appears and survives only under very special conditions.

In modern European history, the centralizing princes had to contend repeatedly with at least two other influential groups: the aristocracy and the third estate. There were countries in which the aristocracy was first transformed and then merged with segments of the middle class (England). And there were societies in which a large part of the third estate was absorbed into the service of the monarch (prerevolutionary France, Prussia). Indeed, in some periods of absolutism, the monarchs came close to stamping out entirely both aristocratic and third estate opposition. But wherever the rule of law idea was upheld, the aristocracy, the third estate, or both together played an important role in circumscribing princely power either by securing government recognition of their rights or by participating directly in government themselves. Thus, in Russia, where the tsar's personal absolutism crushed every sign of independence, the idea of a legal order was to remain, even after Speransky's initiatives and the later 1864 reforms, the largely unfulfilled aspiration of a handful of liberals.[22]

Yet it is not easy to understand the precise way in which the struggle among the monarchy, the aristocracy, and the third estate generated a legal order. For, viewed as separate groups, noblemen and merchants had no more reason to favor the rule of law than did princes and their bureaucrats.

A nobility's major concern is to defend its ancient prerogatives from incursions by other groups. It wants to protect the social privileges and the political rights that accompany its position in the social hierarchy. The traditional principles and practices that establish these entitlements have many of the features associated with custom: they are implicit and unwritten, and they precede any official authorization. Moreover, they are by their very nature contrary to the spirit of formal equality which a legal order must embody, for they belong to a form of social life in which each rank has its own unique rights and duties. So it is not surprising to find that no purely feudal or aristocratic society has ever developed a legal system in the modern Western sense.

The third estate in general and merchant groups in particular would have equally little reason to support the rule of law. It has often been said that one of the factors on which the development of exchange relationships in a market economy depends is the businessman's capacity to trade against a background of established usage and law that allows him to calculate, with some degree of certainty and precision, the economic consequences of violating or keeping his agreements. Market rationality cannot be squared with a situation in which merchants are unable to predict how government power will be used to affect their transactions and their assets.[23] The need for explicit and clear-cut standards is all the more urgent when capitalism develops, as it did in Europe, in the setting of traditional moral standards and religious beliefs that condemn the kind of conduct it requires. For example, exchange value must replace customary prices, and the prohibition against usury must be swept away to allow for the unhampered exercise of the profit motive.[24]

Nevertheless, none of this suffices to explain why merchant groups would make or support legal systems. With sufficient independence from the state to regulate their own affairs, and enough concentration of commercial activity within their own communities, they would have no reason to settle for a law developed by government bureaucracies and government courts. Far better for them to rely as much as possible on rules, tribunals, and informal controls set up within the commercial groups themselves. This merchant law has a better chance of being substantively responsive to the needs of trade than principles laid down by remote rulers and applied by learned judges. And the outcomes of decisions made by merchant tribunals are more likely to be comprehensible to businessmen and predictable by them than any that can be expected from an arcane method of legal analysis or from the balancing of antagonistic social interests by lawyers.

Once again, the hypothetical conclusion agrees with a well-established historical tendency. Wherever merchant communities sprung up and won even a limited degree of independence from central governments—in medieval Europe or the Islamic world, in Japan or in the Mediterranean civilization of Graeco-Roman antiquity—they struggled to develop their own associations and their own law alongside the bureaucratic law of the state.[25] Only in modern Europe did the breakthrough occur that made it possible to fuse the two bodies of law into a legal order that differed from both its parents.

Thus, the interests of rulers and their staffs, of aristocracies, and of the third estate are all insufficient to account for the attempt to institutionalize the rule of law. To find a satisfactory explanation, one must discard the static analysis of the outlooks and interests of different social groups in isolation and move toward a dynamic view of the way these groups reacted and adjusted to one another in the course of their fight for power.

In many of the European societies, the rulers and the third estate jointly opposed the aristocracy and the estate system itself, besides being in competition with one another. Indeed, the very appearance of a relatively powerful middle class may be viewed as a consequence of the fact that political centralization was not sufficiently rapid and extensive to crush the aristocracy before professional and commercial groups had had time to flourish in the interstices of the dissolving feudal order. In some Western European countries, the monarchs were not powerful enough to destroy completely the independence of the third estate, whereas the latter was often too weak to secure or to preserve self-government of its own interests. Moreover, both the prince and the third estate were frequently forced to make concessions to the nobility. All parties to the conflict had to opt for second best, and the liberal state was founded on compromise, more evenly struck in some countries than in others, among monarchic bureaucracy, aristocratic privilege, and middle class interest. This compromise had crucial implications for law.

Princes and bureaucrats may have wanted not to be subject to the vigilance of a watchful judiciary in the administration of the laws nor committed to a program of group accommodation in lawmaking. But, for the reasons previously enumerated, they could not dispense with a system of public and positive rules. Aristocracies may have preferred to maintain their unwritten constitution rather than to come under a legal order that undermined the differences between their privileges and the entitlements of other ranks. But they could not afford to be deprived of legal protection against the princes. Middle class groups may have preferred some variety of self-regulation to the formalities of the rule of law. But, in view of their economic and political interests, they needed safeguards from the ruler's whim at a time when they had not yet themselves become masters of the state. At the least, a wall, though often a winding and transparent one, had to protect the market from politics and the private citizen from personal subordination to the officeholder: this wall was the legal system.

Rulers had to sacrifice a parcel of their discretion and the aristocracies and the third estates a measure of their desired independence from government. Through this reciprocal conciliation and surrender, the legal order was born. When we study the events that produced legal systems in Europe— the struggles between courts and ministries, between juristic technique and remorseless statecraft, between efforts to submit government to society or to subject the latter to the former—we encounter the signs and stages of this process. For all parties concerned, the rule of law, like life insurance and like liberalism itself, was an attempt to make the best of a bad situation.

Natural law

A second major condition for the emergence of a legal order is a widespread belief in what might loosely be called natural law. Natural law consists of principles that combine prescription with description and apply universally to all societies. It has some of the features of custom: a disregard for the fact-value distinction and a claim not to be a product of human deliberation. Yet it differs from custom in the generality of its formulation, in the universality of its alleged scope of application, and in the scholarly or religious character of the authority upon which it is based.

The natural law idea was a major source of the concept of explanatory scientific laws.[26] Its immediate political significance, however, was its capacity to provide a universalist standard by which to evaluate state law and to restrict government.

One possible origin of the conception of a higher law is the experience of cultural diversity. Thus, in fifth-century Greece men came to realize that societies which could not easily be dismissed as primitive cherished different and even conflicting customs. This shattering discovery provoked a search for universal principles of conduct, based upon human nature, that might underlie the variety of customs and serve as criteria for their assessment. The philosophic doctrines fashioned in the course of the quest for these overarching norms were used by Roman lawyers to develop the *ius gentium*. The intimate links of this common law of mankind to natural law doctrines as well as to mercantile needs are well known, though their precise nature remains in dispute.

Another support for natural law notions is transcendent religiosity. Since this factor seems to have been uniquely important in the development of modern legal ideas and institutions, it will be the focus of my discussion of the relationship between natural law and legal order.

The core of a religion of transcendence is the belief that the world was created by a personal God according to His designs.[27] The characteristic dichotomy of transcendent religion is that between God and the world. Because the world was made, rather than generated, it does not fully share the sacred or divine nature of its author. Nevertheless, the lawful universe betrays the hand of a divine lawgiver.

This image stands in clear-cut opposition to modern, antinomian denials of the existence of harmony in nature. But it is also antagonistic to much Chinese, Hindu or Buddhist, and Greek cosmology, which holds that there is an inherent but uncreated pattern in the world. For these views, the fundamental contrast is between the reality of order and the illusion of chaos, the world of hidden truth and the world of appearance, rather than the typical transcendent division of heaven and earth. The Chinese conception of *tao,* the Buddhist dualism of *sunyata* and *miasma,* and the Platonic dichotomy of the science of "ideas" and the war of "opinions" exemplify this simple and powerful doctrine.

Almost always the religions of transcendence have been religions of salvation. By this I mean that they have added to the basic dogma of the divine creation of the world at least two other theological commitments: the belief that all men have an immortal soul made in the image of God, which is distinct though not necessarily separable from the body, and the notion that God deals with mankind in history and makes it possible for at least some of its members to live in His presence forever.[28] Semitic monotheism, represented by Judaism, Christianity, and Islam, is the source and the bearer of this view of the world. But in all these religions there has always been an undercurrent reassertion of immanence, particularly strong in Christian mysticism, the Jewish kabbalah, and Islamic Sufism.

It has often been claimed that transcendent religions in general and salvation religions in particular constitute a stage in the religious evolution of mankind. It might be more accurate to dispense with evolutionary language and to say that some societies seem to remain more or less alien to the transcendent aspect of religion: either they fail to develop it at all, or they assign it a subordinate place.

There is a close connection between such a religiosity and the beliefs or institutions that sustain a legal system. Once we understand the character of this connection, we shall be able to deepen our insight into the more general relationship between types of consciousness and ways of organizing society.

A transcendent religion is both an outlook and a cluster of institutions, rituals, and differentiated groups. Like all things social, it exists both in the mind and in behavior. So I begin by discussing the influence it has exercised on law as a belief. Then I turn to its importance as ritual and institution.

One link between the legal order and the cosmology of transcendent religions is suggested by the concept of law itself. The idea of regularities in nature and in social life is an integral part of the belief that God has made the world according to a plan. Moreover, it does not seem to have arisen except in societies in which this belief was widespread.

The doctrine of the government of the world by divine law may represent an extrapolation to the cosmos of the more ancient picture of the human ruler governing his people according to his commands.[29] But once the transition from human to godly law takes place, the conception of human law can never again be the same. Society must now be seen as part of a cosmic order and its rules as more or less faithful imitations and conclusions of laws laid down in heaven. These divine precepts preexist any act of human will. They both describe what happens and establish what ought to be; they override the difference between description and prescription. Moreover, they hold good for different societies and ages because the heavenly lawmaker stands above and apart from time. Thus, there is a higher or natural law distinct from, and superior to, the customs of particular social groups and the commands of earthly sovereigns. Human positive law makes the abstract dictates of the higher law concrete or adapts them to the peculiar conditions of each society.

This view of the relationship between natural and positive law has crucial implications for the autonomy and the generality of the legal order. Because the higher law derives from a divine source and therefore cuts across space and time, it serves as an Archimedean point from which all social arrangements can be evaluated. It is neither a set of particularistic standards of interaction gradually forged in daily life nor a series of commands handed down by a ruler to deal with more or less specific situations. Instead, it is a normative order that transcends society altogether, just as God transcends the world.

Thanks to the invention of the natural law idea, radical criticism of social arrangements becomes possible for the first time. With the idea of a universal law of nature, a potentially revolutionary principle is born; namely, familiar kinds of organization and existence do not exhaust the varieties of good or possible states of social existence. In order to accept the cosmology of the transcendent religions and the related conception of a higher law, men must commit themselves to standards whose validity is universal and objective rather than a product of their own wills.[30]

Insofar as human law seeks to participate in the character of the higher normative order, it too must be represented as relatively autonomous from the desires of human sovereigns and from the customs of particular societies. It should take account of those desires and customs only as aids in the task of interpreting in each unique historical situation what ought to be made of the more or less abstract laws of nature. Thus, the belief in the existence of God-given standards of conduct may sustain the conviction that the more perfect positive law becomes by approaching its heavenly model, the less it should be determined by the practices of each time or place. Its rules ought to have a measure of critical independence from politics and custom; this independence requires specialized institutions, occupational groups, and modes of discourse. Hence, the way is open for a type of social consciousness that accepts the rule of law ideal.

Transcendent religion also contributes to the extraordinary significance the ideal of generality has for a legal system. Because natural laws are believed to apply to all countries and periods, the precepts they dictate must be addressed to very broadly defined categories of persons and acts. Therefore, generality in stating the rules of positive law and uniformity in applying them serve as a testimonial of fidelity to the higher law rather than as mere administrative convenience. No wonder that the effort to give content to the nebulous conceptions of generality and uniformity should become a major concern of political and legal thought.

Unless the theology of the salvation religions draws distinctions between the elect and the damned, it will tend to assert that all individuals have an equality of essential worth derived from the universal fatherhood of God. This theological doctrine undermines the legitimacy of every system of rules that determines an individual's entitlements and duties on the basis of membership in a social rank. In this sense, it places an extraordinary emphasis on the generality of the laws. Nevertheless, the political and the legal meaning of the religious notion of equal worth is irremediably ambiguous. Its ambiguity brings out the double-edged character of the commitment to generality in law.

On one interpretation, an abstract generality satisfies the ideal of equal worth. The fewer the distinctions the law makes among categories of persons or acts, the greater the respect shown for the ideal of equal worth. Men with similar duties and entitlements under the same rules have been recognized as equals even though their actual social experiences and their degrees of access to power and wealth may differ sharply. Thus, equal worth turns into formal equality.

On another interpretation, however, the moral equality of individuals requires an equalization of their actual social circumstances. To achieve substantive equality, one may have to treat people who are in different situations differently; to give, for example, prerogatives to disfavored groups. Differential treatment of this kind represents a departure from the ideal of formal equality, and it goes against the conception of generality which this ideal implies. The importance of the double meaning of equality and generality will become evident in Chapter Three. For now, we may take it as simply a qualification of the thesis that religious notions of equality lead to an emphasis on formally equal treatment under general rules.

Up to this point, I have suggested relationships between transcendent religions as a mode of consciousness and the beliefs that make a legal order possible. Now let me complete the discussion by pointing out how the institutionalized forms these religions adopt bear on the emergence of legal systems.

The religion of transcendence depends on the availability of institutions capable of maintaining its unity and thereby of safeguarding its survival. Its dogmas must be authoritatively established and propagated. From this need to mediate God's word to mankind there arises both the quest for some kind of stable church organization and the possibility of prophecy.

The prophet articulates God's word. His posture of critical independence vis-à-vis established political and ecclesiastic authority is an outward form of that appeal from historical actuality to divine ideal which the transcendent view opens up to the religious imagination. The conflict between the revolutionary threat posed by prophecy and the stabilizing concerns of the priesthood is, as Weber pointed out, an essential and recurring tension in the history of the salvation religions.[31]

The ecclesiastic institutions and the priesthood or learned men who administer them provide the framework that keeps the religious community together, suppressing the heresies that might tear it apart. What is more significant for our purposes, they systematize the divine commandments. Thus arranged and interpreted by a specialized priesthood, natural law becomes a well-defined body of sacred law. It is to this body of sacred law and to the institutions, methods, and beliefs which support it that we must often look for an understanding of the secular legal system. As a background to this system and as a source of many of its distinctive features, the sacred law surpasses earlier kinds of lawmaking. It is the most common example of an organized body of positive law, distinct from the implicit standards of custom as well as from the more or less discretionary commands of bureaucratic regulation.

The Islamic *sharī'a,* the Hindu *dharmaśāstra,* the Jewish *halakhah,* and even the Roman *fas* illustrate the extraordinary stability and influence of bodies of priestly law, associated or not with a transcendent religion. In most of these cases, however, the sacred law was never made the basis of a secular legal system with the characteristics of autonomy and generality; it never freed itself from its complete identification with religion and its dependence on the priesthood. Instead, it continued to develop alongside a more or less distinct sphere of bureaucratic law that was concerned with matters different from those the sacred precepts addressed and responded solely to the ruler's sense of expediency. Only in the modern West did a system of law develop that assigned duties and entitlements to individuals regardless of their social ranks. This law was thought to rest upon a basis of God-given natural principles from which it was nevertheless distinct by virtue of its secular character.

Thus, though the religion of transcendence may have been a necessary condition of the autonomous legal system, laying the bases for its underlying mode of consciousness, it cannot have been sufficient. One needs to consider the social and the theological factor together, the circumstances of the liberal state as well as the implications of the transcendent religion, to grasp how and why the legal system came into existence. There was both complementarity and tension in the interplay of the two elements.

What happens when the positive rules of the state lose all touch with a higher law and come to be seen as nothing more than the outcomes of a power struggle? Can the ideals of autonomy and generality in law survive the demise of the religious beliefs that presided over their birth? And is the legal system, perhaps, a transitory characteristic of societies in which the divine and the political order are separated yet not wholly estranged from one another?

Liberal society and higher law

Neither group pluralism nor the belief in higher law, justified by a transcendent religion, would have been enough by itself to produce a legal order and to turn men's minds toward the rule of law ideal. But their combination in modern

European history could bring about what either of them alone was powerless to create.

Left to itself, a theology of transcendence may assert that the sacred laws are independent from politics and custom. But it has no reason to carry this autonomy to the extreme by proclaiming the separation of law from religion and morals and fostering the creation of secular courts and of a secular legal profession. Indeed, when positive law remains simply a sacred code in the hands of a priesthood, it may suffer from a rigidity that keeps it from serving as a medium through which compromises among antagonistic social interests can be struck.

Interest group pluralism, if devoid of any conception of universal law or inherent right, need not generate a desire for the rule of law as a solution to the problem of social order. It may suggest instead a preference for a regime that operates through flexible balances of interest, without distinguishing administration from legislation, or adjudication from administration. Under such a regime, there may be no restraints on the power of the majority and no conception of formal equality as desirable in itself. Only considerations of administrative efficiency will limit the particularism of official decisions; every problem, no matter how concrete, may in principle be resolved according to the balance of political forces at the moment.

But when the effects of a transcendent religious consciousness and of a pluralism of groups converge, they can temper each other. The liberal state needs a law sufficiently secular to reflect changing social values and power relations. It presupposes that no one group in the society has a privileged access to religious and moral truth. And, insofar as it is accompanied by a market economy, it requires the abolition of anticommercial prohibitions of a religious sort.

The belief in a higher divine law, especially when associated with the idea of equality before God, holds positive law to a universalist standard. And it sets boundaries to majoritarian choice by lending support to the notion that there are entitlements no political decision ought to disregard.

The classic philosophical synthesis in the West of these two sets of imperatives was the modern doctrine of natural right and the related theory of "public natural law."[32] The natural right doctrine made room for the transcendent element in European civilization through its emphasis on the existence of universal entitlements and rules superior to state power. Yet it also acknowledged the implications of social pluralism, for it came to conceive of natural rights as powers of the individual to act within a sphere of absolute discretion, rather than as entitlements to definite substantive goods. This in turn led to the view that right consisted less of a particular set of social arrangements than of a process for conflict resolution, a view which was to become the core of much Western political and legal thought.

The natural rights synthesis was eventually undone by the contradictions that had vitiated it from the start. Its transcendent, religious aspect demanded that rules be universal and fixed. Its pluralist, secular side required them to be as particularist and flexible as interest balancing might warrant. The former pressed toward the sanctification of law as a realm beyond politics; the latter toward the complete secularization of law as a set of rules whose making and application were wholly at the mercy of judgments about how to achieve desired political objectives.

This tension manifested itself within the system of natural rights in the form of an ambiguity in the concept of right itself. Were the principles that justified fundamental entitlements divine precepts that could suffer no derogation? Or were they, on the contrary, prudent guides that suggested how society should be ordered to attain certain accepted human ends, but should be modified whenever those ends changed or better means were discovered for their achievement?

Even when the natural right doctrine was divested of its religious legitimacy and was succeeded by a positivist insistence on state law as the source of all entitlements, the ambiguity contained in the classical synthesis lived on in a different form. Modern jurisprudence viewed law as a system of rules that conferred stable entitlements and obligations on individuals. Nevertheless, it also increasingly accepted the notion that the meaning of a rule, and hence the scope of a right, must be determined by a decision about how best to achieve the purposes attributed to the rule. But all such purposive judgments are inherently particularistic and unstable: the most effective means to any given end varies from situation to situation, and the purposes themselves are likely to be complex and shifting. Though the encounter of liberal state pluralism with transcendent religiosity contributed to the rule of law ideal, the tension between them was ultimately to compromise the coherence of that ideal and the stability of the institutions that embodied it.

THE CHINESE CASE: A COMPARATIVE ANALYSIS

The hypothesis

The framework I have outlined suggests the beginnings of an answer to the question of why legal orders developed in modern Europe and, more precisely, in modern Europe alone, until taken from there to other parts of the world. We have seen how this new type of normative order was bound up with a unique and coherent way of comprehending the world and of organizing social relations. Two deep features of this historical situation were the breakdown of stable hierarchical relations among social ranks and the view of nature and society as handiworks of God that had become separate or hidden from Him.

Thus, the effort to discover the historical foundations of the legal order forces us to clarify our ideas about the most basic features of the society within which the rule of law took shape. In other civilizations we find social changes that resulted in a certain pluralism of groups or in the assertion of a transcendent view of the world, a view often accompanied by the elaboration of systematic bodies of sacred law. Nowhere else, however, did the two elements coalesce completely and produce through their interaction the modern rule of law.

We could both test and refine this initial hypothesis if we found a civilization that for some time remained alien to the rule of law ideal and contented itself with bureaucratic law. In such a society we would expect to discover the separation of state and society and the disintegration of earlier forms of community, factors that explain the development of bodies of public, positive law. But we would not anticipate the kinds of social order and of belief associated with the liberal state and transcendent religion.

The civilization I have in mind is the Chinese, particularly in the era that goes from the onset of the Spring and Autumn period to the Ch'in unification and the foundation of the imperial state in 221 B.C. Here we seem to have a society that experienced a sudden growth of its reliance on public and positive rules as devices of political control. Moreover, an intense and continuing debate took place between the proponents and the critics of this new tool of social order. Yet the turn to bureaucratic law was not followed by the emergence of specialized courts, lawyers, and legal doctrines analogous to those of postfeudal Europe. And even the defenders of coercively enforced state rules would have nothing to do with the political ideal of the rule of law. Thus, the comparison with China, as a contrast case, promises to deepen our insight into the complex relationship among modes of social organization, types of consciousness, and forms of normative order.

My comparison will be worked out through three stages of analysis. First, I shall consider the characteristics of a period of Chinese history in which public, positive rules (law as regulation) seem to have had little importance. Next I shall suggest the relationship between an emphasis on positive and public rules and changes in the way society was perceived and ordered. This will also serve as an occasion to examine the absence in China of the conditions of an authentic legal order. The third step of the inquiry will be to show how the issue of the social and cultural presuppositions of different kinds of law was brought out in the debate between two schools of thought during this period of Chinese history—the Confucianists and the Legalists.

Custom and "feudalism" in early China

My comparative discussion starts with a contrast between two periods in the history of ancient China. Following a convention, one may term the first period feudal, even though the implied analogy with European feudalism is in many respects inaccurate. This era covered most of the so-called Western Chou (1122–771 B.C.) and part of the succeeding Spring and Autumn (722–464 B.C.), perhaps until around the mid-sixth century B.C. The second epoch may be named the transformation period because it witnessed changes in social organization and belief that produced an extensive revision of the society's normative order. The nature and the implications of the change should be our main concerns. The transformation period began toward the middle of the Spring and Autumn, and it included the succeeding Chan Kuo or

Warring States (463–222 B.C.), until the Ch'in unification in 221 B.C. laid the immediate basis for the imperial state.

In contrasting and comparing these two periods of social history, one can hope to avoid most of the controversies that plague the literature and to focus on the main outlines of standard interpretations. The issue is what we can make of these interpretations if we take them for granted. The aspects of the feudal period most important to an understanding of its typical kind of law are its political organization, the relationship among the social ranks that characterized it, and the religious vision that predominated.[33]

There is dispute in contemporary Sinology about how long political centralization lasted following the beginning of the Western Chou in the twelfth century B.C. But most scholars are agreed that by the start of the Spring and Autumn a form of political order that may loosely be described as feudal was firmly established in China. Thus, there was a large number of hereditary fiefs that expanded as warfare led to territorial concentration. Unable to establish an effective system of political organization or to defend himself against semibarbarian invaders, the king was reduced to a symbolic ruler. The tenants-in-chief who triumphed in the ensuing power struggle became his *pa* or prime ministers.

Fiefs were organized around fortresses that served as both military strongholds and administrative capitals. It is important to note, however, that they were not primarily trade centers and that they lacked any measure of independence. On the contrary, each fortress town was under the control of the local aristocracy and its fate inseparable from that of the fief of which the town was a part.

Feudal organization was set against the background of an extractive agricultural economy, on which the needs for irrigation and defense had already begun to exert a centralizing influence, and of a relatively stylized form of warfare conducted by the noble overlords and their *shih* (knightly) retainers. To grasp how the political order worked, we must consider the second aspect of the feudal period, its rank system.

As in European feudal society and *Ständestaaten,* two broad categories were sharply distinguished: noblemen *(chün tzu)* and commoners *(hsiao jen).* The noblemen were the imperial family, the tenants-in-chief, who as the dominant group in the social order controlled the large fiefdoms, and the *shih* class. The *shih* were comparable to the knights of Western Europe, the *samurai* of Tokugawa Japan, and the *equites* of early Republican Rome, but they probably had even less independence than the first group and assuredly less than the latter two. Nevertheless, they were to play a decisive part in the changes that marked the transformation period.[34]

For our purposes, it is enough to remember that the *chün tzu* were organized internally along hierarchical and hereditary lines. Whether clan organization strictly defined was pervasive or limited to sinicized groups is a matter of debate. But there can be no doubt of the overriding importance of kinship as a criterion for the distribution of wealth and power and as a support for the cult of the family virtues of filial piety, deference, and group harmony.

Below the noblemen stood the mass of commoners, mostly landless serfs who worked in exchange for food and clothing. Little is known about the nature and extent of slavery, but it seems to have become increasingly used as punishment for the condemned and the defeated.

A critical feature of this social system, closely related to the absence of independent urban centers and to the prevalence of agriculture, was the distinctly subordinate position occupied by merchants. Whereas in medieval Europe towns often became the preserve of self-governing commercial groups, in China such groups remained subject to the noblemen.

This preparatory sketch of Chinese feudal society may now be completed with a reference to the typical modes of religious belief. In this as in later periods of Chinese history, one can distinguish four main categories of religious experience: the universal deity, whose adoration was closely connected with the state cult; the functional divinities or spirits of nature; local cults of a mystic or magic nature; and ancestor worship.[35] Beliefs about the universal Godhead are of peculiar relevance to the study of changing conceptions of law.

Even in this early phase of Chinese history, the oneness of the deity was asserted as the result of the unification of the functional spirits that embodied the natural powers upon whose favor society depended. This precocious drive toward a unified conception of the divine may have been encouraged by the experience of rapid linguistic and cultural unity, followed by political centralization.

The religion of the feudal period influenced the idea of universal deity ambiguously. This ambiguity is brought out by the two designations given to God, *Shang Ti* (emperor, lord-on-high) and *T'ien* (heaven). The former was supplanted only gradually by the latter.[36] The name *Shang Ti* emphasizes the personal or anthropomorphic character of the deity and analogizes his relationship to the world to that of a ruler to his society, an analogy made familiar by the Near Eastern transcendent religions. To describe the deity as *T'ien,* however, is to suggest its impersonal or naturalistic character and thereby also to deny, in the fashion of the immanent religions, the distinction between God and the world. At the root of these two views of God lie two fundamentally divergent ways to overcome polytheism and to unify the view of deity: the hypostatization of power and the deification of nature.

When the dominant image of society is that of a centralized polity under a ruler, the cosmos may come to be perceived as an expanded version of the social order. Hence, God becomes the supreme warlord and eventually the lawgiver, typified by the early Jewish Yaweh. The path is open to the religions of transcendence. One of the immediate sources of such a theology is the concrete experience of progress toward political unity.

But the centralization of power must be combined with something else to encourage a truly transcendent monotheism. This additional element may be the perception that the monarch or sovereign body willfully controls and reorders society. Thus, God is the great king. Or the decisive condition may be the economic situation of pastoralism in which man's relationship to the most important aspects of nature, those that determine his own livelihood, is one of surveillance and power. God is to mankind as the shepherd is to his flock. Both factors seem to have played an important part in the development of theologies of transcendence.[37]

If, however, the focus of social consciousness is man's dependence on the forces of nature outside and within himself, the deity may be identified with nature, and pantheism will replace polytheism. The divine expresses nature instead of creating it. In this manner, the religion of immanence lives on, though in a novel form. The elements of nature are perceived as strands in a larger pattern that inheres in an uncreated, timeless, and perhaps hidden reality.

The remarkable fact about this period of Chinese culture is that both conceptions of the deity were present in a preliminary form because both of the underlying experiences were already widespread. There seems to be no reason at this time why China might not have gone on to develop a transcendent religion. To understand how and why the deification of nature prevailed over the hypostatization of power will be a concern of my analysis of the transformation period.

Enough has already been said about the feudal polity, its rank system, and its religion to serve as a basis for the discussion of its normative order. The most striking trait of that order seems to have been its almost exclusive commitment to custom. Written regulations or codes were still unknown, and the discretionary powers of the ruling princes appear to have been kept within the strictest limits.

The law of the feudal society is captured by the concept of *li,* which was to dominate Confucianist thought. Whether or not the idea of *li* was itself a later Confucianist invention, its later uses aptly describe many of the traits that distinguished the normative order of the period. By examining the characteristics of the kinds of norms the *li* notion describes, and by grasping the relationship of these characteristics to feudal society and culture, we can deepen our understanding of interactional law.[38]

First, the *li* were hierarchical standards of conduct; they governed relationships according to the relative social positions of individuals. The hierarchic quality of the *li* responded to the political structure of the feudal society and to its rank system. Thus, the abyss that divided the *chün tzu* from the *hsiao jen* was taken for granted. Even among noblemen the standards of propriety to which an individual was expected to conform depended on his rank. Strictly speaking, only noblemen participated in the system of reciprocal chivalrous duties; when used to describe dealings among commoners or between commoners and noblemen, the original meaning of *li* merged into a broader notion of custom. In its silence about responsibilities owed by the *chün tzu* to the *hsiao jen,* Chinese feudal society resembled its Roman, Japanese, and Ottoman counterparts and differed from the medieval European.

Second, the *li* were perceived as customary forms of behavior intrinsic to particular social situations and positions. No clear lines were drawn between expectations about what persons of a certain rank would do in a given circumstance and views on what they ought to do. Thus, standards of conduct were relational instead of transactional. By this I mean that they governed and defined continuing relationships that occupied a large part of an individual's social life. The bond between a warlord and his *shih* retainers was such a relationship. The contrast is to rules applicable to acts that involve narrowly defined interests of their parties, like the modern executory contract. Moreover, the *li* were particularistic or concrete, rather than universalistic or abstract, standards of conduct; they were addressed to highly concrete situations and categories of persons. Examples are the kinds of services the *shih* were expected to provide their lords, or, even more precisely, the warnings and gestures men owed to one another in chariot warfare.

Third, the *li* were not positive rules; indeed, in a sense they were not rules at all. They lacked the quality of positiveness because they were not understood, formulated, or obeyed as something apart from the concrete relationships that established an individual's identity and social place. No one made the *li;* they were the living, spontaneous order of society, an order that human will, though capable of disturbing, was powerless to create. Therefore, instead of a catalogue of explicit rules, one encounters more or less tacit models of exemplary conduct. These models were transmitted as part of the experience of learning to participate in social relations according to one's rank, and they were formulated, when formulated at all, as moral anecdotes in authoritative literary works like the *Shih Ching.*

A normative order that relies heavily on pointed but unarticulated images of right conduct can operate effectively only in a social context in which there is a firm consensus of values and perceptions. With the aid of such a consensus the structure of society can be so marvelously subtle and complex that no system of made rules would do justice to its richness and refinement. Yet this structure may remain hidden from men's awareness because the fundamental conflicts of vision that might force them to articulate it never arise. All its parts can contribute to one another's vigor without its being the case that any of them is deliberately chosen as a means to conscious ends.

The effortlessness with which this type of system works parallels in the realm of culture the predetermined course of instinct in the prehuman animal world. Yet, unlike rigid instinctual patterns, culturally transmitted standards of this kind may be violated. But their violation is not derived from, nor accompanied by, a conception of their wrongness, nor can it be followed by an appeal to a different or higher set of principles. To be sure, no actual society can completely fit this mold. The existence of consciousness creates the possibility of conflict. And it is at those points at which the implicit consensus breaks down and needs articulation that social change occurs.

The basis for a highly integrated communion of values and understandings was present in the Chinese feudal period. One factor that made this possible was the stability of the rank system. Another was the immanent aspect of early Chinese religion, for it is the tendency of immanent religions to uphold the existing order of nature and society by sanctifying them. Despite signs of a religiosity of transcendence, the influence of the impulse to deify the world was so strong that a separation between nature and society was precluded. Consequently, there was no articulated conception of the social order as a system of relations established by men and capable of being criticized and changed by them. The notion that the basic structure of social life might be manipulated through made law was largely unknown to Chinese feudal society.

The fourth and last major characteristic of the *li* is that they were not public. Being conceived of as unmade, the *li* also were not viewed as products of state institutions. They touched upon all aspects of social life, and each social rank, relation, and position carried within itself its own law.

The social foundation of the fourth attribute of the *li* lay in the absence of a division between state and society during the feudal period. The system of ranks and the distribution of power were indistinguishable. One's place in the rank order almost completely determined one's access to power. No institution stood apart from the hierarchy of ranks as a state authority, for the rulers were simply the highest rank. Nor did the feudal period have the cultural basis for a state-society dichotomy: the view that social life may be arranged or rearranged by the institutionalized will we call government. The few traces of specialized legal agencies and the restricted command powers exercised by rulers, particularly in relation to the conduct of warfare, do not suffice to dispel the impression that in this society the *li* were the predominant and nearly exclusive standards of right.

All in all, the feudal world of ancient China provides us with a wonderful example of a society almost wholly dependent on interactional law and not yet acquainted with other sorts of law. This phenomenon loses its mystery once we understand the social and cultural conditions of each kind of normative order.

The transformation period: from custom to bureaucratic law

Chinese society and culture changed strikingly toward the middle of the Spring and Autumn, i.e., the sixth century B.C. These changes picked up speed with the onset of the Warring States in 463 B.C. and culminated in the establishment of the unified imperial state in 221 B.C. One may call this epoch the transformation period. My aim in discussing it will be twofold. I want to suggest how a significant body of positive and public law emerged because of the kinds of revision in the structure and in the conception of society referred to by my previous remarks on regulatory law. At the same time, the section will address the question of why the society of the transformation period, unlike postfeudal Europe, did not go on to develop the kind of legal order that became the mainstay of the liberal state. Thus, we may hope to rediscover in this historical case study the conditions of a legal system. Once again, it will be useful to distinguish political, social, and religious events before moving on to their implications for normative order.[39]

The political history of the transformation period was a history of the continuing breakdown of the feudal system. Changes in the character of relationships among states interacted with changes within states. On the international scene, the basic trend was toward political centralization. The internecine conflicts of the feudal society led to a rapid reduction of the number of contending countries and to an increase in the size of each. This warfare had important repercussions for the internal organization of the rivals. The states most likely to triumph in the struggle were those that managed to marshal their economic and human resources most effectively for the purposes of production and combat. Hence, a favorable stage was set for an emphasis on the regimentation of society from above and for the development of doctrines of bureaucratic organization and social planning.[40]

Moreover, the enormous dislocations and sudden reversals of fortune brought about by the turbulent situation gave rise to a mobile cadre of diplomats, scholars, and sophists who offered ambitious princes their services as experts in statecraft. Everything in the experience of these advisers brought home to them the importance of exploiting and taming force.

Against this background, an almost revolutionary change took place in the way society was organized. Power began to flow away from the feudal aristocracies and toward the ruling princes and their counselors, drawn largely from the *shih* stratum of the nobility. The internal centralization of power was accompanied by a growing separation between individuals' inherited place in the rank system and their capacity to control the lives of others. These trends make it possible to speak of a developing distinction between state and society.

Implied in this process were basic changes in the relationships among the ranks of society. The internal composition of the nobility was affected by the decline and destruction of the feudal aristocracy and by the rise to prominence of many persons of *shih* origin. The upper strata of the nobility were the chief victims of state warfare, whereas, with changes in the character of political and military organization, governments increasingly had to rely upon men of *shih* rank.[41] The ascension of the *shih* recalls that of *novi homines* of the equestrian order in late Republican Rome, of the cleric humanists at the time of the consolidation of the European nation-states, and of the *noblesse de la robe* in seventeenth-century France. In all these cases, a stratum directly below the aristocracy staffed administrative posts and thereby supported central rulers in their struggle against aristocracies of "feudal" origin.

The new men held office at the ruler's pleasure, and their relationship to him was one of impersonal service rather than of family bond. Because they lacked a power base of their own, their interest and security lay in faithfulness to the princely power with which they had allied themselves. The advance of the *shih* during the Chinese transformation period should be of particular concern to us, because groups like the *shih* characteristically govern the institutions that make and apply bureaucratic law, and it is from them that legal professions have almost invariably grown.

The sweep of social change embraced commoners as well as noblemen. With the buildup of centralized governments and the concomitant rearrangement of the tax system, the "serfs" of the feudal society were transformed into tribute-paying tenants, and land was made more freely salable. Whatever ties of reciprocal loyalty and dependence held together men of different social ranks were loosened.

Taken as a whole, these political and social events had the effect of separating state from society. One may conjecture that they also contributed to a dissolution of the highly integrated community of values and perceptions upon which the feudal order and its pervasive customary law depended. The differentiation of government from society or of power from hereditary rank and the onslaught of social conflict explain how the foundations were laid for a sudden growth of bureaucratic law.

We must, however, look more closely at the social aspects of the transformation period to identify factors that will help account for its failure to develop a European-type legal order. A crucial feature of the transformation period, which contrasts sharply with the experience of pre- and post-Renaissance Europe, was the lack of a "third estate" relatively independent from the governments of the centralizing monarchies.[42] Merchants had neither the incentive nor the chance to assert their own interests and to develop their own law; the *shih* drawn into the nascent state bureaucracy were unable to sow the seeds of an independent legal profession. The same conditions that account for the nonexistence of an independent merchant community also explain why no legal profession arose during this era.

It remains to describe the directions taken by religion. With respect to the image of the supreme deity, the most important trend was the increasing characterization of divinity as *T'ien* (heaven) rather than *Shang Ti* (lord-on-high). As a result, the notion of deity became more impersonal and naturalistic. The wavering of early Chinese religion between the quest for transcendence and the commitment to immanence was definitively resolved in favor of the latter. Confucianism appealed from the present historical situation to a mythical golden age in the past, and Taoism distinguished between the chaos of appearances and the invisible reality of order. But neither Confucianism nor Taoism, nor the later

Buddhist theology, allowed a marked separation of God and world. Consequently, none of the many forms of ancient Chinese religion viewed the world as something made by God according to a design that could be at least partially apprehended by the human mind. Indeed, even the idea, so important to the evolution of Greek theology, that the deity begot the earth through biological generation remained foreign to Chinese religiosity.

Though the reasons for this turn in the evolution of belief in China are surely obscure, a few considerations ought to be kept in mind. Such was the predominance of agricultural work in everyday life that the motivation for nature worship continued to be strong. Moreover, the concentration of governmental power and the corresponding subordination of all aristocratic or third estate groups—commercial, bureaucratic, or scholarly—to the interests of the state, made it difficult for prophecy or an independent priesthood to emerge. But it is only through the interplay of prophetic discovery and priestly ritualism that religions of transcendence are likely to develop. In China, religious learning was put at the service of government and most ritual functions were performed by the rulers themselves or, in the case of ancestor worship, by household heads. Moreover, there was little contact with other societies to provide the experience of cultural diversity that might have replaced transcendent religion as a basis for natural law.

Whatever the reasons for religious naturalism and for the weakness of ecclesiastical bodies in ancient China, the impact on polity and law was enormous. It became impossible to develop the view that nature and society are governed by universal laws of divine making. Another consequence of the Chinese religious evolution was the absence of a doctrine and of a prophetic or priestly tradition that might have operated as an effective check on governmental power. Lastly, the lack of a conception of the relationship between a personal God and the unique souls made in His image denied theological support to beliefs that could have emphasized the independence of individuals from one another or from the groups and societies to which they belonged.

Hence, the religious experiences of China in the transformation period and of Europe in the Renaissance diverged radically, a contrast that parallels the one we have already discovered in the political and social history of the two post-feudal societies. For in Europe science and political philosophy alike started off from the idea of universal principles; government had to contend with the conception of God-given natural laws and with powerful churches; and religious belief emphasized the capacity of individuals to transcend their social circumstances just as their Creator transcends His creation.

I have sketched a few of the political, social, and religious features of the transformation period, suggested their reciprocal links and implications, and pointed out some ways in which they differ from the events that resulted in modern European society. If one now turns to the repercussions these changes had on Chinese law, with the Western experience again as the point of comparison, he is struck by the occurrence of one development and by the absence of another. There was a remarkable expansion in the use of the kind of law the Chinese called *fa,* yet nothing appeared that resembled the distinctive legal systems established in Europe. The analysis of the transformation period has already supplied us with the tools to understand why this was so. Some elementary facts about the legal history of the time will be useful to support my point.

Toward the end of the seventh century B.C., written codes of law began to appear in the Chinese states. By the time of the Ch'in unification in the third century B.C., government was regulating myriad aspects of social life through written laws. There was a willingness to make the laws public and to enforce them coercively. Traditional institutions of social management like the "Bureau of Records" and the "Director of Crimes" widened their influence. Organized administrative staffs were established with many of the traits that came to characterize imperial Chinese and modern Western bureaucracies.[43] Above all, governments struggled to bring an ever broader range of social activities under their control and guidance; to politicize what had previously been accepted as part of the self-regulating order of society.

These developments should strike a responsive chord in the mind of a student of the European nation-state. But the analogies must not be allowed to obscure how much more relentless the Chinese process was than the Western one; the former remained relatively unfettered by the kinds of legal constraints that played so important a part in the shaping of Western government. No clear lines were drawn between administrative commands and rules of law; no identifiable legal profession became separate from the rulers' staffs; no peculiar modes of legal discourse stood out from other kinds of moral or policy argument.

The legal differences between the two societies simply reflect the contrast we have already encountered in polity, social structure, and religious belief. To see this, one need only consider the type of law to which governments turned during the transformation period, and which the Chinese described as *fa,* in contrast to *li.*[44] The *fa* possessed the defining qualities of bureaucratic law: they were positive and public. Yet reliance on them did not represent a commitment to legal generality save as a sometime stratagem for the organization of power. Moreover, the *fa* were not meant to be autonomous in any of the substantive, institutional, methodological, or occupational senses previously indicated.

First, the *fa* were positive; they were made rules. The tendency to write them down and publicize them calls attention to the more basic premise that the laws arise from the human will rather than from a pattern underlying the reciprocities of social life. The need for positive law was a byproduct of the process described earlier as the disintegration of community. In a setting of rapid dissolution of the established rank system and of the shared values and insights with which that system was bound up, it became increasingly more difficult to rely on custom. With such a deep rearrangement of social relations, the unreflective consensus upon which the effectiveness of interactional law depends would have to diminish in its extension, concreteness, coherence, and intensity. As a result, the law loses the subtlety of standards that remain below the threshold of awareness, but it does not yet acquire the artificial refinement that produces the multiplication of distinctions in an elaborate system of legal doctrine. Hence, the appearance of positive law in the history of a society's normative order always has a shattering significance, the understanding and criticism of which becomes an obsession of social thought. Not only do people discover that they can create social order, but they encounter this capacity in its crudest and most threatening form.

Second, the *fa* were public as well as positive; the new laws of the transformation period were made by government alone. The unique and superior status of these public rules was indicated by the fact that they were used to distinguish the issues to be resolved directly by government agencies from those that fell under the primary or sole jurisdiction of other social bodies, like the village, the family, or the guild. Thus, if the first revolution brought about by bureaucratic law was the passage from the conviction that social order is given to the belief that it is constructed, the second was the change of the normative order into a relatively formal hierarchy of rules, with state law at the top. The historical basis for this change was the growing separation of state and society. Now let us turn to the negative attributes of the *fa,* for they go directly to the differences between European and Chinese legal history during the periods I have chosen for comparison.

A third characteristic of the *fa* was that they could be as general or as particular as the policy objectives of the rulers might require. Undoubtedly, there were frequent references in Legalist tracts to the importance of leveling all subjects before uniformly applied laws. However, generality was always approached as an expedient with which to secure the sovereign's hold over the populace, to keep his own agents in line, and to deprive any social groups outside government of privileges that might enable them to resist state policy. There was no recognition of generality and uniformity as unconditional requirements for the achievement of justice or of social welfare, commitments so important to both the social contract and the utilitarian tradition in modern Western political thought. Consequently, the basis was missing for the dichotomy between commands and laws, or of administration and adjudication, which was the cornerstone of European legal theory and led to the rule of law or *Rechtsstaat* idea.

A fourth and related feature of the *fa* was their lack of autonomy. The refusal to draw clear lines between mere "policy" and law was a corollary of the denial of any distinction between administrative commands and legal rules. The agencies that applied the *fa* were by and large the same ones responsible for maintaining order and executing government policy in the territories under their jurisdiction; specialized courts did not exist. The modes of argument employed in the making and application of the *fa* were the same as those used in all sorts of policy decisions. There was a lack of constraints associated with the appeal to methods of legal reasoning or to the peculiar competence of legal institutions, themes that were to loom so large in Western thinking about law. Finally, no profession of lawyers, as distinct from policymakers and experts in statecraft, emerged from the public administration.

Thus, we see that despite the similarity between the courses of legal history in the Chinese transformation period and in modern Europe, fundamentally diverse tendencies were also at work: in one case toward the imperial bureaucratic state and its regulatory law; in the other case toward a liberal society in which a legal order appeared alongside the administrative machinery of government. The understanding of the reasons for this difference of directions holds the key to an appreciation of the significance of law and of the nature of social order in the modern West. The decisive factors were those emphasized by my sketch of the transformation period.

Because no social groups, ranks, or institutions managed to assert their independence from government, the dissolution of the Chinese feudal order was unable to produce, as it did in the West, a liberal state and a liberal doctrine. There were no objective social conditions for a denial of the superiority of the interests and ideals of any one social group to those of any other group. Thus, there could be no demand for laws that would somehow be neutral among conflicting values or capable of reconciling them in a justifiable way. But, if my account of the historical conditions of legal order is correct, this quest for neutral or objective laws is one of the presuppositions for the tendency to uphold the ideals of generality and autonomy.

The failure to develop a transcendental religion and a body of sacred law deprived Chinese society of the other condition of legal order. Neither the conception of universal law itself nor the narrower idea that human power is limited by divine principle found support in Chinese religious belief and practice.

Confucianists and Legalists

We have seen how the experience of ancient China throws light on the connections among types of law, social structure, and consciousness and advances an understanding of the conditions of the legal order in our own society. The focus of my discussion has been the interplay of legal, social, and religious history in preimperial China. A reference to the debates that took place among schools of thought will carry the argument one step further.

The main doctrinal conflict of the transformation period was the struggle between the disciples of Confucius and the *fa chia,* the so-called Legalists.[45] Both traditions arose out of the same circumstances and appear to have drawn their proponents from similar social groups, yet their responses to the problems of the age were irremediably opposed. It is true that from the outset many thinkers tried to bridge the gap between the two positions and that Chinese imperial practice was built upon a mixture of the two, in which Legalist policies were often clothed in Confucianist language.[46] Neither fact, however, diminishes the truth of the remark that each of the two traditions included a view of man, of society, and of law that was both internally coherent and sharply critical of the ideas of the other.

What makes the controversy of peculiar interest to us is the way it bears on the problem of normative order. A crude and preliminary statement of the debate might be that the Confucianists advocated a return to the proprieties of custom, instilled by moral example, whereas the Legalists were committed to the expansion of bureaucracy and to coercively enforced bureaucratic law. Both schools worked on tacitly shared assumptions that forbade them to defend the rule of law in the modern Western sense or indeed even to conceive of it.

Legalism and Confucianism each had a core in which description and prescription were intermixed and which included an account of human nature, a view of the proper relationship between government and social groups, and a doctrine of normative order. A study of the relationship among these elements reveals the theoretical premises, as distinguished from the social conditions, of commitments to different types of law. Such a study may also highlight, by contrast, the concepts of the individual and of society characteristic of modern Western legal theory.

With respect to the view of human nature, Confucianism emphasized the existence of a natural economy of sentiments. It held that the moral sense exists in man either as a general disposition toward humanity *(jen)* and righteousness *(i),* from which standards might be drawn, or as a tacit code of conduct. Under the proper conditions of upbringing and of government, this moral sense could develop so as to ensure harmony in the individual, in society, and, according to the later writings of the Neo-Confucianists, in the cosmos itself. The aim was to elicit latent, preexisting notions of propriety.[47]

The Legalists, for their part, claimed that men had an insatiable ego, enslaved by the passions. They either denied that a potential benevolence existed in human nature or disbelieved that it could ever prevail over pride, envy, and greed.

Just as the Confucianists argued that there was a natural pattern of moral sentiments waiting to be developed, so too they trusted in a natural order of society. Society was perceived as an association of groups, generated by a limited number of basic relationships, like those of ruler and subject or master and disciple. Each group had its own valuable and well-defined place within the broader scheme of society; each relationship, its own inherent rights and wrongs. The task of government was to orchestrate and protect this immanent order rather than to destroy and supplant it.

The Legalists, on the contrary, wanted nothing more than to extend the powers of government. As advisers to princes, they viewed this policy as an end in itself, though they might also have justified it as a requirement of successful economic and military administration without which the state would disintegrate in times of trouble. Institutions or potentates outside government were rivals of the government's power and therefore threats to its sovereignty. Consequently, traditional bodies like the extended family, the village, or the guild should be stripped of most of their powers, their tendency to develop centers of authority checked, and all men equalized by the fear of the ruler and his agents. The imposed order of the state would replace an imaginary natural order of society.

These contrasting views of personal and social life led to utterly different conclusions about law. If there is a natural harmony of moral sentiments, the cultivation of such sentiments by means like the imitation of exemplary conduct would be the mainstay of the social order. Thus, the Confucianists accepted and reinterpreted the *li* of the feudal age as the way to resolve the conflicts among and within individuals that had become rife during the transformation period. They argued that the *fa,* as coercively imposed positive rules, affected the symptoms rather than the causes of social ills. Because they disregarded the true basis of social harmony, such rules could lead only to greater dissension. The Confucianists viewed society as an organic whole of groups and relationships, each with its own indwelling harmony; consequently, they declined to emphasize the law of the state.

In its distaste for positive and public rules, Confucianism showed its devotion to customary law. Its program was to restore and to refine the order the events of the transformation period were destroying, but at a higher level of moral reflection than had previously characterized that order. This explains the constant appeal to a mythical golden age of the past.

From the Legalist view of human nature, it followed that people had to be kept in line by external, coercively imposed constraints. The Legalist doctrine of the relationship between government and society implied that laws had to be made by the former for the latter. Thus, the Legalists turned to the positive and public rules of bureaucratic law for a way of dealing with the trials of their historical situation.

Though the theoretical assumptions about man and society made by Confucianists and Legalists may have steered the two schools in opposite directions, both tendencies were incompatible with a rule of law doctrine. The Confucianist and the Legalist view of human nature and social order have surely had analogues in Western political thought. One need only think of the conservative notion of hierarchical community or of the modern theory of statecraft as represented by Machiavelli. But the mainstream of thought has flowed in different channels. The effort has been to reject doctrines of natural benevolence and community as dreams while avoiding as nightmares the bestial view of human nature and the ruthless *raison d'état*.[48]

In the central tradition of modern Western social thought, men lack an innate goodness whose cultivation might secure a just social order, but they deserve to be respected as individual persons, and they are capable of arriving at common understandings about right and wrong on the basis of their mutual respect. Though spontaneously generated social arrangements are neither always available nor inherently just, they ought to be protected as manifestations of individual and collective will. The laws should complement and police rather than smash the internal rules of private institutions.

These were the building blocks of the doctrines of human nature and society from which modern European jurisprudence developed. It saw the legal system as both a device for reciprocal constraint through fear and a repository of shared understandings and values, as both a framework imposed upon private associations and an order emerging from them.

LIMITS OF THE CHINESE COMPARISON: THE EXPERIENCE
OF OTHER CIVILIZATIONS

The comparison between the legal experience of ancient
China and modern Europe leaves many questions open.
These two traditions represent extremes of the spectrum of
presence or absence of the rule of law. Both societies underwent changes that led to the proliferation of bureaucratic law,
yet in only one of them did a true legal order take hold. Most
civilizations, however, have occupied an intermediate place
along this spectrum. A brief review of some of these halfway
cases might begin to suggest how the insights gained from the
Chinese comparison could be qualified and developed.

To this end, it may be useful to single out two main kinds
of situations that approached the rule of law ideal in some
respects while falling short of it in others. The first of these
includes the sacred laws of ancient India, Islam, and Judaism;
the second, Graeco-Roman legal history.

The sacred laws of ancient India, Islam, and Israel

Despite enormous differences, the Hindu, the Muslim,
and the Jewish sacred law have several important features in
common.

First, all these systems of sacred law were believed to
have a suprahuman authority, as the will of a personal God or
as the reflection of an impersonal order. The Hindu *dharmaśāstra* worked out the implications for human conduct of
dharma. The *dharma* was the proper way of life, which fixed
the virtues and duties of each *varna* (the major castes) within
the cycle of existence and which coexisted with *artha* (material advantage or power) and *kāma* (pleasure) as one of the
great aims of human striving.[49] Thus, it was more than a
statement of what people should do; it was also a description
of what, in the nature of things, they must do. For men could

stray from their appointed path only for a short while before they were dragged back onto it. Even the gods were subject to this eternal decree, whose source was pictured more often as an objective process than as a person with whom one might have a personal encounter.

The *sharī'a* set out Allah's commands to humanity. It was divine revelation, as determined by the text of the Koran, supplemented by the sayings of the Prophet preserved in tradition *(sunna)*, the consensus of scholars *(ijmā')*, and analogical reasoning *(ḳiyās)*.[50] To master this law was to possess knowledge itself *(fiḳh)*.

Similarly, the Jewish *halakhah* represented a comprehensive order for human life. The primary source of this order was the Torah, God's revelation at Sinai to His chosen people. At least from the time of the Second Commonwealth, it became clear that the *halakhah* might have other sources: tradition, including the prophetic injunctions; the interpretation of the Torah by the scribes *(mi-divrei soferim)* or the positive and negative enactments of the great sages (the *takkanot* and *gezerot* of the *bet din*); and custom *(minhag)*.[51] As important as these supplementary sources of law might be, all gained force by their presumed fidelity to the will of a personal deity. Even custom received its validity from the righteousness *(ṣedeq)* by which the people affirmed its submission to God's commands.[52]

The ultimate social and religious bases of these systems of sacred law might be brought out by a contrast between two conceptions of law in the ancient Near East. In Egypt, the king was the personification of deity: he possessed the faculties of recreating social relationships through speech *(hu)*, of understanding them through his divine intelligence *(sia)*, and of maintaining order *(ma'at)*.[53] The ascension to the throne of each new king signified the re-creation of the world. The ruler might have had to contend with oracles that claimed to represent divine will directly as well as with the ambitions of his own aides. But, for the most part, there was no group sufficiently independent from the Egyptian autocracy to restrain its power, and, at least until the Fifth Dynasty, no belief in a divine order distinguishable from the monarch's whim. Hence, positive law was free of any requirement of generality or autonomy; it could take the form of highly individualized commands *(hap)* issued as part of the managerial activity of government.

But in early Sumerian Mesopotamia, a very different situation may have existed. The king's power seems to have been limited at first by independent assemblies and by a belief in a higher cosmic order *(kittum)*. It was his task to preserve this order and to adopt it equitably to changing conditions *(mēšarum)*. [54] Thus, in principle, the monarch's decisions were at once justified and restricted by the higher law. Though the content of this Sumerian legal tradition has been described as characteristically secular and though it may not have had the support of an independent priesthood, it contained the basic elements from which sacred law was to emerge.

If the idea of divine authority was the first shared attribute of the traditions of sacred law, the second was the interplay among divine precepts, royal edicts, and custom. This interplay operated both as a distribution of competences and as a process of mutual influence: the holy law, the prince's commands, and social conventions applied to different, though overlapping, areas of life; they also affected each other's content. Thus, a set of rules may have relied on divine authority and still have been permeated by customary or bureaucratic law. Moreover, the balance between the ruler's commands and the law of the priests always remained unstable; either may have prevailed decisively over the other.

Throughout the history of Hindu law, one witnesses an accommodation among the *dharmaśāstra,* the king's power to issue edicts *(kṣatra),* and custom *(ācāra).* So, too, there was a tension between the study of *dharma* and the *arthaśāstra,*

which taught the ruler how to achieve power and prosperity
for himself and his people, much in the style of the European
Renaissance literature of advice to princes.[55] Any distinction
among the three kinds of law was blurred, for each intruded
repeatedly upon the others. The *ksatra* often represented the
imposition of bureaucratic law by a territorial sovereign who
was himself politically unaccountable. Hence, it contrasted
with the *dharma,* which consisted of rules that were supposed
to apply to everyone and that imposed special obligations
upon the high as well as the low. Nevertheless, in the course
of conflicts between the princely rulers and the Brahmin
aristocracy, the *dharmaśāstra* both imposed limits on the
king's discretion and frequently reinterpreted to suit his
aims.[56]

An analogous process occurred in the relationship of the
sacred law to custom. The *dharmaśāstra,* as a literary law
elaborated by an elite, seems to have had only an oblique
influence on most of the customs that governed everyday life.
Yet local customary practices may often have imitated Brahminic standards in the same way that in Japanese Tokugawa *bakufu,* the law of each estate emulated *bakufu* law
itself.[57] Conversely, the *dharmaśāstra* gradually incorporated
norms that acquired the authority of the sacred law but arose
more from customary practice than from textual interpretation.[58]

The Muslim *sharī'a,* for its part, was bounded on one
side by administrative discretion: the discretionary power of
the caliphs *(siyāsa)* manifested itself in secular ordinances (the
kānūn, or the *nizām* and the *marsūm* of the Hanbali school).[59]
The *sharī'a* judge himself might occasionally award a discretionary punishment *(ta'zīr)* instead of the foreordained
sanctions of the sacred law *(hudūd).* On the other side, custom *('urf, 'āda)* circumscribed the holy rules.[60]

Neither of these two boundaries was ever fixed. Usually,
a sphere of administrative discretion was thought to be

authorized by the *sharī'a* itself. Because of the importance often attached to "public interest" as a criterion for the interpretation of the sacred law, the distinction between divine command and secular edict rarely exhibited in practice the sharpness it might have in doctrine.

Custom was never recognized as the official source of law, even by the Maliki school, which was the most favorable to it. But it is said to have exercised a powerful influence upon the development of the *sharī'a* and to have served often as a basis for freewheeling interpretations of the sacred law *(istiḥsān)*.[61]

Throughout the history of Islam, there were reactionary movements that attempted to suppress or to disguise the roles of bureaucratic and customary law. One thinks of the North African and Spanish Almoravids during the eleventh and twelfth centuries, of the West African Fulanis during the nineteenth century, and of the Arabian Wahhabis in this century. But these tendencies departed from the mainstream in Islam, which has always been characterized by the coexistence and interpenetration of divine law, secular edict, and popular custom.[62]

It is perhaps in ancient Israel that one finds it hardest to distinguish these three kinds of law. For here the authority of priests and prophets was often so great, and the merger of religion and polity so complete, that both custom and edict were viewed as of a piece with the *halakhah.* To be sure, it seems certain that during the monarchy, the king had authority to legislate about governmental matters, like taxation and military service. Nevertheless, he was regarded as bound by a double covenant, with God and with the people. He could not easily overstep the limits imposed by the sacred law, and he was subject to priestly and prophetic challenge.[63]

As for custom, it came to be recognized as modifying the *halakhah* in those areas of private life in which the sacred law operated as a *ius dispositivum,* a set of rules that applied only when the parties had not disposed otherwise. But, unlike the enactments *(takkanah)* of the learned, custom was powerless to change the law on matters of ritual.[64]

We can now turn to a third common characteristic of sacred laws: their dependence on a particular group and on a set of methods. In each case, the existence of distinctive techniques for the elaboration of law reinforced, and was reinforced by, the distinctiveness of the groups that used them. In all three traditions, the custodianship and the interpretation, if not the actual application, of the law was in the hands of a body of scholars, at once jurists and moral or religious teachers.

Together with this occupational specialization went a preference for textual exegesis, the glossatorial method.[65] The sacred law was embodied in a tradition of holy books. These texts were viewed as the supreme fount of authority. Yet they were often vague or reticent about matters on which the holy law had to be brought to bear. Reverence for the written word combined with the need for constant readaptation and elaboration to produce layer upon layer of commentary on the original writing. These glosses may have made ample use of analogy to extend or restrict the literal scope of rules in light of presumed intent or ascribed purpose. But the commentator was not free to impart his own abstract systematization to the material with which he worked.

The foremost source of the sacred Hindu law were written texts, the *smṛtis* and *śāstras*. These writings were organized and interpreted by Brahmins who maintained a greater or lesser measure of independence from the ruler. The autonomy of the Brahminic elaboration of law was compatible with strong monarchic power precisely because the *dharmaśāstra* was always viewed more as a social ideal and as a factor in deciding cases than as a binding code of law.

In the characteristic fashion of systems of sacred law, large numbers of commentaries and digests were produced.

And an elaborate method of textual exegesis, the *mīmāmsā,* was established.[66] The interpretive techniques adopted were very much shaped by the dominant cosmology. Islam and Judaism both conceived of their sacred laws as primarily the work of a personal God, who had purposes in promulgating them. Insofar as the human mind resembled, or participated in, the divine intelligence itself, men might hope to apprehend part of God's intentions as a lawmaker. Thus, a religious basis existed for the effort to interpret rules according to divine purpose. And this concern with God's aims might in turn suggest an interest in human goals as determinants of the meaning of laws. But in India, there was little outside the *bhakti* tradition to suggest that God was a person whose purposes might be intelligible to man. Consequently, it became necessary to devise a series of formalistic maxims of interpretation that dispensed as much as possible with references to intent.

In both classic Islamic and ancient Jewish law, we find judges with a substantial degree of independence from the ruler. Most important, there were learned men charged with the elaboration of the sacred law: the Muslim *'ulamā'* and the Hebrew sages and scribes. The authority of scholarly comment might be contested: Ibn Taymiyya's attack on the validity of doctrinal consensus *(ijmā')* as a source of law during the fourteenth century and the Sadducee criticism, in the post-Hasmonean period, of the Pharisees' use of Oral Law come readily to mind. But the opposite view prevailed, and doctrinal exegesis exercised, as it would have to, a decisive influence on the development of the law.

For the reasons indicated, Islamic and Jewish theologian-jurists were able to use interpretive methods whose suppleness and audacity surpassed anything available to the Brahminic exegetes. In particular, we find in both cases a liberal use of open-ended analogical reasoning (the Jewish *gezera shava* and *hekkesh*[67] and the Muslim *kiyās*)[68] and of "fictions" to evade the inequities of strict law (the Hebrew *ha'aramah*[69] and the Islamic *ḥiyal*).[70] (Indeed, in both cases, the Judaic device seems to have contributed directly to the Muslim usage.) At the extreme, there was an effort during the Second Commonwealth to justify deviations from the *halakhah* in terms of "the need of the hour"[71] and the recognition during the Umayyad Caliphate of a power to break the rules of analogical reasoning in response to political preference *(istiṣlāh, maṣlaḥa).*[72]

In the two traditions, however, the struggle to preserve the unity of the religious community and the vested interests of established scholars resulted in a narrowing of the area open to inventive legal reasoning. In Islam, this happened quite early, with "the closing of the gates of independent reasoning" in the ninth century.[73] In Jewish history, it happened relatively later, with the completion of the Babylonian Talmud by the mid-sixth century.[74]

Now that some of the similarities and differences among ancient Hindu, Islamic, and Jewish law have been indicated, it may be possible to understand how and why each of them differed from the modern Western rule of law. All three civilizations lacked some of the indispensable preconditions of a legal order, though this may be less true of Islam than of India, and still less true of Israel than of Islam.

Ancient India never developed the kind of group pluralism that encouraged the growth of a legal order in the West. It is true that the Hindu system allowed for a considerable amount of decentralization and that the Brahmin aristocracy often exercised enough power to constrain, or even to subjugate, the prince.[75] But this was not enough to offset the consequences of the sacred law's intimate involvement with the caste system and of its control by an unsupervised priestly cadre. For these factors meant that the law would take the form of standards that set particularistic duties and entitlements for each caste, rather than of general rules conferring formally equal rights on broadly defined categories of persons.[76] There was no impulse toward moral and legal universalism in the sacred law; hence no reason to impose constraints of generality on royal ordinances. The same circumstances prevented the laws from serving as a flexible medium in which the outcomes of group conflicts might be expressed. And they also explain why it was impossible to disentangle legal rules from religious and moral precepts.

Indian religion contributed to this situation. Hinduism always maintained an ambivalent attitude toward the conception of the personality of the ultimate Godhead. Hence, it never arrived unequivocally at an idea of the universal laws that a personal Creator might have set over His creation and that human reason might discover. The *dharma* was more a set of obscure interdependencies latent in things than a rational design imposed upon them from the outside. Moreover, Hindu religion in the main, far from asserting the equality of all persons before God, stressed a hierarchy of worth and gave it a cosmological foundation. It was left to the *bhakti* strain within Hinduism to affirm both the personality of God and the possibility of personal salvation.[77]

In Islam, we find a system that more nearly resembled a legal order. The *sharī'a* is a universal law that reflects God's will and establishes a measure of equality among all men. But the societies in which Islamic law developed characteristically lacked an authentic group pluralism.[78] Despite the rise of a commercial bourgeoisie,[79] the structure of power was sufficiently stable to leave the elaboration of the sacred precepts in the hands of a scholarly elite and the power to legislate at the mercy of rulers whose discretion had few effective limits. Hence, there was little impulse to treat either the sacred or the royal ·law as a tool of group compromise, though an adaptable law merchant might be allowed to develop first alongside and then within the *sharī'a*.[80]

Given these circumstances, the characteristic liberal separation of legislation, administration, and adjudication could not fully emerge. Instead, the political rulers and the religious or scholarly elite were each, in its own way and within its own sphere, at once lawmakers, administrators, and judges.

Finally, the Jewish *halakhah,* as it had developed by the end of the Second Commonwealth, seems to have come closer to a legal order than any other body of sacred law. The divine provenance of the Torah provided support for belief in the universalism of the sacred law, and biblical doctrine emphasized the essential equality of all members of the nation. Moreover, throughout the history of the ancient Jewish sovereign state, there was a significant degree of group pluralism.

Political centralization, even under the monarchy during biblical times, never became as extreme as in the large empires in which other systems of sacred law appeared. For the king had to contend with the independent power of local oligarchies, and of priests and prophets. In the Second Commonwealth, this relative weakness of the central rulers manifested itself in the rivalry of the king, the Great Synagogue, the Council of Elders, and the Sanhedrin.[81] The basis of this institutional competition was a social circumstance in which aristocratic notables, the priesthood, and the scholarly corps of scribes and sages were all able to maintain a measure of independence from the central ruler, be he prince or high priest. Thus, a sovereign might be constantly reminded by his partners in power of his duty to obey the sacred law and threatened with overthrow if he appeared to defy the Torah.

Despite the fact that many of the features and conditions of the rule of law were present in ancient Israel, a true legal order never emerged. Both princely or priestly rulers and the assemblies that shared authority with them had responsibilities that were simultaneously legislative, administrative, and judicial. Hence, it was impossible for the ideals of legal generality and autonomy to win the prominence they did in modern Western legal systems.

My thesis about the historical bases of legal order suggests an explanation for this fact. Both the First and the Second Commonwealth had aristocratic and theocratic features.[82] There was a pluralism of elites rather than of society as a whole. The basic structure of power was sufficiently well defined and stable to be self-legitimating. In the absence of broader social conflict, the *halakhah* could remain under the control of an oligarchy, belief in its sacred character both strengthening the established social order and being strengthened by it.

Under such circumstances, there was no need to devise a system that seemed to accommodate the divergent interests and ideals of many social groups and to guarantee the impersonality of power. Hence, little pressure existed to embrace a rule of law ideal. And whatever tendencies may have been at work to transform this condition were stifled by the political destruction of the sovereign state.

In brief, then, the sacred law systems of ancient India, Islam, and Israel all fell short of becoming legal orders. In the first case, both the religious and the social bases of the rule of law were largely absent. In the second case, the religious requirements were satisfied, but the social ones were not. In the third case, society as well as religion came close to providing a context for the creation of law in our modern European sense.

The Graeco-Roman variant

Greek and Roman legal history offers another example of a tradition that stood in between the ancient Chinese rejection and the modern European acceptance of the rule of law. Despite enormous variations among periods and places, the legal experience of the classical Western world had a continuing identity, an inner unity that distinguished it from the holy laws of the Near East, as well as from the legal order of liberal society.

To bring out the additional perspective on my argument this form of legal life provides, it may be helpful to concentrate on the social and religious background of law in Greece, and particularly in Athens, from the mid-seventh century B.C. to the conclusion of the Peloponnesian War. For this period saw changes in consciousness and social organization that were analogous in many ways to those that marked the breakdown of aristocratic "feudal" societies in preimperial China and preliberal Europe.

Consider first the social factors. In Greece, unlike China, political centralization was never powerful enough to suppress, or even to control, group conflict. By the early seventh century in much of Hellas, the power of monarchs had long been in decline to the benefit of aristocratic oligarchies. There was neither an economic basis nor a military excuse for the establishment of very large territorial units and the assertion of monarchic absolutism. The type of agriculture practiced did not call for the management of large-scale irrigation works nor for an intense concentration of rural estates. Moreover, from the end of the Dorian invasions to the coming of the Persian threat there was no imperative of external defense that might have encouraged the merger of Greek city-states.

From the seventh century to the beginning of the fifth, the economy became increasingly monetized. Agriculture and commercial specialization both fostered and drew upon a growth of mainland and Mediterranean trade. In many parts of Greece, commerce overshadowed agriculture. But most important of all was the rise of numerous and powerful merchant groups,[83] a phenomenon strikingly absent in ancient China.

The reasons that have been proposed for the appearance

of these groups suggest why ancient Greek society was so much more favorable a setting for group pluralism than ancient China. The agnatic tribal organization typical of societies dependent upon large-scale agriculture was unknown in Greece. Ancestor worship, traditionally associated with sedentary food-raising peoples and a powerful support of extended family links, played a minor role. Moreover, the economic predominance of the cities over the hinterland may have contributed to the severing of kinship ties between rural and town dwellers.[84]

Many aristocrats engaged in trade or allied themselves with merchant families. Others betrayed their estate and became leaders of the popular parties of small farmers, workers, and tradesmen. The ensuing group struggles contributed to the downfall of some aristocratic oligarchies and to their replacement by "tyrannies." The revolutionary despotism of the "tyrants" prepared the way for the "democratic" orders of the fifth century, based upon independent commercial and farmer sectors of the community.[85]

"Tyranny" was a decisive stage in the evolution of a relatively pluralistic social order. Thus, the Peisistradid regime in Athens played the foreign merchant community (the *metikoi*) against the Eupatrids, just as the Etruscan dynasty in Rome manipulated the commercial plebs in its struggle against the patriciate.

Even the peasantry achieved a measure of power. During the seventh and the sixth century, commercialization, monetization, and demographic pressure had driven large numbers of farmers into debt.[86] Unable, as their Chinese counterparts, to meet successfully their personal and tax liabilities and to pay exorbitant rates of interest, they lost their land to urban financiers. But they found allies in the "tyrants," many of whom came to power with a program of freeing the peasants from financial obligations.

A similar, though less far-reaching, pattern of conflict and change can be discerned in the history of Republican Rome. It is evidenced in the rivalry of patricians and plebeians,[87] the appearance of a powerful "equestrian order,"[88] the emergence of small but influential groups of speculative capitalists within this order, and the bitter internal rivalries of the new consular nobility.[89]

Thus, it might seem that one of the bases of legal order— a strong degree of group pluralism and group conflict—had been created in Athens by the time of the Peloponnesian War or even of the Cleisthenic reform and in Rome before the demise of the Republic. Indeed, at the time of Cleisthenes the whole conception of law seems to have changed from an idea of imposed order *(themis)* to one of rule based on consent *(nomos)*.[90] And the Roman Republic produced an elaborate system of secular legal doctrine.

Nevertheless, in neither case did an authentically liberal society emerge. For one thing, there was the continuing prominence of slavery. For another thing, there was the use of the privileges of citizenship to exclude large numbers of foreigners who resided in the state or were subject to its jurisdiction. Before being swallowed up by the Hellenistic or the Roman empire, the ancient state was a community in which social privilege was inseparable from political right. The entire citizenry formed, in a sense, an aristocratic estate, jealous of its prerogatives and anxious to maintain its separation from all other estates. The shared ideals and interests of citizenship imposed a limit to the range, if not to the intensity, of social conflict and reinforced the overall hierarchic order.[91]

Within and outside this elite, every social rank continued to have a corporate ethos that defined the rank's place in society. Because economic power remained attached to the religious and political entitlements or disabilities of each group, the ancient republic was one in which "status consciousness masked class consciousness."[92] As a result, an ideal of formal equality, and together with it a commitment to generality and autonomy in law, could not fully develop.

Let me now turn to the presence in Graeco-Roman society of the other major basis of legal order: the belief in a higher, universal law. Both political thought and religious speculation contributed to a theory of universal natural law. But by the time this natural law had been shaped, the triumph of absolutist imperial states and the rigidification of hierarchy had already destroyed the social bases of legality. Moreover, because of its origins, the Graeco-Roman natural law tradition lacked the support of a powerful independent priesthood.

Natural law ideas in Greece were in part a byproduct of encounters with other civilizations. As Greeks came into more frequent contact with "barbarians," they were forced to confront the issue of the conventionality of their practices and they were encouraged to search for overarching principles with which to evaluate divergent standards of conduct.

Thinkers became sensitive to the way similar moral ends might be expressed by different rules. At first, the made rules of each society might be devalued in favor of what was "natural"; *nomos* was contrasted unfavorably with *physis*.[93] But this critique of convention was usually followed by a quest for the universal element in human nature and for the unwritten law to which that nature gave rise.[94] This trend in political thought, which had roots in the Atomist, the Sophistic, and the Hippocratic tradition, was paralleled and reinforced by philosophical inventions and religious changes.

Pre-Socratic philosophy inaugurated a rationalistic inquiry into nature that had no true analogue in China. It set out to elaborate an account of natural phenomena that might show how they related to each other and to underlying substances or principles. Thus, it contributed to a view of the world as a system governed by universal laws.

At the same time, Hellenic religion moved to a unification

and a personification of deity. The poets and philosophers groped toward an idea of the oneness of God. And, though nature spirits continued to play a role in Greek religiosity, the gods were seen more and more as superior to the constraints of nature. The natural order itself could be viewed as a divine creation.[95]

Despite these tendencies and the significance of the ecstatic salvation cults, Greek religion fell short of transcendent monotheism in two crucial respects. First, it never fully overcame its initial polytheism.[96] Second, cosmogony was seen as a process of begetting rather than making; the world was viewed as an offspring, not an artifact.[97] This ran counter to the idea of universal laws implanted in nature by a Creator and to the notion of God's transcendence over the world. Indeed, the whole tendency of Graeco-Roman theology was to make the image of the divine increasingly impersonal.[98] There is, thus, a sense in which much of ancient Western religiosity stood midway between Chinese naturalistic pantheism and the salvation religions of the West.

Moreover, natural law ideas lacked the support of an independent church organization. With the exception of the Panhellenic oracles, there was no powerful priestly group that might have served as the bearer of the doctrine of universalistic divine law.[99] In Rome, as in Athens, the sacred law was bypassed by, or transformed into, a secular law. Religious life remained bound up with the worship of the state; only private conscience could appeal from public power to otherworldly authority. The Roman state religion could be manipulated, successively, in the interests of the senatorial oligarchy, the rival factions of the late Republic, and the emperor.[100] Thus, even when natural law thinking became a major preoccupation of jurisprudence under the Roman principate, it lacked a social or a religious basis from which to resist the assertion of imperial will.

Looking back, we can now see how the conditions for

the emergence of a legal order were satisfied only imperfectly in the Graeco-Roman world. The level of group pluralism and group conflict achieved was never quite sufficient to transform the society into a liberal one. And to the extent that natural law ideas developed, they were too late, too shaky in their theological foundations, and too destitute of social reinforcement to be a significant influence on the organization of power.

To be sure, we find elements of the rule of law in Cleisthenes' Athens and in Republican Rome. In Athens, differences in the methods and institutional settings of legislation, administration, and adjudication began to take shape.[101] The ideal of equality before the law also became a concern of political thought,[102] though its implications could never reach as far as they might in a liberal society. In Rome, these same developments were accompanied by the ascension of a "status group" of jurists who went well beyond the Greek rhetors in creating a distinctive body of legal doctrine.

These achievements were nevertheless fragile and limited for they rested on half-baked foundations. The same aspects of society and culture that impeded the free development of a legal order also facilitated the replacement of the city-state by the personal absolutism of the Hellenistic kingdoms and the Roman empire. Once these imperial states had been established, they undermined much of what had been accomplished by way of establishing the rule of law: legislative, administrative, and judicial functions were concentrated in the ruler and his agents, and imperial edicts were freed of the requirement of generality. In the late empire, a new law of estate privileges and disabilities was built up, reflecting the fact that the relatively pluralistic and conflictual society of earlier times had given way to a better entrenched hierarchy of ranks.[103] By then, the possibility of legal order had disappeared.

LAW AS A RESPONSE TO THE DECLINE OF ORDER

It remains to point out some of the implications of the argument of this chapter for the problem of social order. The discussion of this problem in Chapter One concluded with the hypothesis that some social settings might best be understood in light of the doctrine of consensus and others from the perspective of the theory of instrumentalism. If so, we must try to find out the circumstances to which each of the conceptions is most applicable. Once this is accomplished, it might be easier to determine how the conflict between the two modes of consciousness and conduct that these views of social order describe might be resolved.

The situation portrayed by the consensus view of social order is the basis of interactional law. Custom flourishes to the extent that there is a closely integrated community of understandings and ideals—widely shared, coherently inter-related, concrete in their dictates, and intensely held. The existence of such a community makes it possible to rely on implicit standards rather than on explicit rules and to view these socially accepted norms as determinants of the rights and wrongs of individual conduct.

The context in which bureaucratic law emerges is one in which at least the ruler or the ruling group is able to view society from the standpoint of the instrumentalist doctrine. In this new setting, social order must be ensured through some device other than the internalization of tacit guidelines of reciprocal obligation. Public and positive laws become the means by which social relations are manipulated in behalf of the policies deliberately chosen by the ruling groups. The separation of state from society creates the institutional vehicle for this control. Power is justified by religion, but this religious authority is tested by government's success in guaranteeing public order and material prosperity.

Thus, the consensus-oriented view of social order applies best to those societies in which custom is the only significant type of law. The instrumentalist thesis comes into its own with the growth of bureaucratic regulation. The conflict between the two modes of order becomes most acute in the form of social life that produces the rule of law.

In such a society, two distinct and even antagonistic modes of experience coexist in the minds and in the behavior of the same persons. On one side, there is the experience of pursuing one's own ends and of seeing other persons as aids or obstacles to the achievement of those ends. On the other side, however, there is the equally pervasive experience of acquiescing in the practices of the collectivities to which one belongs and of following their rules as criteria of right and wrong. This second experience relies on the shared assumptions that survive group conflict, as well as on the belief in transcendent, universal principles of right.

The two tendencies conflict in every area of conduct and belief. From the standpoint of a person's concerns with his own individually defined aims and with the choice of means to their attainment, acceptance of group values can never be more than a constraint on freedom. From the perspective of the individual's loyalty to the groups to which he belongs, the single-minded instrumental pursuit of his own goals appears as a threat to the possibility of all association.

Thrown back and forth between these two manners of organizing their lives and of viewing their places in society, men are unable to arrive at a coherent definition of self. Thus, the contrast of the instrumentalist and the consensus doctrine is more than a puzzle about the best way to describe the social bond; it is also a struggle carried on in daily life. This struggle manifests itself in a variety of related ways. At one level, it is the opposition of personal autonomy to community, or rather the compulsion to perceive them as contradictory rather than complementary. At another level, it is the alternative between treating the social context of one's life as a source of helps and hindrances to the satisfaction of individual desires and treating it as a preexisting order, inherently worthy of respect.

These cross-currents are well reflected in the dilemmas faced by a legal order. The conditions of liberal society require that the legal order be seen as somehow neutral or capable of accommodating antagonistic interests. Each individual or group must be able to view the rule of law instrumentally as the best means to promote over the long run its own ends. Yet every choice among different interpretations of the rules, different laws, or different procedures for lawmaking necessarily sacrifices some interests to others. Obedience to the laws could not survive if it depended solely on even the most enlightened calculus of efficiencies by private groups and individuals. For there is always the chance that the advantages to be gained by any given party in disobeying the law or subverting the legal order itself outweigh the risks of loss. Thus, the legal system must be able to draw upon a consensus and upon a corresponding sense of obligation that rise above any calculus of costs and benefits.

If it is true that the theoretical problem of social order arises from a moral and a political situation, this problem can be resolved only by changing the situation. But which changes are possible, and which are necessary? Can one overcome the conflict between these two different ways of dealing with social existence without retreating to the unreflective acceptance of the collective values expressed by the tacit reciprocities of custom or to a bureaucratic welfare tyranny that treats all social arrangements as subjects for governmental manipulation through regulatory law? An answer to this question would require a deeper insight into modern society than the present stage of my inquiry permits. Nevertheless, the argument contains a suggestion for further progress.

For millennia, men viewed nature and society as expressions of a sacred order, self-subsisting if not self-generating, and independent of the human will. According to this out-look, the test of wisdom was the capacity to apprehend the hidden harmony of the world and to submit to it. Persons perceived their relationships to others as set within the same predetermined and eternal boundaries that circumscribed their transactions with the life-giving elements of nature.

As long as this mentality prevailed, the social order could not be treated as something to be built and rebuilt and on occasion to be defied. The possibility of intentional, far-reaching change was ruled out by the acceptance of the naturalness of social relations in general and of a social hier-archy in particular. The fact that the abiding cosmic order manifested itself in a fixed pattern of interpersonal relation-ships ensured that reliance on group standards would over-ride and suppress independent individuality. Both diver-gences among periods and differences among individuals must have seemed then like surface variations on unchanging themes. Consequently, the sense of historical time and that of the radical separateness of persons were equally unfamiliar. Such, in brief, was the kind of society and culture in which custom reigned supreme.

It is only within a relatively recent compass of history that a truly different form of existence and of consciousness appeared. The new vision was inspired by the discovery that order could and indeed had to be devised rather than just accepted ready-made. This discovery had several aspects, which one might separate if only to clarify their relationships to each other. People distinguished society from nature. They began to treat the latter as something to tamper with in their own interests and the former as an artifact of their own efforts. One consequence of this view was that time turned into history; it became possible to conceive of progress and decline as characteristics of entire societies rather than merely of individuals and to contrast an era with those that had preceded or followed it. Another result was to bring out the conventional and contingent character of every form of social hierarchy so that the exercise of power had to be justified in new and more explicit ways.

Wherever this crisis in the understanding and in the institutional forms of social order arose, it evoked two alternative responses, which are nicely illustrated by the diverging courses of Confucianism and Legalism in China. The first answer consisted of attempts to reassert the earlier conception of the unity of nature and society as the basis of a natural social hierarchy and thereby to reestablish the rule of custom. The second path led to a frank recognition that nothing in nature predetermined how society ought to be arranged and that its arrangement was solely a matter of human convenience.

But *whose* will was to replace nature as the source of social order? Because the crisis was bound up with ever widening disparities among social ranks, the source had to be the will of the rulers, of the particular social groups in control of the agencies of government. Thus, an implicit and spontaneous order was displaced by an explicit and imposed one, whose tool was bureaucratic law. This is what we see in the doctrines of the Chinese Legalists and in the politics of the great empires of Oriental antiquity.

Neither in theory nor in practice did either of the two major responses to the crisis of order ever prevail to the exclusion of the other. The processes of specialization and stratification, which weaken custom, make it impossible to dispense with a measure of imposed governmental control. Conversely, even the most relentless scheme of bureaucratic regulation may directly affect only a minute area of social life. Much social activity may continue to be governed by customary patterns of conduct, still viewed as extensions of the regularities of nature.

Moreover, each of the attempted solutions to the crisis of order has a limited ability to legitimate social arrangements.

The attempted remarriage of a natural order and a social hierarchy, whether we find it in the Confucianists, in some of the European natural lawyers, or in latter-day versions of conservatism, imposes on men a burden of tradition they can no longer support unreflectively as good and necessary. On the other hand, the imposition of an order whose sole basis is the will of the ruler or of the ruling groups may ultimately subvert both social organization and personality. It undermines the former by destroying the opportunities for the justification of power. It attacks the latter by depriving people of any firm sense of how they fit into the world around them.

Without such a sense, as the critics of bureaucratic law were quick to point out, people are made to feel homeless in nature and left at a loss to judge and to justify the conduct of their own lives. As beliefs about what ought to be done are dissociated from understandings of what the world is like, these beliefs are deprived of support. In each moral or political choice, an arbitrary decision takes the place of a natural necessity.

The inadequacy of the two major responses to the crisis of order is highlighted by their significance for social stratification. Both views have characteristically been used to support, and have been fostered by, rigid hierarchical relationships among ranks. But in this they have rarely been successful for long. Once the perception of the conventionality of all social arrangements enters people's minds, it threatens the foundations of social hierarchy.

The crisis of social order and the failure of attempts to resolve it throw men into a condition that may revive in a higher form a predicament faced by certain nonhuman primates. Lévi-Strauss once suggested that the behavior of these animals has lost the unreflective determinism of instinct without acquiring the conscious determination of conduct by learned rules; the genetic program is silent where the cultural one has not yet begun to speak.[104] Hence, their acts seem without rhyme or reason, presenting to the observer the image of a restless bafflement forever incapable of hitting upon an order of group relations that would allow them to ascend the evolutionary ladder.

In even the earliest societies that can be identified as human, the regularities of instinct were not only greatly restricted but also replaced by custom. Like the "instincts" and "drives" of animals, customary patterns of behavior are relatively rigid, largely unreflective, and common to whole associations of individuals, whose dealings with one another they structure. Unlike the regularities of conduct based on the genetic code, these patterns are taught. Though neither deliberately made nor articulated as rules, they become shrouded in symbol and attached to belief. Because it can never be wholly dissociated from reflection, custom is always on the verge of falling prey to distinctions between regularity and norm, or between social practice and individual conscience.

Whenever the certainties of interactional law begin to dissolve, human beings seem relegated to the situation of the nonhuman primates—denied the experience of an unreflective order, they are yet powerless to create another. But there is a crucial difference between the nonhuman and the human predicament: what other primates encounter as an unspeakable fate, men must confront in the terror of consciousness.

If bureaucratic law fails to provide the structure that both society and personality demand and that the breakdown of custom shatters, what can be put in its place? Can the need for organized power be satisfied without a hierarchy of ranks? Can the awareness of the capacity to create social arrangements, an awareness associated with the decline of custom, be somehow reconciled with the experience the disintegration of custom has not yet ceased to destroy: that life receives weight and direction from an order that precedes the human will?

3

LAW AND MODERNITY

THE PERSPECTIVE OF MODERNIZATION

The preceding chapter suggested some of the conditions under which bureaucratic law and a legal order emerge as alternative responses to the crisis of order that the weakening of custom represents. This chapter focuses more specifically on the rise and decline of the rule of law in the West. Up to this point, modern European civilization and its law have been viewed from without, through comparison with other societies. Now the inquiry turns inward, toward the relations between law and other aspects of social life within the West. At a still more general level, the change is from an emphasis on the issue of social order to a concern with the problem of modernity. It may therefore be useful to consider once again the definition of this problem.

All the classic social theorists worked within what might be described as the perspective of modernization. They held that the civilization in which they lived was the outcome of a revolutionary break with its predecessors, a break that introduced something genuinely novel in world history. Modern society might be analyzed in radically different ways, but its uniqueness remained undisputed. Together with this notion went the belief that all aspects of modernity are inseparably interconnected. Social hierarchy, economy, politics, and culture were all thought to be parts of a whole, though there was little agreement on the relative priority of the factors that made up the whole or on the precise nature of their interdependency.

Perhaps the most important common ground was the insistence on seeing modern society as a form of social life that had to be understood as the product of a particular interplay between that society's ruling self-image and its external forms of organization. The social theorists declined to accept the idea of modern society as an association of independent if not equal individuals, whose security and freedom were guaranteed by impersonal law. But, for the most part, they also refused to treat this ideology of the dominant groups as a mere crust that might obscure, but could not illuminate, the nature of modernism. Their deepest insights had to do with the process by which both social organization and social consciousness were transformed through conflict with each other.

I have already called attention to some of the ways in which the perspective of modernization began to be attacked and dismantled, almost from the time of its appearance. Today, it is widely recognized that the reformation of our ideas about modernity has become imperative. Changes in the form of social life call for untried explanations and offer a new outlook on history. The proliferation of societies that share a commitment to industrialism, but seem to differ in all other respects, makes one wonder whether the idea of modernity has any real substance at all. For it suggests that there was never any necessary link among the elements of post-Renaissance European civilization.

The need to reconstruct the perspective of modernization without losing the insights it made possible determines the questions this chapter seeks to answer. What in fact was the dialectic of belief and experience in early modern or, as I shall call it, liberal society? What is the relationship of that society to the form of social life which follows it? And what is the significance of the similarities and differences among the main types of contemporary industrial society?

These issues will be studied with regard to their bearing on legal history. The transformations of law provide a viewpoint from which to survey the panorama of modernity. This theme is all the more appropriate because of the central place occupied by the rule of law ideal in the most influential justifications of the liberal state.

To carry out the program outlined, we must first have a framework within which to compare societies. With the help of this comparative scheme, we shall be able to inquire into the origins and the nature of the modern liberal state and to understand the type of law and of legal thought with which that state was peculiarly associated. Once this is accomplished, it will be possible to investigate the ways in which the transformation of liberal society is revealed in the evolution of its normative order. We can then go on to the broader issue of the relationship among the different types of modernity and among their respective kinds of legality. What we learn about the fate of the rule of law may enable us to define some of the major prospects and responsibilities of modern society.

Throughout the argument, historical illustration and detail will be at a minimum. For the effort is to identify, on the basis of more particular historical studies, the "deep structures" of different forms of social life and the possibilities of change or conflict within these basic patterns. These patterns may stand as tentative guides to further research, ready to be corrected and superseded.

THE COMPARISON OF SOCIETIES: A PRELIMINARY FRAMEWORK

Elements

To formulate a rudimentary grammar for the comparison of societies, I shall contrast three forms of social life: the tribal, the liberal, and the aristocratic. Each of these will be distinguished by the way it deals with three basic problems of human association. For the moment, it is enough to treat these types of society as categories of analysis that may be useful in clarifying the principal options faced by a society even though they may not describe any historical situation in particular. Lastly, it should be clear that the concepts of tribal, liberal, and aristocratic society are meant to be parts of a comparative scheme rather than stages of a universal evolutionary sequence.

In all but the smallest and most isolated societies, individuals interact in two different kinds of contexts. The first type of encounter is the one in which an individual, the subject, meets a person he is able to identify as a member of a group to which he himself belongs. The person who appears to the subject as a co-member in a significant group is the insider. The significance of a group can be loosely defined as the importance membership in it has for the way the subject defines his self-image and therefore his place in society.

The insider is often someone with whom the subject has face-to-face encounters: a relative, a friend, or a colleague. In this case, the group has to be small. But not all the persons the subject habitually deals with join him in a significant group, nor are all significant groups predicated on direct interaction. Thus, to illustrate the latter point first, the subject may view members of his own race or religion as insiders without ever having met them, as a Jew might distinguish between Jew and Gentile. On the other hand, though two persons of different castes could have worked side by side in traditional Hindu society, they might not have considered themselves bound by any tie of common membership in a significant group. Each would have been a stranger to the other.

The stranger is the opposite of the insider. He is someone whose relationship to the subject is a more or less open question; there is no firm setting of group life to cast that relationship in a definitive mold. The subject must always view the insider as a person like himself, as one capable of participating in the same sorts of social relations the subject recognizes as indispensable to his own personality.[1]

As long as the insider remains an insider, he may be hated, but he can never be completely denied by the subject the kind of humanity the latter attributes to himself. The stranger, by contrast, may be seen and treated, though he need not be, as a being with none of the decisive attributes that make the subject what he is. In consciousness, in actuality, or in both, the subject can easily reduce the stranger to the condition of a tool of his own ambitions or of an obstacle to their attainment. When this happens, the stranger is likened to the impersonal forces of nature, beneficent or dangerous, which establish the circumstances of the subject's life and choices.

Several qualifications are in order. Because social relations may be equivocal and asymmetrical, one who views another as an insider may in turn be viewed by the latter as a stranger. Moreover, a person who encounters another as a stranger in one context may meet him as an insider in another.

Finally, the distinction between strangers and insiders, which is never absolute, may tend to disappear under conditions I shall later enumerate.

A second general question one can ask about a society is a follow-up of the first. On what basis do members of significant groups hold together and how do insiders deal with strangers? The previous issue goes to the anatomy of groups; this one has to do with the very nature of the social bond. It draws our attention to the fundamental correspondence between the ways in which social relations are in fact ordered and men's images of self and others. Every society will have groups that may be viewed as characteristic of it in the sense of exerting the greatest influence on the quality of everyday life. If, for example, a certain kind of family community turns out to be the typical significant group in a society, it will be especially important to discover the principle of association that governs its internal life.

Were we able to answer the two preceding questions with respect to any given society, there would remain a third matter that would require elucidation before we could be said to have understood the meaningful core of a society's organization and culture. This third aspect is the way people tend to define the relationship between what their experience is and what it ought to be, between actuality and the ideal. Just as the second problem grows out of the first, the third issue is suggested by the second.

When I distinguished the varieties of law, I pointed out that to comprehend the specifically social aspect of human conduct, we can never stop with the description and explanation of factual regularities. The character of a set of social relations remains misunderstood until we elucidate the ideas or sentiments of obligation by which men shape their reciprocal dealings and praise and blame one another. A study of the social bond calls for an appreciation of the sorts of normative order that surround social relations with precepts, symbols, and beliefs. Sometimes this normative order will be all but completely identified with social practice: actuality will be idealized and the ideal actualized. This is what we have seen happen in customary law and in the immanent religions. At other times, however, the ideal and actuality will be contrasted, as they are in the other types of law and in the transcendent religions.

The distribution of individuals among significant groups, the character of their relations to each other as insiders or strangers, and the interplay between conceptions of the ideal and understandings of actuality constitute the elements of a framework for the comparative study of forms of social life. What can this framework help us learn about tribal, liberal, and aristocratic societies?

Tribal society[2]

Imagine a society in which every individual belongs to a very small number of significant groups but in which each of these groups occupies a large part of his life. Thus, activities that in a different kind of social life might be connected with a variety of distinct groups are in this society concentrated within a few collective bodies. At first, the only significant group may be one whose membership is determined by real or hypothetical kinship ties. But in almost all societies, other significant groups, such as territorial entities, have also acquired a measure of relative independence from the family group.

A consequence of the paucity of significant groups is that the contrast between insiders and strangers can be drawn with a sharpness that would otherwise be impossible. If every individual belongs to a multiplicity of specialized groups, he is likely to encounter persons who are insiders in one context yet strangers in another setting. In this way, the images of familiarity and strangeness, attached to the same persons, easily become confused and weakened in the subject's mind. Besides, the more narrowly defined the scope of each of the significant groups that make up a society, the less is each of them likely to engage the whole personalities of its members. As a result, strangeness or familiarity may be attributed more directly to roles or activities than to the persons who perform them. The strong contrast of strangers and insiders, together with all this contrast implies about the nature of significant groups, is the first characteristic of tribal society.

Not even in the most extreme cases of tribalism is there ever an absolute line between insider and stranger. The universal prohibition against incest offers the classic demonstration of this thesis. The set of persons of opposite sex whose sexual relations with the subject fall under the incest prohibition always partially overlaps the kinship group as it is defined for nonsexual purposes. For example, the mother may belong to the latter, but not to the former; in one context she is a member of her son's group, whereas in another she is excluded from it. Thus, the separation of significant groups arises from the most elementary and universal facts about the family.

Let me now pass on to the second part of my scheme: the nature of the way insiders in the society's characteristic groups are drawn together and the quality of their encounters with strangers. The chief point to grasp is that in tribal societies very different standards of behavior are imposed on relations among insiders and on those between insiders and strangers.

Along these lines, much was made in the literature of social theory of the way premodern (read nonliberal) societies distinguished between the intragroup and the intergroup exchange of commodities. Thus, whereas dealings among insiders might be tied to some seemingly inalterable standards of reciprocity, one's economic relationships with strangers could be governed by a purely predatory conception that allowed each party to take as much as he could get from the other. Communal solidarity in one sphere of life is opposed to unharnessed economic warfare in another.[3] An example of this phenomenon, which became famous because of its importance to the development of capitalism, was the history of the prohibition against usury in the West.[4] The Deuteronomic precept, which forbade the charging of interest to fellow Jews, allowed interest to be charged Gentiles.

The organization of capitalist markets required that profit-guided trading take place within groups from which it was previously banned. But capitalism also depends on an individual's being able to trade with strangers in the assurance that they will abide by well-defined rules. The profit motive, if it is not to destroy the institutional foundations of a market society, must work itself out within constraints that preclude the taking of goods by material force and that permit a relatively impersonal price system to develop.

At the heart of the difference in the way insiders treat each other and the way they deal with strangers lie two utterly different kinds of social relations. Insiders do not recognize strangers as persons with whom they share anything important. In contrast, the members of the group believe themselves tied together by a deep and lasting communal bond. Typically, this bond rests both on a natural fact and on a sharing of common beliefs or ideals. The natural fact is the fate of being born into a family, a territory, a religion, or a race. But this predetermined circumstance is important only insofar as it contributes to a mental experience, which is the very core of tribal community: the sense of having a view of the world and of the good in which others participate, a view whose hold over the group is so strong that it need never be spelled out. Communal solidarity is precisely the condition of extensive, coherent, concrete, and intense moral communion identified earlier as a foundation of custom.

Thus, the stage is set for putting to the tribal society the third question suggested by my conceptual map. How will individuals who relate to each other in the manner described tend to conceive of the place of the ideal in actuality? Surely, they will have no conception of the right or the good as something towering above the natural and the social world that surrounds them. Their tightly bound community of sentiments and ideas will encourage them to identify what ought to be with what is by denying them the experience of moral doubt. Hence, their law, their religion, and their art will all express the view that the ideal and actuality are at root inseparable. Indeed, the very notion that nature and society might undergo a basic change must remain alien to a people who have not yet broken the nearly closed circle within which everything in the tribal society moves.

Liberal society

Take now a society that stands at the opposite pole from the tribal and call it liberal.[5] In such a society, every individual belongs to a large number of significant groups, but each of these groups affects only a limited part of his life. Thus, personality is carved up into a long list of separate or even conflicting specialized activities. The reverse side of this specialization is that the whole person comes to be seen and treated as an abstract set of capabilities never tied together in any one context of group life.

Such a mode of association undermines, though it does not abolish, the tribal contrast of strangers and insiders. As significant groups grow in number, they intermesh more and more. Hence, the frequency with which men who are insiders for some purpose become strangers for another increases.

The extent to which a subject can define himself and his fellows by reference to their shared experience in a group diminishes. At the same time, as individuals interact more often in impersonal contexts, like markets and bureaucracies, the position of the stranger is itself robbed of much of the foreignness, hostility, and fear with which it is connected in tribal society. Thanks to these convergent trends, impersonal respect and formal equality edge out communal solidarity toward some and suspicious hostility toward others. In place of the insider and the stranger, there emerges the abstract other to whom one shows neither love nor hate.

The distinction between strangers and insiders never wholly disappears under liberalism. It persists in the form of national, ethnic, and local attachments, and, above all, as a contrast between the public world of work and the private life of family and friendship. Yet the impersonality of the public realm and the communal character of the private one are always changing positions. On one side, there is the search for colleagueship in the workplace and the tendency, within and outside state law, to apply standards of good faith and fairness to commercial dealings, for the sake of business needs. On the other side, familial relationships are abandoned to the exploitation of power advantages within the family under the guise of respect for the integrity of the family group. In liberal society, the law of communal solidarity is repeatedly imposed upon public life in the name of the law of the jungle, and the law of the jungle upon private life in the name of the law of communal solidarity.

What precisely is the nature of the social bond that relegates intragroup community and intergroup enmity to subordinate positions? I shall call this intermediate tie the association of interests. The basic premise of the association of interests is that men will abide by relatively stable standards of interaction because they believe it to be to their mutual advantage to do so rather than because they participate in an identical vision of the truth and the good. In other words, the subject accepts and obeys a structured framework for reciprocal dealings with others as a means to the achievement of his own ends. Such a system cannot work by its own motion; what moves it? One traditional answer is that conduct violative of the rules will be so sanctioned by governmental punishment or informal social controls that most people in most circumstances will find that it pays to play by the rules. The trouble with this response is that it leaves unexplained why obedience to the rules continues even when overt sanctions seem inadequate or unimportant to the agent.

To gain a deeper understanding of how the association of interests works, one must inquire into the conception of personality and into the psychological experience bound up with this form of social life. In tribal society, individual consciousness tends faithfully to reflect collective culture. The mechanism by which the passions are stopped from wreaking havoc upon the established arrangements of society is an unthinking obedience to the official culture; order in society presupposes and evokes order in the soul. In this sense, Plato's doctrine in the *Republic* and the Confucianist social ideal were both attempts to work out the conditions under which the tie between personal and political harmony might be reestablished at a higher level of consciousness and refinement. But what is to hold the passions in check when the moral community on which tribal society depends has fallen apart? To this question various answers, none of them entirely satisfactory, have been offered in the theory and practice of liberal societies.

First, it is pointed out that allegiance to common values lives on in liberal society under new disguises. Groups like the family may continue to approach the condition of communal solidarity and even the society as a whole may move upon the shared though shifting ground staked out by its collective past. Nevertheless, it remains true that the greater the independence of the passions from the common culture, the more urgent the need to find an alternative basis for order among and within men.

Proust's remark that "our social personality is the creation of other people's thoughts" suggests the master device for the guarantee of social and psychological stability under liberalism. Each individual occupies a place in the various specialized groups to which he belongs. The parts he plays and the way he plays them determine the content of his desires as well as the means available to him to satisfy them. By shaping how others view him, his roles shape his view of himself. This social image of the self steps into the vacuum created by the chaos of the passions. It gives the individual an illusion of coherent personality in exchange for his submission to the demands of the group. Among these demands is the need to strive for mastery of the skills required for the performance of his roles. In this manner, each individual's supreme interest in the image of self becomes the linchpin of social order; he is led, indeed forced, by that interest to keep the savage passions at bay.

Against the background of what has been said above about the nature of group life and of the social bond in liberal society, it is possible to infer the kinds of beliefs about the relationship of the ideal and of the actual fostered by this society. As interest association replaces community solidarity, the basis for seeing social arrangements as expressions of the good, the beautiful, or the holy collapses. No longer is there a living and all-inclusive tradition that can be perceived as instinct with the ideal. On the contrary, the most pervasive experience of life becomes that of the diversity of conceptions of good, beauty, and holiness, and the main puzzle of social thought, that order can prevail despite this diversity.

In tribal society, reason is the awareness of a highly concrete ideal implicit in reality. Reason of this kind knows no distinctions between *is* and *ought* or between theory and practice. But in liberal society, a different view of the link between the ideal and actuality, and thus of the nature of each, carries along with it a change in the conception of mind. Reason must now be broken up into distinct faculties: the choice of means for the achievement of one's interests and the perception or statement of abstract ideals; the former devoted to what is, the latter to what ought to be; one instrumental, the other contemplative. Between them stands still a third faculty whose relationship to the other two remains obscure and ambiguous: the theoretical knowledge that, though concerned with the actual world, is pursued for its own sake rather than as a handmaid to interest.

Aristocratic society

The last form of social life in my comparative framework is in many ways a synthesis of the two previous ones. The task is to determine just wherein the synthesis lies. Many societies commonly described as feudal or oligarchic approximate the features of what I shall call aristocratic society, though perhaps its most perfect example remains the European *Ständestaat*. It is a unique category in the logic of social types, as unified in its internal structure as tribal or liberal society and as irreducible as they to one of the other types.[6] If this hypothesis is correct, a reconstruction of the category of aristocratic society is an indispensable part of any effort to work toward a general social theory and to understand with its help the modern social world and its vicissitudes.

Liberal society tends toward universalism; it is inclined to draw people together under the rule of formal equality. Tribal society is particularistic; the subordination of the individual to the group and the rigidity of group differences suppress the acknowledgment of a common humanity in which native and foreigner alike participate. Aristocratic society is best understood as a peculiar combination of universalism and particularism. Both its strengths and its weaknesses spring from this alliance.

The commonest form of the synthesis is a secular one. Each individual belongs to a specific group, his estate, that confers on him a broad range of entitlements and obligations and largely predetermines his outlook on society, on nature, and on himself. These strata, sharply divided from one another and decisive in setting the quality of individual life, constitute the particularist element in aristocratic society.

The significant social groups are not on a relatively equal footing, as they tend to be in tribal society. They are steps on a single, continuous hierarchic ladder rather than coequal partners or antagonists. Precisely because of this configuration, the plan of an aristocratic order is relatively simple and clear. Hence, it constantly brought home to individuals no matter what their rank. In belonging to a particular estate that stands apart from all other estates, each person is also aware of fitting into a universal order of society. Up to a point, the members of each estate are strangers to the members of other estates. But they are also joined together by the ties of superiority and subordination typified in the feudal bond. They recognize each other as complementary parts of the same society and, in this sense, as joint insiders within a broader community.

In European feudal societies and *Ständestaaten,* the blend of particularism and universalism was given a still more dramatic form by the dominant theological beliefs. A tribal society identifies the sacred with itself—with arrangements, objects, or forces it believes peculiar to its own experience. It will abandon its view of the immanence of the divine in actuality before it stops seeing itself as God's preferred stage for His deeds. The history of Judaism exemplifies this pattern. In liberal societies, by contrast, religious universalism is the reverse side of social universalism. People will begin to think of God as a universal person without special commitments to any one nation, and they will develop a relativistic view of the worth of the religious beliefs of different countries and ages. Both traits were brought out by the rationalist deism of the European Enlightenment.

The Christianity that so pervaded life and thought in pre-Enlightenment Europe found a middle position between the extremes of religious universalism and particularism. Though it acknowledged in principle a universal brotherhood of man, it emphasized the separation of Christendom from the surrounding pagan world or from infidels within Christian lands. Thus, it was possible to believe that all men were called to membership in the same Christian community while acting on the fact that all were not yet members of it. The denial of the absolute strangeness of another person, required by the idea of the common fatherhood of God, could be reconciled with the element of distance in the Christian's posture toward the religious outsider.

The secular and the theological combination of particularism and universalism in aristocratic society tell us a great deal about how people treated with each other under that regime. A rigid hierarchy of ranks presupposes and implies the breakup of any closely knit and all-inclusive community of values, for its exposes each rank to a distinct experience and imposes on it unique responsibilities. Yet the same social circumstances that dissolve the tight moral community also preclude what I described as the association of interests. Such an association is based on the premise that individuals can come to view themselves as persons who transcend the groups to which they belong and who, despite their class differences, encounter one another on a footing of relatively equal worth, expressed by their formal equality of political rights. Neither assumption holds in aristocratic society. Much of the individual's life plays itself out within the confines of a single group, his estate. Moreover, by virtue of his rank, he has privileges and duties that establish his unalterable hierarchic relationship to men of other ranks.

The leading principle that holds the aristocratic order together is honor rather than communal solidarity or interest association.[7] Honor is the recognition by others that one excels in the virtues peculiarly suited to one's rank in view of the entitlements and obligations that attend it. Every individual is caught forever within the same social circle that limits what he can do, know, and feel. Thus, for example, rather than being a person *with* a nobleman's jobs, he *is* a nobleman. For himself and for others, his social place exhausts his humanity and is inseparable from it. One can be a good serf or a good cleric, but one cannot be simply a good man. Hence, the struggle for self-expression and approval by others must appear in aristocratic society as the desire to realize in one's own existence the peculiar mode of humanity proper to one's rank. The force of this desire gives life to the paraphernalia of estate privileges and obligations, making each individual see their preservation as self-defense.

Because the aristocratic order has a single stable hierarchy, in contrast to the multiple unstable rankings that distinguish liberalism, its top stratum, the aristocracy, plays a uniquely important part in determining the character of the entire society. The aristocracy's preeminence over all other estates gives it the independence necessary to perfect the relation between individual and group that the principle of honor implies: the assertion of the corporate spirit of the estate in the deeds of its members. The same independence explains the peculiar loftiness of ambition and the self-assured possession of self that set the aristocratic ethos apart and have often been identified with the idea of honor itself. The non-aristocratic estates, however, are all more or less under the political control and cultural tutelage of the aristocracy. Insofar as they serve and emulate the nobility, they can never fully work out the modes of consciousness and of existence that express their own corporate nature.

Here lies the deep contradiction in their circumstance. When trying to assert their own modes of communal organization, they are constantly frustrated by the power interests of the aristocracy. Yet their own identity as estates is inseparable from a hierarchic order in which the nobility occupies the dominant position. This is precisely the contradiction that dominated the relationship between peasants and merchants, on one side, and nobles, on the other, during the emergence of the European nation-state and during its passage from the aristocratic to the liberal type of social life. The peasants rebelled and the merchants plotted for greater privileges of self-government within aristocratic society. They could not get what they wanted, however, without crippling the aristocracy. They thereby transformed the character of social life in such a way that they ceased to exist as separate corporate groups, a result no one may ever have intended or wanted. The free development of commerce, for example, helped create a mercantile society in which the market was open to everyone rather than being the meeting place of a distinct category of persons.

Each type of society has a focal point of tension, a hidden flaw in its characteristic way of defining the social bond. When, for whatever reason, the weakness becomes manifest and has clear-cut consequences, the society disintegrates and takes on a new form. For tribal society there is the danger that the community of shared values may fall apart, victim to group conflict. Liberal society is vulnerable to the implications of its uniquely unstable system of ranking: some groups in fact have more power than others, yet no group seems entitled to dominate the others. Hence, a continual struggle takes place between the quest for equality and the need for authority. The analogous tension in aristocratic society is the conflict between the power of the aristocracy and the struggle of the other estates to affirm their autonomous identity and to develop their own internal community. History shows us the consequences of the disintegration of tribal and aristocratic societies. But to what other form of social life does the decline of liberalism lead? The answer to this question remains only partly known, and will be a theme of later sections of this chapter.

The last step in my analysis of aristocratic society is to suggest its typical way of dealing with the relationship of the ideal to the actual. In this, as in all other aspects of its existence, we should expect to find an intermediate position, a point midway between the tribe's identification of *ought* with *is* and liberalism's remorseless contrast of the two. Once again, the issue may be usefully approached from the standpoint of the reconciliation of universalism and particularism in group life.

The particularist element in aristocratic society encourages each estate to equate the good, the beautiful, and the sacred with its own honor, that is to say, with the strivings and virtues that mark it off from other ranks. At the same time, however, the universalist component leads each social stratum to seek, and allows it to grasp, a more inclusive conception of the ideal, which rises above the estates and applies to them all. When aristocratic society accepts the claims of a transcendent religion like Christianity, the antagonism between the tendency to sanctify existing social arrangements and the tendency to oppose them to a higher heavenly perfection becomes still more intense. As a result of this tension, we can expect to find in the culture and in the everyday experience of aristocratic society an oscillation between a joining together of ideals and actuality and a breaking apart of them.

Take, for instance, the place of the Christian vision in medieval European society. One of the most striking features of this period was the aristocracy's attempt to identify its own ethos with the Christian life by carrying the latter down to earth and taking the former up to heaven. The product of this double ascension and descent was the Christian knight and his code of chivalry.[8] Nevertheless, an aspect of social life at least as prominent pointed in the opposite direction. This contrasting feature was the radical disjunction between the brutality of everyday existence and the serene Christian purity displayed in monastic communities as a way of life and in Christian liturgy as an episode in everyone's life. Thus, there was a constant swing between the practice of otherworldly detachment and the quest for mundane comfort, power, and glory.

For all its semblance of ordered hierarchy, aristocratic society is the stage of a war, carried out within individual souls, among visions of the good, the beautiful, and the holy. Therein lies that society's peculiar pathos and the chief inspiration of its highest accomplishments.

Social change

Though this typology is not offered as a scheme of universal evolution, it has certain implications for the understanding of social change. The degree and character of significant change, far from being identical in all societies, vary with each form of social life. The deepest root of all historical change is manifest or latent conflict between the view of the ideal and the experience of actuality.

In liberal society, there is a constant and overt struggle

between what men are led to expect of society and what they in fact receive from it. The high point of this conflict is the combination of an intense need for organized power with a baffling inability to justify any kind of power at all. Another aspect of the conflict is the adversary nature of the relationship between high culture and society. Still another is the tendency of material demands vastly to exceed the resources available for their satisfaction. Because of this many-sided antagonism between ideal and actuality, change in liberal society is rapid and pervasive in comparison with other types of social life.

In an aristocratic society, aspiration and experience are felt to be more at home with each other. The gap persists in half-veiled forms: the ambitions of the nonaristocratic estates cannot be harmonized with the social order, and the moral or religious vision of the society seems both to legitimate and to condemn the established hierarchies. In such a society, change may be both slower and less apparent than under liberalism.

Finally, in tribal society there is merely the possibility, seldom realized, that the communal consensus will disintegrate, making it possible for beliefs to emerge that challenge familiar ways. But, for the most part, such change as exists tends to be noncumulative and unconscious. Structural change is an aberration rather than a normal fate.

The view of social change I have sketched poses, but does not answer, two questions—dark riddles at the outskirts of social theory. First, how could tribal society, which is surely the type most applicable to the earliest forms of human association, ever change? Second, are there any general reasons why one form of society turns into another?

To answer the first question, one must postulate that in any society that can be characterized as human there is always a potential rift between ideal and actuality. This inherent possibility is simply a particular manifestation of that more general power to transcend the forms of one's existence which is a defining attribute of humanity.

If there is a solution to the second problem, it might be a speculative hypothesis about the relationship between the way societies change and the way human nature develops in history: each type of social life would at once reveal and invent new sides to human nature, and the historical succession of societies, when viewed as a whole, would show a movement toward a more perfect reunion of conflicting impulses in humanity. It is not my purpose here to elaborate or to justify this frankly evolutionary idea. I mention it only to suggest the form of a possible answer and thereby to indicate once again how the problems of social theory may force one back to a more basic puzzlement about human nature and its relation to history.

LAW AND EUROPEAN ARISTOCRATIC SOCIETY

Between feudalism and liberalism

The framework outlined in the previous section provides us with the beginnings of a language through which to compare societies. More specifically, it gives us a vantage point from which to approach for our own purposes a theme that loomed large and appeared under many guises in classic social theory: the way modern liberal society developed out of aristocratic society in European history. Sometimes the inquiry was given a still broader evolutionary scope to include a theory of the passage from tribal to aristocratic orders. Almost always it focused on how the novel society recast the relationship of consciousness to existence and on what it portended for mankind's future.

If we are to retain any hope of progressing beyond the point where the classic social theorists left off in the analysis of modernity, we might do well to begin where they did: with an interpretation of what was involved in the emergence of modern European society from the preexisting mode of social life. Such an interpretation is already implicit in my earlier contrast of aristocratic and liberal society. The task now is to make it more concrete and to relate it to law without dissolving the theoretical discussion into a morass of historical particulars.

It has become commonplace to describe the sort of European society that followed the feudal order, but preceded the liberal state, as the society of estates, or *Ständestaat*. Both medieval feudalism and the *Ständestaat* may be considered species of aristocratic society, but it was the latter that served as the immediate forerunner of Western liberalism. A good way to define the *Ständestaat*'s place within the broader category of the aristocratic order is to recall some familiar characterizations that emphasize the arrangement of power.

First, the society of estates was marked by two basic splits. One was the rift between the mass of the people, composed largely of the peasantry, and the elite. The other cleavage separated the different social ranks or estates within the elite from the princely power.[9] Both dichotomies—mass and elite, estates and prince—were indispensable to the *Ständestaat* though neither was peculiar to it. Distinctions within the elite were shaped mainly by hierarchic yet reciprocal ties of military and political obligation. The coexistence of elite and populace, though also colored by such factors, could more accurately be described as economic domination.

Second, the estates that made up the elite were corporately organized into assemblies, like the French *états,* the Austrian and German *Stände,* the Italian *parlamenti,* and the Spanish *cortes.*[10] Within these assemblies, each estate spoke for itself, rather than for some alleged general interest; each defended its own peculiar privileges against the pretensions of the other estates. In the zealous defense of corporate privileges, identified with unchanging law *(ius)*, lay, as Montesquieu and Tocqueville were to point out, the kind of freedom typical of this aristocratic society.[11]

Third, the system of estates developed against the background of the commercial capitalism of the trading towns and of bureaucratic centralization in the service of princely power. Wherever merchant interests gained the upper hand in their own right or through alliance with the aristocracy, the estate assemblies moved toward parliamentarianism. Whenever, on the contrary, the prince succeeded in retaining control of government and drew upon the third estate to set up an elaborate bureaucratic staff, the estate assemblies withered into puny judicial adjuncts of an absolutist state. The repeated attempts of commerce and bureaucracy to tame each other and the relentless encroachment of both upon the traditional hierarchy of ranks constituted a third feature of the *Ständestaat*.

Of these three characteristics, the first links estate society to feudalism and the third to liberalism, whereas the second describes its unique institutional nature and defines its special place within the genus of aristocratic orders. Hintze has shown how the *Ständestaat*'s distinguishing feature, the corporate organization of the estates, took two main forms.[12] It is worthwhile to dwell on the differences between them because they will turn out to be useful in explaining the double path that led from the *Ständestaat* to liberal society.

The oldest type, the one least influenced by the feudal system and closest to tribal roots, was the bicameral system that developed in England, Scandinavia, and much of Eastern Europe. The wealthiest and most powerful nobility sat in an upper chamber; other elite groups, like gentry and free cities, were represented in a lower chamber. The high chamber almost always began as the king's great council, whereas the lower chamber had the character of a general convocation of the privileged elements of the nation.

The second type of estate structure was tripartite. Nobility, clergy, and professional-commercial groups were organized into corporate bodies with an indissoluble set of legislative, administrative, and judicial prerogatives. Such a system became characteristic of France, much of central Europe, and the Kingdom of Naples. In these countries, most of them within the orbit of the former Carolingian empire, the feudal system had disrupted, to a still greater degree than in the other countries, the clannish nature of tribal life and had opened the way to a centralist territorial reorganization of society. Princely ambition had brought into existence a group of scholar-bureaucrats, increasingly trained in the Roman law, who had their own corporate identity and occupied, together with merchant groups, an important position within the third estate.

These were the specific institutional features of the *Ständestaat*. If we now combine these traits with the attributes of consciousness and existence I ascribed to aristocratic orders in general, we shall have a basis upon which to grasp the nature of law in this preliberal society.

Law in the Ständestaat

Remember that bureaucratic law usually includes two sharply contrasting components. The first is a profane realm of discretionary commands, an area in which the ruler is more or less free to move according to his conceptions of princely expedience or social welfare. The second aspect is a sphere of social life immune to the ruler and subject solely to some sacred, suprapositive order. This law, allegedly higher than politics, ought not to be mistaken for tacit custom; most often it takes the form of God-given precepts whose exegesis is entrusted to a cadre of learned priests or scholars.

Several examples have already been given of civilizations that superimposed such a double-layered normative order upon custom. Sometimes, as in certain epochs of ancient India or Islam, the sacred element in law prevailed so decisively over the profane that even the exercise of princely discretion was judged by religious standards. In these societies, which developed under the overwhelming impact of a shared religion and under the influence of priestly or scholarly groups, the prince was expected above all to perpetuate the sacred law, to season its rigors in extreme cases, and to adapt its principles to changing circumstance. At other times, however, as in the China of the Warring States period, no coherent religious tradition or well-entrenched social groups checked princely power. In these latter cases, discretionary command, enforced through bureaucratic domination, best characterized the law.

From the perspective of this scheme, the law of European feudal societies and *Ständestaaten* was notable for its balance: in many European societies, over a long period of time, royal discretion and higher law complemented each other. Their very equilibrium created a situation in which the barrier between them broke down. But rather than one side's triumphing over the other, both changed into a wholly novel kind of law, and the premises of consciousness and existence on which normative order had previously rested were revised. To understand this seemingly paradoxical process of balance and transformation must be the chief task of any study of postfeudal law in the West.

The contrast of the two faces of preliberal law is underlined by the traditional distinction between *Polizeisache* and *Justizsache*. The former were the matters that fell under the prince's competence to keep the public peace, supervise his subordinates, and gather the resources necessary for the perpetuation of his power. This activity, in which the modern categories of legislation, administration, and jurisdiction were confounded, took the form of edicts, *ordonnances,* or *Landesordnungen.* The royal law constituted the discretionary part of the normative order.

Over against it stood the *Justizsache,* the matters pertaining to the privileges and obligations of the estates of the realm. Portions of this corporate law might come to be written down in a variety of ways: as royal charters recognizing entitlements that were supposed to preexist them, as anonymous popular compilations, or as scholarly treatises. But regardless of the form, the principle persisted that the written word described a law that preexisted it. The two parts of the system, represented in the contrast of *lex* (police regulation) and *ius* (fundamental law), came together in the person of the king, who was both maker of edicts and protector of the constitutional order of the estates. Any attempt by him to violate that order in the exercise of his police powers entitled the estates to resist his incursions.[13]

The elements that make up a legal order—the attributes of positiveness, publicity, generality, and autonomy—were therefore distributed in such a way that no real legal system could exist or even be conceived. The law of princely ordinances was neither general nor autonomous in the modern sense, and the law of estate privileges neither public nor positive. Let us now look more closely at each of these statements and piece out their relationship to my earlier remarks about the nature of aristocratic societies in general and of *Ständestaaten* in particular.

The lack of a commitment to the ideal of generality in the royal law manifested itself in that law's freedom from the modern contrast between legislation and administration. The prince's commands within the boundaries of his police power were not meant to promulgate or to execute general rules applicable to abstract categories of persons and acts. The same type of order, with the same kind of justification, might be addressed to a single individual or to the entire realm, without any stopping point on the continuum from individualized directive to universal precept other than respect for the law of the estates. At the outset, the conditions were not yet at hand that would make generality an indispensable requirement rather than an accidental characteristic of law and thereby separate administration from legislation.

The law of edicts was likewise alien to the modern dualism of administration and adjudication. Such a dualism, with its characteristic contrast of institutions, methods of discourse, and occupational groups, reflects a sustained effort to protect the authoritative interpretation of law, as a sphere of rule-determined decisions, from politics, as a realm of prudential judgments. The chief problems of modern jurisprudence involved showing how prudence might be disciplined by law in administration and law tempered by prudence in adjudication. In the period we are discussing, however, the prince's discretion was unhampered by a commitment to general rules, and it could therefore dispense with a technique for their uniform application. Moreover, the royal police power was already limited by the privileges of the estates. Another limit would be sought only after this one began to crumble.

Throughout the history of the *Ständestaaten,* rulers were engaged in a struggle to expand the scope of their power into areas of social life formerly the domain of the suprapolitical prerogatives of the estates. The revolutionary significance of this struggle is shown by the fact that it resulted in the development of a positive and public law at a time when such law was still considered a special or even extraordinary device.

Insofar as it was positive, the king's regulation asserted the principle that ever broader ranges of social experience might be manipulated by acts of political will. Because it was public, a law that only the central government could lay down, it presupposed and fostered the separation of state from society and of political right from social status.

The law governing estate prerogatives presented a reverse picture of the king's ordinances. This fundamental, constitutional law, a system of *ius* rather than of *lex,* already had the beginnings of a commitment to generality and autonomy. As the law of an aristocratic society, it could not admit a formal equality that cut across distinctions of rank, nor could it allow the free development of specialized legal institutions, personnel, and arguments.[14] Yet it established the obligations and entitlements of broad categories of individuals; it was perceived as beyond the reach of politics; and it was expected to be applied impartially. Thus, it was from the start something more than mere custom.

This part of the law also differed from monarchic command in its initial lack of a public and positive character. It was not at first made by the central government, for it preceded the state's appearance and limited its power. And though it might occasionally be articulated and written down, it was seen as an order whose existence and validity preexisted human deliberation.

The neat line between royal and corporate law faded away. But the social forces behind both aspects of the law were so matched that the distinction collapsed in both directions, and this fact is of the utmost significance in understanding the later history of law in the West.

On one side, the prince was increasingly held to standards of legal generality and autonomy. An ever larger area of his police power became subject to the demand that individual interests be regulated only under the authority and within the limits of preexisting laws, addressed to broadly defined categories of persons and acts. Thus, the contrast of administration and legislation gained a foothold. The separation of administrative and legislative power made it important to establish an independent judiciary, with its own personnel and procedures, to oversee the administrative use of legislation. This might be done through a differentiation of tasks within the prince's staff or through the assumption of more specialized judicial responsibilities by the corporate assemblies.

Some aspects of these developments seem to have been largely unintended consequences of the growth of bureaucracies designed to serve the prince's interests. But this alone would not have been enough, as the Chinese comparison suggested. It was crucial in Europe that the aristocracy, the third estate, or both together always remained sufficiently powerful to restrain the prince.

While the law of ordinances was being organized and domesticated in this fashion, the law of estate privileges underwent a remarkable transformation of its own. The institutionalization of corporate assemblies and the rivalry of estates with each other and with the prince encouraged even sharper and more explicit formulations of the entitlements and duties of each estate. It became steadily more important for all parties to determine where royal authority stopped and fundamental law, above politics, began. If these determinations were not made by the state, they nevertheless constituted the social compact that defined the structure and limits of national government.

Thus, the law of estate prerogatives began to acquire a public and a positive character without entirely losing its earlier identity. For it continued to be viewed as an order that was higher than government itself and that ought not to be meddled with lightly. In this way, the law of privileges became the core of modern European constitutional law and remained so, at least until the French revolutionists' assertion of omnipotent popular sovereignty introduced a rival tradition of constitutionalism.[15]

The development to which I have referred did not occur everywhere at the same pace or with the same emphasis. There were countries in which the centralizing impetus of the monarch prevailed over the autonomy of the estates and the defense of their law. The idea of fundamental law was almost wholly destroyed, despite occasional rebellion and resistance by the estates. The prince bent large parts of the aristocracy and of the third estate to his own service and created from their midst a numerous corps of state servants. In these countries, the *Ständestaat* was followed by bureaucratic absolutism.

In other societies, however, a renewed aristocracy, often in alliance with enriched merchants groups and with professional people, captured a major part of the state machine. Princely power suffered accordingly. And the doctrine of fundamental law was enshrined as the safeguard of the established social hierarchy and as an assurance of the limits on the ability of groups in government to use their position against groups outside government. A large public staff was slow to develop. In these societies, parliamentary constitutionalism succeeded the *Ständestaat.*

Bureaucratic absolutism and parliamentary constitutionalism were the two main routes of transition from the society of estates to liberal society. They might be illustrated, respectively, by Prussia and England.[16] Bureaucratic absolutism flourished chiefly in the territories characterized by a tripartite *Ständestaat,* where the imprint of feudal organization, as a premature bid for a centralized state system, was deepest. Parliamentary constitutionalism appeared within the area of the bicameral type of *Ständestaat,* in which the estates had always retained a greater measure of independence. Russia is an altogether different case, a society in which imperial authority was so absolute and personal from the start that no true system of estates can be said to have ever existed.[17]

Bureaucratic absolutism provided the context for the nondemocratic variety of liberalism, which offered the middle classes protection from governmental "arbitrariness," but largely denied them direct participation in government affairs. Parliamentary constitutionalism led to liberal democracy. The passage from bureaucratic absolutism to the liberal democratic state might be accomplished, as in France, through revolution.

The contrast between bureaucratic absolutism and parliamentary constitutionalism should not, however, blind us to the features that, in contrast to other civilizations, both had in common. In no *Ständestaat* was the prince powerful enough to impose his ordinances on the basic activities of social life without satisfying in some measure the requirements of legal generality and autonomy. In this sense, he had no choice but to uphold the rule of law.

The reasons for this astonishing development are surely difficult to surmise. Yet the argument of Chapter Two suggested some of the factors that may have been involved. Among these, two were singled out for special attention: the complex of circumstances that allowed a broad spectrum of groups to maintain or to assert their identities in the face of state centralization and the acceptance of religious ideas and institutions that invoked a universal moral order to which even state law was subject. My earlier discussion of these factors may now be offered as a tentative explanation of the evolution I have just traced.

The pluralism of groups and the vision of society associated with it made the untrammeled assertion of bureaucratic law impossible. It contributed first to the persistent, though often ultimately unsuccessful, defense of estate prerogatives, then to the modern outcry for formal equality and impartial justice under law. The belief in a God-given natural order, whether accompanied or not by an independent church, gave a cosmic support to the confinement of state power by the fundamental law of the *Ständestaat* or by liberal constitutionalism. The modern rule of law emerged from the double-edged process by which the law of edicts acquired the trappings of generality and autonomy and the law of estate privileges became public and positive.

LIBERAL SOCIETY AND ITS LAW

My comparative framework and my analysis of the *Ständestaat* provide tools with which to begin the study of liberal society and its law. The intention of my approach is to emphasize the relationship between prevailing belief and external organization. Thus, I begin by discussing the situation of consensus in liberal society as a way to uncover the central paradoxes of a dominant ideology. Then, the argument points to the roots of these paradoxes in a unique form of social hierarchy. The proposed understanding of the interplay between commitment and experience under liberalism permits a reinterpretation of the place of law in liberal society. And this reinterpretation in turn advances our insight into modernism. Finally, some of these themes will be illustrated by reference to German legal history. For the moment, I shall use the concepts of liberalism and modernity synonymously, though it will turn out that the former is only a special case of the latter.

Consensus

The comparison of forms of social life suggested that the central theme of consciousness and existence in liberal society is a peculiar set of interdependencies among three factors.

The first element is the multiplication of significant groups with the diminishment of the area of individual life dominated by each group. Roles are specialized, but every person occupies a variety of them. The second basic feature of liberal society is the disappearance of a sharp distinction between strangers and insiders. The social order becomes an association of interests that plays on men's need for each other's approval. Third, ideals are opposed to actuality.

Taken as a whole, these aspects of modern society give new urgency to the question of how persons with conflicting views of the good and of reality can live at peace with each other and with themselves. Even peace is not enough; society must be set up in a manner capable of justification in the eyes of its members. Without such a justification, an ordinary life, lived in obedience to the conventions of its time and place, loses the overwhelming reassurance on which it can count when social practices seem to embody natural necessity or holy right. As a consequence, the experience of the arbitrariness or meaninglessness of existence invades the routines of work, play, and family, routines which had previously been the bulwarks against that experience. How does this predicament, the deepest and most frightening hallmark of modernity, arise from the defining attributes of liberal society, and how does it bear on society's preferred forms of law?

Universalism, interest association, and the estrangement of ideals from actuality have two major effects on consensus. They endanger the possibility of extensive, coherent, concrete, and intense agreement about the rightness or goodness of social arrangements. More importantly, they undermine the willingness to accept the fact of agreement as a sign that one has discovered the good or the right.

The universalism of liberal society lies precisely in its tendency to multiply the number and to diminish the individual importance of the group settings in which each person lives. A traditional example is the parceling out of tasks once concentrated in the family. Individuals expose only a limited portion of their humanity to their fellows in each of the narrow strips of life on which they meet. The associations one belongs to lack the breadth of similar experience with which to fashion a common moral vision. Thus, people can share certain purposes or interests, but they cannot make their groups into communities. For the first key to community is the capacity to perceive and to deal with others as whole persons rather than as jobholders, and the second key is joint participation in a shared universe of discourse about man and his good.[18]

The replacement of tribal solidarity and aristocratic honor by the bond of interest and approval is another aspect of the same disruptive movement. Because people lack the grace of community, they can be held together and kept in place only by their need to use each other as means to the satisfaction of their own desires. And because they cannot expect love, they must settle for esteem.

Nevertheless, there are also forces at work in a liberal society that reinforce moral agreement. An aristocratic order may in fact be more favorable to extreme differences of vision and commitment than a liberal one; this is the sense in which the latter comes closer to the tribal type of social life than the former. Each estate in an aristocratic society has its own honor: its code of conduct and its favored image of man. Among the nobility in particular, the cult of individual distinctiveness may be precisely the means through which the honor of one's rank is expressed. Liberalism may undermine the bases of community, but, by tearing down the barriers among significant groups, it also creates the conditions for a pervasive uniformity of desires and preconceptions. Here, however, the analogy between tribal and liberal society stops. Whereas in the former custom can be revered as holy, in the latter it is open to constant attack.

Thus, the narrowing of the range of agreement is not in and of itself the decisive fact about normative ideas in a liberal society. Despite the shattering of earlier kinds of solidarity, the basic structure of belief and power may remain surprisingly stable. But even when liberal society fails to increase the actual diversity of individual circumstances and beliefs, it corrupts the persuasive authority of the consensus it generates. Men may increasingly cease to view that consensus as a reliable source of criteria for the justification and criticism of social arrangements.

One can begin to see why this might be so if he remembers the last defining attribute of liberal society, its tendency to destroy the foundations of the idea that what ought to be somehow inheres in what is. The loosening of the ties of community fosters a particular mode of consciousness and is fostered by it. This outlook begins with the insight that conventions of behavior are shaped by history; it goes on to the denial of their intrinsic goodness; and it ends in the conviction that they are based upon the naked acts of will by which people choose among conflicting ultimate values.

Established practices must be robbed of their claim to be the measure of goodness or rightness if they are to be approached in the manipulative, instrumental fashion which the liberal style of interest association implies. At the same time, every step in the disruption of community adds to the sense that no one way of arranging society is either stable or self-justifying. The awareness that interpersonal relations may assume an almost endless variety of forms, each with its own peculiar causes and effects, sends men searching for higher, comprehensive principles of justification and criticism. But, by an irony that overshadows much of modern culture, the same conditions that make this search necessary also render it futile.

To the extent that moral, religious, or aesthetic ideals

lose the support of communal authority, they have to be redefined as private concerns and preferences for choice among which there are no public criteria. The consequence of this privatization of ideals is that whatever consensus does persist in liberal society seems groundless. Unmasked as products of circumstance and tradition, conventional morality and taste have lost the appearance of inevitability; they must be measured against some independent standard. Yet no standards with which to evaluate agreed upon conventions remain; even religious revelation is now regarded as an experience of the individual conscience, over which government has no say and from which it can infer nothing. At last there comes the despair of the worth of everyday tasks, a despair that may start off as an experience of the intelligentsia, but which reaches little by little into every sector of the population.

How, then, can there be consensus without authority, stability without belief, order without justification? This is the puzzle one confronts in trying to understand the core experience of modernity. To grasp the place of law and of the state in liberal society, we must solve this puzzle. To solve it, we must shift the focus of inquiry from consensus to hierarchy.

Hierarchy

A rank order is a hierarchical distribution of social groups with respect to access to wealth, power, and knowledge. There are two clear-cut forms a society's rank order can assume, opposite poles along a single spectrum.

At one extreme, there is the closed and inclusive sort of ranking. Its closure has to do with the stability of the place occupied by each of its members. Its inclusiveness describes its importance in shaping the individual's social position. Inclusiveness strengthens closure: the more all embracing a social place becomes, the harder it may be to change it.

Ranking in an aristocratic society is closed and inclusive. Each person occupies a position fixed more or less forever at birth. And a single hierarchy outweighs all other criteria of preference in the society; one's membership in an estate directly influences every aspect of his social existence.

The alternative type of ranking is open and partial. Openness refers to the ease with which individuals can change places in the rank order. Partiality describes the multiplicity of different ranking systems. The more a society tends toward partial ranking systems, the more it relies on a variety of different hierarchies of access to wealth, power, and knowledge. These hierarchies may be only loosely connected. Partiality facilitates openness just as inclusiveness favors closure.

In comparison to an aristocratic order, a liberal society has a ranking system that is relatively open and partial. The social position of his parents is less significant in determining the individual's opportunities. Moreover, he participates in a variety of social hierarchies. Though his position in each of them reinforces or limits his station in others, the different hierarchies are more likely to be incongruous than they would be in an aristocratic society. Inherited wealth, political influence, educational attainment, and job all hang together, but often in more or less shifting and untidy ways. A man high up in one hierarchy may more easily find himself low down in another.

A relatively open and partial rank order creates the possibility of a widening gap between the existence and the felt legitimacy of hierarchy. This is precisely the situation one finds in liberal society. The subordination of classes and roles is sufficiently closed and inclusive to determine, and to be perceived as determining, much of the individual's social condition. Yet it is also open and partial enough to be viewed as something contingent and indeed arbitrary, ultimately without any basis in the nature of things.

There is a dominant and rather stable structure of dependence and domination in liberal society. Nevertheless, the individual may be sufficiently capable of changing his position in that structure, and sufficiently aware of discrepancies and tensions among the different criteria that establish his place within it, not to take the established rank pattern for granted.

This way of looking at the issue of hierarchy in liberal society puts great weight on the ties between objective relationships of dependence and the consciousness people have of these relationships. Indeed, it insists that the former are inseparable from the latter—which does not mean they are the same. In fact, it is only the lessening of the relative closure and inclusiveness of the rank system that allows men to become more fully conscious of the nature of the hierarchic arrangements in which they are involved. Consciousness requires distance, the capacity to imagine oneself outside a circumstance and to wonder about how one ought to deal with it. Thus, it is only superficially a paradox that the awareness of hierarchy should be associated with the weakening of the rank system.

This hypothesis about ranking in liberal society is consistent with the recognition that there may be important differences in the objective measure of closure and inclusiveness of a rank pattern, as well as in the degree to which any given level of hierarchy becomes conscious. With these provisos in mind, we can reconsider the issue of illegitimate consensus and power in liberal society.

The same process that diminishes the scope and stability of the rank order also decreases the likelihood that the remaining amount of inequality will be accepted as justified. Every conventional criterion for the allocation of social advantages falls under the suspicion that it, too, is arbitrary. Even reliance on merit becomes suspect when its dependence on the distribution of genetic endowments is taken into account, for people may begin to doubt whether a man's social place should be determined by a fact of which he is not the author.

Thus, the more varied and moderate distinctions of rank become, the less tolerable do the remaining differences seem. By a paradox which Tocqueville first described and whose source in the very structure of modern society we are now able to identify, the love of equality increases with every step toward the equalization of circumstances.[19] Yet it is precisely in these conditions of dissolving hierarchy and moral confusion that the need to find a basis for the exercise of power, and to distinguish its legitimate uses from its illegitimate ones, appears most urgent. The progress toward equality both destroys and craves authority.

What is less remarked though just as important is that every consensus or tradition begins to be tainted in the eyes of its adherents with the failings of the hierarchic social circumstance from which it arose. In the course of the transition from more closed and inclusive to more open and partial rankings, people become increasingly sensitive to the influence of past or present distributions of power on accepted ideas about right conduct. What seems at first glance the outcome of a long tradition of agreement turns out, on closer inspection, to represent the beliefs and interests of the dominant groups who shaped the tradition.

Perhaps the most visible aspect of this phenomenon is the tendency in modern culture to criticize beliefs or ideals by uncovering their origins in a sort of political or personal domination. (Think of Nietzsche, Marx, and, in a sense, Freud, perhaps the most characteristic, if not the most profound, social thinkers of the modern age.) To "unmask" an idea becomes a surrogate for the proof that it is false or evil. What makes this trend so persistent and pervasive is its association with an experience that ever wider groups undergo in their everyday lives.

The core of this experience is the increasingly common perception that our practices are products of the very forms of ranking they are used to justify. Thus, a vicious (or liberating) circle of demoralization of existing social arrangements starts on its way. Each weakening of the legitimacy of the rank order undermines trust in conventional practices, while each successive departure from belief in the rightness of tradition upsets still further the felt legitimacy of established hierarchies.

My thesis about hierarchy and consensus in liberal society may be broadened into a commentary on theories of social order. The political economists believed that men could be bound together by their divergent and complementary interests; this was to be the great civilizing mission of the market. Conservative and Romantic critics of liberalism argued that stable interpersonal relations could be restored only if people lived in settings that encouraged allegiance to common values. In a sense, both doctrines were fanciful solutions to a mythical problem. They both took seriously the Hobbesian view of society as a set of individuals with relatively equal strengths, as well as with conflicting ends, so that no one was sufficiently more powerful than his fellows to impose his will upon them. Hence, the possibility of order became mysterious.

But once we conceive of society, as Marx insisted we should, as an association more of groups than of individuals, the mystery disappears. For among groups—classes and organizations—there are clearly enormous disparities of power. This structure of group domination ensures that an order will in fact be imposed.[20]

There is, nevertheless, a flaw in this criticism of traditional doctrines. For the reasons suggested, the power system of liberal society is one that becomes increasingly unable to retain its authority. By its very nature, it destroys its own legitimacy in the eyes of dominators and dominated alike. Thus, the parcel of truth contained in the liberal and the conservative conception of the problem of order in modern life is the nonexistence of an order men can accept. The aspect of truth in the Marxist attack on those views is that, given objective disparities of power, it does not necessarily follow that because people reject the legitimacy of the hierarchic system they will be able to overthrow it or even to discover something to replace it.

We can now understand the puzzling coexistence of resignation and disbelief, unequal power and egalitarian conviction, that marks consciousness in liberal society. There is indeed a structure of domination. But it affects people's outlooks on society and on themselves ambiguously. It cuts away its own ground by overturning faith in the naturalness of the established hierarchy. But by the same process through which it saps its own foundations it also poisons all other moral and political beliefs. People lose confidence in their own judgments and they lose hope of discovering criteria for common judgments. All their conceptions begin to seem mere prejudices of an age, a society, or a faction, whims produced by social arrangements for which no independent justification can be found. The resulting moral skepticism encourages either a despairing acceptance of the existing order or an aimless shifting from one pattern of inequality to another.

Thus, we can account for a basic, common experience in modern society that would otherwise remain unintelligible: the sense of being surrounded by injustice without knowing where justice lies. This condition is the political side of that more general sentiment of arbitrariness and even absurdity which gradually enters into the consciousness of every group.

A crucial factor in the resolution of this predicament must therefore be the extent to which and the manner in which people manage to overcome their disorientation over values. The need to discover a good that has become hidden gives speculative thought and political practice a mission they must carry out jointly if it is to be carried out at all. To change the situation one must see the good. To see the good one must already be in a situation that would permit one to have confidence in the worth of one's moral inclinations. Hence, the search for moral understanding becomes inseparable from the struggle to create a society whose arrangements do not irremediably distort the moral vision of its members.

Law and the state

The preceding discussion of liberal society furnishes the elements to develop further an understanding of the directions taken by modern legal and political thought. And this reconsideration of the social basis of theory will carry us into the study of the actual place of the legal order in liberal society.

The basic issues of jurisprudential and political speculation arise from the twofold experience of the unjustifiability of the existing rank order and of the corruption of moral agreements or traditions by the injustice of their origins. Insofar as people have this experience, they struggle to avoid or diminish enslavement to each other in the rank order and to establish the most far-reaching power, the power of government, upon a basis that overcomes the arbitrariness of ordinary social hierarchies.

A major form of this struggle is the striving toward the rule of law. Earlier in my argument I characterized the rule of law by its commitment to generality and autonomy. For my present purposes, it is useful to distinguish between a looser and a narrower conception of the rule of law. The former is always characteristic of the dominant response to the situation of liberal society, whereas the latter arises in special circumstances only.

In the broadest sense, the rule of law is defined by the interrelated notions of neutrality, uniformity, and predictability. Governmental power must be exercised within the constraints of rules that apply to ample categories of persons and acts, and these rules, whatever they may be, must be uniformly applied. Thus understood, the rule of law has nothing to do with the content of legal norms.

As long as the lawmaker must manifest his will through general rules, he is stopped from directly punishing or favoring particular individuals and therefore from bringing them under his immediate personal control. The administrator, for his part, deals with individuals but only within the constraints laid down by rules he did not make. Thus, he too, according to this mode of thought, is kept from using public power to achieve personal ends. For the administrator to act within the boundaries set by the laws, there must be some other person with final authority to determine what the laws mean, and to do so by a method different from the administrative one. This official is the judge.

If the administrator were also the judge, it would be possible for him to twist the meaning of the rules to whose execution he is committed so as to suit his own purposes. Moreover, he might end up confusing the administrative and the judicial method, each distinct in its emphasis and each indispensable for the proper management of the state.

The administrator focuses on the most effective means to realize given policy objectives within the constraints of the law. For him, rules of law are a framework within which decisions are made. For the judge, on the contrary, the laws pass from the periphery to the center of concern; they are the primary subject matter of his activity. Adjudication calls for distinctive sorts of arguments, and its integrity demands specialized institutions and personnel.

Thus, even the narrowest view of the rule of law includes a differentiation of the procedures of legislation, administration, and adjudication. We shall see later how and why first the distinction between the administrative and the judicial method and then the difference between both of these and the legislative method became less and less tenable.

If the uniform application of general laws by separate administrators and judges is enough to characterize the rule of law ideal in a loose sense, a stricter version of that ideal makes certain demands upon the method of legislation itself. It requires that laws be made by a procedure to which everyone might have reason to agree in his own self-interest. More especially, it insists that each person participate somehow in the process of lawmaking. It is therefore expected that the legal order will possess the attribute described earlier as substantive autonomy: it will represent a balance struck among competing groups rather than the embodiment of the interests and ideals of a particular faction.

There is a rough correspondence between the two forms of the rule of law and the familiar contrast of the nondemocratic and the democratic variety of liberalism. Which of the two kinds of legal order have prevailed in a society seems to have depended largely on whether the third estate was sufficiently powerful to demand participation in the central government, as in England, or only influential enough to limit princely will by general law, as in Germany. A later discussion of the German case will refine this hypothesis and point out other pertinent factors.

In either of its two main variants, the rule of law tries to deal with the predicament of liberal society by ensuring the impersonality of power. Its capacity to achieve this objective rests, however, upon two crucial assumptions.

The first assumption is that the most significant sorts of power can be concentrated in government. As long as the hierarchies of class or role in society fail to affect the basic freedoms of the individual and to tyrannize over the most central aspects of his existence, the problem of unjustified ranking can be kept within manageable bounds. Government must stand above or outside the system of social ranks. This independence of the state from social hierarchies may be brought about by the democratic selection and control of public officers or it may rely on the notion of a monarch or bureaucracy whose position supposedly safeguards it from the influence of party interests.

The second key assumption of the rule of law ideal is that power can be effectively constrained by rules, whether the rules operate as limits on administration or as the substance of choice in adjudication. The generality of the rules and the uniformity of their application guarantee that those who, unlike legislators, exercise power over particular individuals will find it difficult to turn their offices to personal advantage. Still more important, the private citizen need not experience his relationship to the administrator or to the judge as one of personal dependence, for the law creates a buffer between him and them.

The cumulative thrust of these two premises of the rule of law is to distinguish sharply the dealings of officials in their official capacities with private citizens from the dealings of private citizens with one another. The former relationship is subordinative, but it involves no personal subjection of one man's will to another's. The second relationship is mainly coordinative; at least it imposes only secondary or transitory forms of subordination. The difference between the two situations corresponds to the traditional division of public and private law.

Each of the two basic assumptions of the rule of law turns out to be largely fictitious. In the first place, it has never been true in liberal society that all significant power is reserved to government. Indeed, the hierarchies that affect most directly and deeply the individual's situation are those of the family, the workplace, and the market. These inequalities are neither undone nor effectively redressed by the commitment to formal equality before the law. Nor are they subverted, at least in the short run, by the devices of political democracy.

The other critical premise of the rule of law doctrine—that rules can make power impersonal and impartial—is just as shaky. Take the issue of legislation. There are two reasons why no possible method of lawmaking in liberal society could be accepted as truly neutral. First, procedure is inseparable from outcome: every method makes certain legislative choices more likely than others, even though it may often be difficult to spot its bias on any given matter. Second, each lawmaking system itself embodies certain values; it incorporates a view of how power ought to be distributed in the society and of how conflicts should be resolved. It cannot without circularity be used to justify the view upon which it is founded.

Rules could ensure the impersonality of administrative power only if there were indeed a way to determine their meaning independently of the administrator's preferences. Thus, the problem of administrative legality turns into a question of whether judicial power can be adequately controlled by rules. Can judges make use of a method that purges their decisions of personal whim? If we admit that words lack self-evident reference, that meaning must ultimately be determined by purpose and context, and that the intent of prior lawmakers is always more or less incomplete, it becomes doubtful whether a truly impartial method of judging could ever be fashioned within the conditions of liberal society. The sense of the precariousness and of the illegitimacy of consensus makes it difficult for the judge to find a stable authoritative set of shared understandings and values upon which to base his interpretations of the law. Hence, every case forces him to decide, at least implicitly, which of the competing sets of belief in a given society should be given priority. And it requires him to rely on an accepted morality that, even if it can be identified, is increasingly revealed as the product of a social situation itself lacking in sanctity. To this extent, adjudication aggravates, rather than resolves, the problem of unjustifiable power.

Thus, the very assumptions of the rule of law ideal appear to be falsified by the reality of life in liberal society. But, curiously, the reasons for the failure of this attempt to ensure the impersonality of power are the same as those that inspired the effort in the first place: the existence of a relatively open, partial rank order, and the accompanying disintegration of a self-legitimating consensus. The factors that make the search necessary also make its success impossible. The state, a supposedly neutral overseer of social conflict, is forever caught up in the antagonism of private interests and made the tool of one faction or another. Thus, in seeking to discipline and to justify the exercise of power, men are condemned to pursue an objective they are forbidden to reach. And this repeated disappointment accentuates still further the gap between the vision of the ideal and the experience of actuality.

Law, bureaucracy, and liberalism: a German example

This section reexamines, in the setting of modern German history, some of the points previously made about liberal society and its law. Besides providing examples, the references to Germany may help connect my present study of the place of law in liberal society with the discussion in Chapter Two of the bases of legal order. Moreover, legal and social developments in Germany departed in important respects from the simplified scheme with which I have interpreted liberalism and the rule of law. Thus, the German case challenges my argument, forces me to qualify it, and allows me to elaborate it. It will be useful to begin again with a broad historical background before moving on to the specifically German trends.

Nowhere was the *Ständestaat* a more enduring and deeply rooted phenomenon than in central Europe. Here, as in other European regions, the corporate system of estates was in many ways the outcome of the feudal aristocracy's reaction against the early centralizing tendencies of the twelfth and the thirteenth century, just as feudalism had been the fallback position of a premature effort at centralization on a large territorial scale.

Three characteristics of this *Ständestaat* are particularly relevant to our present concerns. First, judicial and administrative functions were inseparable; both were exercised together by prince and estates as part of their joint responsibility for the administration of justice and the maintenance of the fundamental law of the realm. Second, public and private law had not yet been distinguished, which is another way of saying that political right and social status were still an indivisible whole. Third, there was no staff of bureaucrats charged with a public office that might be clearly distinguished from a private privilege. This last matter demands closer scrutiny.

Since the early twelfth century, Europe had witnessed the growth of professional administration in a number of contexts. Each centralizing monarch began to surround himself with trained clerks who might assist him in his major preoccupations: extending his control through the administration of justice, exacting tribute from his subjects, and amassing wealth from his domains.[21] Thus, the royal courts established institutions like the Chancery and the Exchequer in England, the *parlements* and *cour des comptes* in France, or the Sicilian judicial and administrative agencies under Roger II.[22] The men who staffed these bodies might have had special training and significant power of their own, but they remained members of the king's household and tools of his policy. They drew no distinction between the prince's own patrimonial interests and his political aims.

The free cities of the late Middle Ages provided a somewhat different atmosphere for the rise of administrators. The town bureaucracies might have had a clearer sense than the king's servants of occupying a public office. Yet their loyalty to, and their remuneration by, a private clientele was considered a normal aspect of their position.

In the state-building monarchies of the fifteenth, sixteenth, and seventeenth centuries the separation between private service to the prince and government work gradually became clearer. Nevertheless, the tendency was still to treat the administrative office as a private asset to be exploited and even sold in the interests of its owner.[23] One thinks in this regard of the *officiers* in a French kingdom that was perhaps the most full-blown example of bureaucratic absolutism in Europe before the ascendancy of Prussia.[24]

From the mid-seventeenth century onward, these characteristics of the *Ständestaat* began to be undermined in Prussia. Though the immediate agent of this change was the Hohenzollern dynasty, its greatest beneficiary became the bureaucracy itself and the classes from which the bureaucracy was drawn and with which it was allied.

Administrative and legislative power were separated from judicial authority. This separation served a variety of purposes. It disentangled monarchic initiative from a setting of judicial responsibilities and rituals that had set limits on the king's authority in the past. And it deprived the estates of the substance of their political power while allowing them to retain some of their traditional adjudicative prerogatives.

The new dichotomy also contributed to a subtle but significant change in the conception of law. The corporate law of the *Ständestaat* had both a territorial and a personal connotation: it was the law of a *Land,* a place where different groups lived together, each according to its own law. Once the legislative and the administrative tasks were centralized, it became possible to make law, and to perceive it, as a universal order applicable to all the inhabitants of an area. The legal order became associated with the idea of state sovereignty, and this idea was given a territorial emphasis.[25]

The same factors that allowed the concentration of administrative and legislative power in a central government also gave rise to the modern contrast of public and private law. The immediate significance of this division was to separate clearly the area of life over which government had a more or less free hand from the one it surrendered to civil society. At first, private law was simply an extension of the corporate law of the *Ständestaat*. Thus, the earliest codifications, like the *Preussische Allgemeine Landrecht* of 1794, were still permeated by the spirit of estate privilege.[26] But, in time, prerogatives began to be sacrificed to the program of formal equality, though never as completely in Germany as in many other European countries. Public law started out as a counterpart to the undisciplined law of royal ordinances, but it too was to be subject to universalistic standards after the triumph of the *Rechtsstaat* idea.

Another basic current in the evolution of the Prussian state was the creation of a bureaucratic corps, forbidden, with increasing effectiveness, to treat public offices as private assets.[27] This development culminated in the acceptance of an ideology that defined the public purpose the bureaucracy should serve as a universal interest—the welfare of the state as an organic whole rather than any factional advantage. The heyday of the notion of the administrative class as a neutral power was the period of the Stein-Hardenberg reforms after the expulsion of Napoleon.

This idea of devotion to a universal interest had an element of truth as well as a surfeit of mystification. It marked a time in which the bureaucracy had become, together with the landed aristocracy and the monarch, a partner in power. In its first impetus of liberalism, the bureaucracy could undermine the structure of corporate society by freeing the serfs, thus preparing the way, often unwittingly, for a vast agricultural and industrial capitalism. Yet it combined these apparent assaults on the aristocracy with concessions to the aristocracy's interests and with strenuous attempts to emulate its ethos and to join its ranks. At the same time, it served as the hammer of dynastic ambition, beating down the Hohenzollerns' foreign and domestic foes with a state apparatus of unprecedented efficiency. Nonetheless, this enormous bureaucratic machine began to set its own goals and eventually to impose them on the prince for whose service it had been created. Thus, the ideology of bureaucratic universalism was the leading doctrine of a state in which the governmental staff had risen from the position of hireling to that of coregent.

In retrospect, one may say that bureaucracy in Europe as a whole, and in Germany in particular, passed through four typical, overlapping stages: a phase in which the administrator was no more than a private servant of the prince; a period in which he conceived of his charge as a public one, distinct from the king's household, but nevertheless continued openly to manipulate the office as private patrimony; an epoch in which the officeholder forswore any direct use of governmental power to advance his personal ends; and finally an era in which the bureaucracy presented itself as the custodian of a universal interest.

Now that we have before us the outline of the changeover from *Ständestaat* to bureaucratic absolutism in Germany, we can understand how this bureaucratic order came to be redefined as a liberal state and what this redefinition implied for the theory and uses of law. The central concept here is that of the *Rechtsstaat,* the German interpretation of the rule of law ideal.

The doctrine of the *Rechtsstaat* was first developed in southwest Germany rather than in Prussia. It dates to the triumph over Napoleon. Its political core was the notion of a compromise among the prince, the *Stände,* and the bureaucracy. This compromise was expressed by the formula of constitutional dualism: power would be shared by the king and the bureaucracy, on the one hand, and by the corporate estates, through their diets, on the other. Both conservatives and liberals dreaded the absence of legal restraints on the exercise of legislative and administrative power. Conservatives feared this lack because it might mean a surrender of all limits on popular sovereignty; liberals, because it offered no safeguards against princely caprice.[28]

When the *Rechtsstaat* idea was embraced in Prussia after the 1848 debacle of democratic liberalism, it took on the form that was to characterize it until the overthrow of the monarchy.[29] The liberals and the middle classes were granted security without meaningful participation. The rule of law was defined as the reign of a legal order that was administered by an independent judicial bureaucracy; that bound government to act under general rules; and that conferred fixed entitlements and obligations on individuals. Within the sphere of private life protected by the legal system, the merchant could trade in peace and the scholar could state his opinions more or less freely.[30] Thus, the impersonal bureaucratic order was accepted by politically conscious though powerless groups as a way to satisfy their longing for liberation from relationships of personal dependency.

This commitment to a modest ideal of legal generality and autonomy was as much the outward expression of a compromise among the ruling groups as a concession to the middle classes. It left the landed aristocracy, the upper level bureaucrats, and the monarch free to exercise their condominium over the state. The devices with which the liberals had hoped to gain a measure of participation in government—the control of the budget by the *Reichstag* and the right to impeach ministers for failure to execute the laws faithfully—soon proved ineffective.[31]

The social and political trends whose broad lines I have sketched suggest why the dominant modes of administrative and judicial reasoning evolved as they did in Germany. At first, there was little distinction between the judicial and the administrative bureaucracy. Both were expected to adhere strictly to rules and to interpret them more or less literally. This insistence on mechanical formalism was one of the ways the monarch had to ensure his control over the bureaucracy and to guarantee its faithfulness to his policies. At the same time, formalism protected the nascent bureaucracy against the king and the aristocracy by allowing bureaucrats to justify their decisions as impersonal applications of rules.

In a second stage of development, the bureaucracy won a large measure of independent power. With the institutionalization of the *Rechtsstaat,* the judicial and the administrative bureaucrats began to perform more clearly distinct tasks. This functional differentiation was reinforced by a social cleavage: the judges were drawn mainly from the bourgeoisie, whereas the top administrators increasingly merged with the nobility, as did the successful parvenu industrialists. During this period, the effort to circumscribe narrowly judicial discretion served a double purpose. In one sense, it satisfied the middle classes' desire for certainty, and hence security, in the application of law. In another sense, it assured the administrative elite that the judges would adhere closely to the laws and decrees, whose making the top bureaucrats often controlled.

In its struggle to relegate the judiciary to an inferior position, the administrative cadre also used other weapons.

One of these was to make the Ministry of Justice a court of appeal. Another was to remove certain issues from the judicial sphere altogether, subjecting them to special administrative procedures. Still another move withdrew the right of indictment from the courts and gave it instead to the state prosecutors.[32]

Whereas the judiciary was confined to a formalism of rules, the administrative bureaucracy, no longer dominated by the monarch, could adopt a relentless instrumental rationality. Only the balance of political forces within Germany and among the major powers limited the ends that might be pursued or the means that could be used to promote them.

Toward the late nineteenth century, and more clearly in the Weimar Republic, when industrialization had already set its mark upon German society, a third period in the history of the forms of bureaucratic reasoning began. This epoch was distinguished by a transformation in the ideals of legal theory and, to a lesser extent, in the actual modes of judicial discourse. Under the impact of intense economic concentration, the bourgeoisie was increasingly divided into two groups with different concerns: the salaried and essentially powerless middle class and the great capitalists, closely allied with the military and bureaucratic leaders.[33]

This latter group, a managerial elite, no longer depended on the judiciary for anything important. It could achieve its objectives through its direct influence on government and through cartels that created a vast body of nonstate law, almost wholly beyond the reach of the judiciary. The security and predictability it wanted were acquired through its position in the structure of power.

The employed middle classes might at any moment become interested in freewheeling judicial constructions of laws on whose making this salaried bourgeoisie could have little impact. Given the fact that the judges were themselves drawn mainly from this stratum and shared its outlook and interests, they could be expected to tilt the exercise of their discretion toward middle class interests. This they were to do in the boldest fashion during the Weimar Republic through the use of the good faith clause of the Civil Code to "revaluate" debts whose real worth had been all but annihilated by the hyperinflation of the early twenties.[34]

There is a more general reason why long before the crisis of the Weimar years merchant groups were likely to favor "constructive interpretations" on the part of the judiciary. In its attitude toward the legal order, a commercial class is normally torn between two demands. It wants judicial decisions to be predictable enough not to interfere with the calculation of the economic consequences of transactions. But it also desires the law as applied to be sensitive to trade usage and to adapt constantly to the needs of commerce. The former longing usually militates against the increase of judicial discretion whereas the latter favors it. In late nineteenth-century Germany, however, this conflict was resolved because the judges, drawn from the merchant groups or sympathetic to them, could often be counted on to exercise discretion in a manner that would be both substantially predictable and responsive to the needs of the merchant class.

It was in the context of the situation brought about by the breakup of the bourgeoisie into two groups, one indifferent to the judiciary and the other anxious for its equitable intervention, that the social basis for a jurisprudence of mechanical rule application was destroyed. The turn to policy-oriented styles of judicial reasoning was hastened by intellectual movements that had begun to undermine the entire view of knowledge and language upon which earlier conceptions of the judicial decision rested.

The decline of rule formalism in law application, a decline that brought judges' reasoning closer in style and method to the instrumental rationality of the administrative bureaucracy, presented the defenders and spokesmen of the working classes with a Hobson's choice. If they attacked rule formalism, they opened the way for the adventures of a judiciary unsympathetic to their interests. If, on the contrary, they opposed the enlargement of judicial discretion, they contributed to the maintenance of a legal order whose class nature was strengthened, rather than weakened, by the pretense of neutrality. Thus, socialist legal thinkers hesitated between the defense of formalism and opposition to it.[35]

From this discussion of certain trends in the history of the German state one can draw some inferences of more general relevance to my argument about law in liberal society. First, the *Rechtsstaat* was the manifestation of a compromise between state sovereignty and the corporate order of estate society. The same was true, to a lesser extent, of the English rule of law. But a liberal order that tends toward monarchic and bureaucratic absolutism can perpetuate many of the characteristics of aristocratic society more easily than a liberal state that adopts the forms of parliamentary constitutionalism. The rule of law in England was both cause and effect of the direct participation of the middle classes in government. The legal counterpart to the nondemocratic variant of liberalism in Germany was the narrow interpretation of legal generality and autonomy as pledges of security for both the powerful and the powerless.

The German case suggests that the bureaucracy, as a "universal class," is likely to play a crucial role in the creation of nondemocratic liberalism. Today, the bureaucracy has survived its aristocratic and monarchic allies and it has become a major influence in all industrial societies. The basic impulse of top bureaucrats remains everywhere and always the same: to ensure maximum leeway for their own instrumental rationality and to limit the discretion of other groups, either by confining them to rule formalism or by allowing them to choose among a small number of means to preestablished ends.

A second set of conclusions one might infer from the German example has to do with the legal order's relationship to authoritarianism. The mere commitments to generality and autonomy in law and to the distinction among legislation, administration, and adjudication have no inherent democratic significance. They can help promote an oligarchic or dictatorial monopoly of power. Tocqueville was surely right when he observed: "if he [the prince] entrusted despotism to them [the lawyers] under the form of violence, perhaps he would find it again in their hands under the external features of justice and law."[36] Not only can the legal order embody a well-arranged authoritarianism, but it can coexist indefinitely with the use of pure terror to crush the enemies of the regime by individualized unbridled violence. Indeed, the fact that liberal society is one in which the specialization of roles impresses upon everybody the deepest gaps among the different spheres of social life may make the coexistence of law and terror all the easier to accept.

Lastly, German history illustrates clearly the dilemma the ideal of legality presents to the proletariat in a state which the working classes do not effectively control. The proletariat depends on a centralized bureaucracy to serve as a counterweight to local oligarchies and to nationwide interest groups. It also needs a universalistic legal system to restrict arbitrary domination by social superiors in and outside the workplace. Nevertheless, centralized bureaucracy restricts democratic participation. And the equal treatment of unequal situations by the judiciary simply confirms, if it does not aggravate, their inequality.

It might seem that the one solution to this dilemma is to seize power. But, as the experience of many socialist societies shows, the seizure of power can never in and of itself resolve the problem, for as long as there is a commitment to centralized bureaucratic organization, the issue will remain. Later we shall see that the same ideological and social tendencies that might begin to dismantle bureaucracy also undercut the legal order and ultimately bring the very idea of public and positive law into jeopardy.

THE DISINTEGRATION OF THE RULE OF LAW IN POSTLIBERAL SOCIETY

Postliberal society

An understanding of liberal society illuminates, and is illuminated by, an awareness of that society's legal order and legal ideals. For the rule of law has been truly said to be the soul of the modern state. The study of the legal system takes us straight to the central problems faced by the society itself.

If this hypothesis, which underlies my argument, is correct, then any revision of the nature and uses of law will reveal changes in the basic arrangements of society and in men's conceptions of themselves. At the same time, whatever we can learn about these social changes will help us reinterpret the transformation of the legal order. In this spirit, I discuss on the following pages some aspects of the way certain countries, the Western capitalist social democracies, have become postliberal societies.

The characteristics of these societies undermine the rule of law and they strengthen tendencies in belief and organization that ultimately discourage reliance on public and positive rules as bases of social order. These startling trends will force us to reexamine our view of the situation and the prospects of postliberal societies. For my immediate purposes, it is enough to emphasize two commonly observed sets of features of this novel form of social life.

The first group of features refers to the overt intervention of government in areas previously regarded as beyond the proper reach of state action. The response to the problems of unjustified hierarchy, a response the rule of law failed to provide, is now sought from the government. The rank order itself increasingly moves to the center of political debate and political action. As the state becomes involved in the tasks of overt redistribution, regulation, and planning, it changes into a welfare state.

The other notable set of attributes of postliberal society is but the reverse side of the events just enumerated: the gradual approximation of state and society, of the public and the private sphere. For one thing, the state's pretense to being a neutral guardian of the social order is abandoned. For another thing, private organizations are increasingly recognized and treated as entities with the kind of power that traditional doctrine viewed as the prerogative of government. People may become more conscious of what was always partly true, though perhaps less so in earlier periods: society consists of a constellation of governments, rather than an association of individuals held together by a single government. The state that has lost both the reality and the consciousness of its separation from society is a corporate state.

Now let us see how these welfare and corporatist tendencies affect the society's normative order.

The welfare state and the decline of the rule of law

Welfare state developments influence the legal order of postliberal society in a variety of ways. But two kinds of immediate influence seem particularly significant.

The first type of effect is the rapid expansion of the use

of open-ended standards and general clauses in legislation, administration, and adjudication. For example, the courts may be charged to police unconscionable contracts, to void unjust enrichment, to control economic concentration so as to maintain competitive markets, or to determine whether a government agency has acted in the public interest. Such indeterminate prescriptions have always existed in the law, but they grow rapidly in prominence because of the transformations to which I refer.

The second major impact of the welfare state on law is the turn from formalistic to purposive or policy-oriented styles of legal reasoning and from concerns with formal justice to an interest in procedural and substantive justice. Before further discussion, these terms should be defined.

Legal reasoning is formalistic when the mere invocation of rules and the deduction of conclusions from them is believed sufficient for every authoritative legal choice. It is purposive when the decision about how to apply a rule depends on a judgment of how most effectively to achieve the purposes ascribed to the rule. The difference between these two types of legal reasoning is one between the criteria thought appropriate to the overt justification or criticism of official decisions; it does not pretend to describe the actual causes and motives of decision.

An ideal of justice is formal when it makes the uniform application of general rules the keystone of justice or when it establishes principles whose validity is supposedly independent of choices among conflicting values. It is procedural when it imposes conditions on the legitimacy of the processes by which social advantages are exchanged or distributed. It is substantive when it governs the actual outcome of distributive decisions or of bargains. Thus, in contract law, the doctrine that bargains are enforceable given certain externally visible manifestations of intent exemplifies formal justice; the demand that there be equality of bargaining power among contracting parties illustrates procedural justice; and the prohibition of exchanges of two performances of unequal value, however value may be assessed, represents substantive justice.

A formal view of justice requires, to be coherent, a belief in the possibility of formalistic legal reasoning. And it is likely to be most persuasive in the realm of exchanges among individuals rather than in that of governmental distribution, which inevitably involves choices among conflicting interests. Thus, it tends to distinguish sharply between an impersonal justice of reciprocity that dispenses with distributive premises and an arbitrary justice of distribution whose pronouncements are never impartial and general enough to have anything more than the appearance of law.

Procedural or substantive notions of justice become important as purposive forms of legal reasoning are adopted, and they in turn give impetus to those varieties of argument. For policy-oriented legal discourse forces one to make explicit choices among values, and the pursuit of procedural or substantive justice requires that rules be interpreted in terms of ideals that define the conception of justice. Hence, every decision about the principles that govern exchange is seen to rest upon procedural or distributive premises and to have procedural or distributive consequences.

Postliberal society witnesses an escalating use of open-ended standards and a swing toward purposive legal reasoning and procedural or substantive approaches to justice. This is a change of emphasis rather than a sequence of clearly differentiated stages. In few societies have these shifts followed a line of uninterrupted progression. Periods of greater stress on formalistic legal reasoning and formal justice have followed eras of a more policy-oriented mode of legal discourse, as in nineteenth-century America. Even during the hegemony of formalism, there has often been a widespread awareness of the fact that the legal order was redistributing resources among groups and classes. Nevertheless, I shall argue later that present-day tendencies differ from their earlier counterparts not merely because of the more pronounced, persistent, and universal character of the contemporary developments, but, above all, because of the emergence in the welfare-corporate state of a unique relationship among problems of formality, equity, community, and equality in law.

The immediate causes of the postliberal moves toward purposive legal reasoning and procedural or substantive justice are directly connected with the inner dynamic of the welfare state. These moves appear as ways to deal with concentrated power in the private order or to correct the effects of a system of formal rules. As government assumes managerial responsibilities, it must work in areas in which the complexity and variability of relevant factors of decision seem too great to allow for general rules, whence the recourse to vague standards. These standards need to be made concrete and individualized by persons charged with their administrative or judicial execution.

The reasons for the greater emphasis on purposive legal reasoning and on procedural or substantive justice are more obscure and less amenable to a comprehensive interpretation. Changes in the theoretical understanding of language, in the character of common beliefs about the basis and scope of legitimate state action, and in the structure of the rank order all seem to play a part. Language is no longer credited with the fixity of categories and the transparent representation of the world that would make formalism plausible in legal reasoning or in ideas about justice. In the absence of belief in the naturalness of existing hierarchies of power or distribution, the legitimacy of governmental, including judicial, activity comes to depend increasingly on the welfare consequences of that activity. Finally, the vicissitudes of class struggle strip the state of every pretense to impartiality and transform it into an acknowledged tool of factional interest in a social situation in which the dictates of justice are still believed to be unknowable.

Whatever the causes of the trends I have described and however much they may vary from one country to another, their chief effects on the law seem clear. They repeatedly undermine the relative generality and the autonomy that distinguish the legal order from other kinds of law, and in the course of so doing they help discredit the political ideals represented by the rule of law.

Open-ended clauses and general standards force courts and administrative agencies to engage in ad hoc balancings of interest that resist reduction to general rules. One of the corollaries of generality in law is a severe limitation of the range of facts considered relevant to the making of official choices. If the number of pertinent factors of decision is too large, and each of them is constantly shifting, then categories of classification or criteria of analogy will be hard to draw and even harder to maintain. But the kinds of problems to which comprehensive standards characteristically apply tend to defy such limitations. They involve the conflict of numerous and inchoate interests against the background of a refusal to sacrifice any one of these interests completely to the others.

When attempts are made to codify standards, to reduce them to rules, their character is distorted. Either a large area of uncontrolled discretion and individualization subsists under the trappings of general norms, or the flexibility needed to make managerial decisions or to produce equitable results is lost. The same dialectic of illusion and petrification can be observed in the analogous processes by which Roman praetorian law was overtaken by imperial legislation,[37] English equity lost out to common law,[38] and the customary or sacred laws of non-Western societies were codified by colonial administrators.[39]

Purposive legal reasoning and nonformal justice also cause trouble for the ideal of generality. The policy-oriented lawyer insists that part of interpreting a rule is to choose the most efficient means to the attainment of the ends one assigns to it. But as the circumstances to which decisions are addressed change and as the decisionmaker's understanding of the means available to him varies, so must the way he interprets rules. This instability of result will also increase with the fluctuations of accepted policy and with the variability of the particular problems to be resolved. Hence, the very notion of stable areas of individual entitlement and obligation, a notion inseparable from the rule of law ideal, will be eroded.[40]

The quest for substantive justice corrupts legal generality to an even greater degree. When the range of impermissible inequalities among social situations expands, the need for individualized treatment grows correspondingly. No matter how substantive justice is defined, it can be achieved only by treating different situations differently. Thus, for example, it may become necessary to compensate for an existing inequality with a reverse preference afforded by the legal order to the disadvantaged group. Priorities among groups in turn shade imperceptibly into preferences among individuals and individual situations.

The history of the law of obligations and of liability rules in many Western social democracies illustrates another way in which the insistence on substantive justice enters into conflict with established notions of generality. Classic theories of contractual and delictual liability drew a sharp line between the allegedly impersonal justice of reciprocity, with which they were concerned, and distributive justice, which, if it existed at all, was the province of politics and the marketplace. At the same time, they confined liability to areas of conduct that seemed amenable to general rules and they asserted its absolute character within those confines.[41]

In the era of the welfare state and of policy-oriented legal discourse, there is a firmer recognition that exchange rules do have a distributive significance. Nonetheless, the attempt to take distributive criteria into account in an adjudicative setting unavoidably forces the courts into fields in which the complexity of relevant factors and the lack of widely shared standards of justice make generalization hard to come by and to stick with. The situation is aggravated by the impulse to extend liability, in response to equitable considerations, to areas where the same sorts of problems arise. And the difficulty is compounded still further by the willingness, in criminal as well as in private law, to admit a growing list of exculpatory conditions within this enlarged sphere of liability. For the granting of an excuse turns on judgments about particular persons and individual situations, judgments that resist statement as rules.

The same events that subvert the generality also tend to destroy the relative autonomy of the legal order in its substantive, methodological, institutional, and occupational dimensions.

Overarching standards invite their appliers to make use of the technician's conception of efficiency or the layman's view of justice. If, for example, one seeks to give content to the conception of good faith in contract law, one must go outside the narrow confines of lawyers' learning to consult the practices and enter into the thought patterns of a certain social group.

As purposive legal reasoning and concerns with substantive justice begin to prevail, the style of legal discourse approaches that of commonplace political or economic argument. All are characterized by the predominance of instrumental rationality over other modes of thought. Indeed, policy-oriented legal argument represents an unstable accommodation between the assertion and the abandonment of the autonomy of legal reasoning, just as procedural justice mediates between formal and substantive justice.

The decline in the distinctiveness of legal reasoning is connected with the need administrators and judges have of reaching out to the substantive ideals of different groups, of drawing upon a conventional morality or a dominant tradition. These changes in the substance and method of law also help undercut the identity of legal institutions and of the legal profession. Courts begin to resemble openly first administrative, then other political institutions. Thus, the difference between lawyers and other bureaucrats or technicians starts to disappear.

The cumulative impact of the movements discussed in the preceding pages is to encourage the dissolution of the rule of law, at least insofar as that form of legality is defined by its commitment to the generality and autonomy of law. To be sure, autonomy and generality could never be meant as completely actualized descriptions of the legal order in liberal society; they are no more than ideals which the liberal form of social life makes necessary to entertain and impossible to achieve fully. What distinguishes the law of the postliberal period is primarily the turning away from these ideals, a change of course that, despite its apparent insignificance, indicates important shifts in human belief and social order.

The corporate state and the attack on public and positive law

The corporatist tendencies of postliberal society have potentially an even more dramatic effect on the law than the welfare state trends. If the latter contribute to the disintegration of the rule of law, the former ultimately challenge the more universal and elementary phenomenon of bureaucratic law, law that is public and positive.

The spearhead of corporatism is the effacement both in

organization and in consciousness of the boundary between state and society, and therefore between the public and the private realm. As the state reaches into society, society itself generates institutions that rival the state in their power and take on many attributes formerly associated with public bodies. It is doubtless true that much of the earlier separation of government and society may have been more a matter of vision than of reality. But here one must tread carefully. The images people hold of their social situation are an integral part of those situations; indeed, they establish their specifically social meaning. Thus, a modest change of emphasis in forms of organization may be important if it is accompanied by a transformation of belief. The corporatist developments, like the welfare state ones mentioned earlier, seem to exemplify this principle.

Corporatism's most obvious influence on the law is its contribution to the growth of a body of rules that break down the traditional distinction between public and private law. Thus, administrative, corporate, and labor law merge into a body of social law that is more applicable to the structure of private-public organizations than to official conduct or private transactions.[42] But though this development undermines the conventional contrast of public and private law, it does not necessarily destroy the broader difference between the law of the state and the internal, privately determined regulations of private associations. Insofar as private law is laid down by the state, it too is, in this more comprehensive sense, public.

The deepest and least understood impact of corporatism is the one it has on the very distinction between the law of the state and the spontaneously produced normative order of nonstate institutions. As private organizations become bureaucraticized in response to the same search for impersonal power that attracts government to the rule of law principle, they begin to acquire the features, and to suffer the problems, of the state. At the same time, the increasing recognition of the power these organizations exercise, in a quasi-public manner, over the lives of their members makes it even harder to maintain the distinction between state action and private conduct. Finally, the social law of institutions is a law compounded of state-authored rules and of privately sponsored regulations or practices; its two elements are less and less capable of being separated. All these movements, which tend to destroy the public character of law, carry forward a process that begins in the failure of liberal society to keep its promise of concentrating all significant power in government.

The tendency of large corporate organizations to become bureaucratized and to produce a body of rules with many of the characteristics of state law should not be confused with an increasing regulation of the corporation by the state. In fact, quite the opposite may be true: the bureaucratization of corporate institutions may be associated with their ability to become relatively independent power centers with decisive influence over government agencies.

Corporatist tendencies are often associated with demands for the change of public and private organizations into democratic communities. These demands are still usually encountered as ideologies rather than as institutional realities. Nonetheless, they are just as much rooted in the structure of the postliberal order as the rule of law ideal is in the nature of liberal society.

Sometimes the communitarian aspirations are part of a radical attack on the corporate bodies. At other times, they present themselves under the guise of a reformist politics of participation. But whatever their immediate source or objective, they all betray a dissatisfaction with the nature of hierarchy and therefore of personal existence under liberalism. They all attempt to show how the fundamental experience of unjustified power and arbitrary consensus can be dealt with when the rule of law fails to dispose of it. And they all look for an alternative to the ideal of legality in the notion of a community bound together by a shared experience and capable of developing its own self-revising customs or principles of interaction. The profound and irreconcilable differences between rightist and leftist interpretations of the communitarian program have to do with the extent to which they envisage the community as arising from a preservation and strengthening, or from a destruction, of the rank system of liberal society.

An integral part of the search for community in both its conservative and its revolutionary variant is the aim of avoiding the manipulation of social life by imposed rules and of respecting the spontaneously produced internal customs of each communal group. This longing is heralded by the currents in social thought and jurisprudence that emphasize the "living" or "inner" law of associations in contrast to the made rules of the state.[43]

What is ultimately at issue is therefore the positive character of law itself: whether or not significant reliance will be placed upon made and articulated rules as opposed to immanent and implicit custom. And behind this conflict of types of law lies a more general antagonism between forms of social life—one for which order is a spontaneous byproduct of interaction; another for which it represents authority imposed from above or outside.

Formality, equity, and solidarity

Legality as formality. There is an issue that overpowers and encompasses all others in the history of the modern Western rule of law. It is the problem of formality in law.[44] To understand this problem is to perceive at a single glance the relationship among the different attributes of the legal order, the sense in which they are threatened by the historical trends I have discussed, and the opportunities and dangers that accompany their subversion. Thus, my discussion of formality will allow me to summarize the analysis developed thus far and to make it more comprehensive.

In the most general sense, formality means simply the marks that distinguish a legal system: the striving for a law that is general, autonomous, public, and positive. The idea of formality emphasizes the deeper motives that inspire this quest for government under law. Formality views the core of law as a system of general, autonomous, public and positive rules that limit, even if they do not fully determine, what one may do as an official or as a private person. Standards are seen as dangerous tumors on the body of formality; principles as rules with a higher degree of generality than other rules, a more indeterminate range of application, and a variable degree of force within that range.

A system of rules is formal insofar as it allows its official or nonofficial interpreters to justify their decisions by reference to the rules themselves and to the presence or absence of facts stated by the rules, without regard to any other arguments of fairness or utility. This definition seems tautologous; it spells out what it means to abide by rules. Everything will depend on where one draws the line between the factors of decision that are intrinsic to the system, and therefore worthy of consideration, and those that are not. Yet this restatement of the idea of legality has the merit of calling attention to the fact that the very identity of such a system of rules depends on the possibility of distinguishing what it would be best to do in a particular case if there were no applicable rules from what one ought to do given that the rules exist and that he is committed to apply them.

In a narrower sense, formality is the willingness to allow the rights and duties of the parties to be determined by the presence or absence of external solemnities like the seal. Both formality as rules and formality as ceremony appear to make it possible to ascertain entitlements and obligations without evaluating the goodness or badness of particular results. This intention to find the legal antidote to the subjectivity of values is what unites the two senses of formality.

Some precautions are needed at the outset. First, formality is always a matter of degree: law is never purely formal, nor can formality ever vanish. Second, the problem of formality has to do with the kinds of justifications that are publicly given for legal doctrines and decisions rather than with their actual causes or motives. Indeed, the more formal a style of legal reasoning becomes, the easier it may be to manipulate on behalf of interests the lawyer pretends to disregard. Nonetheless, these methods of justification will be of concern to one who believes that the most basic characteristics of a society can be illuminated by studying the relationship between what people do in fact and what they claim to be doing or say ought to be done.

One way to examine the place of formality in the history of modern law is to see how formality contrasts with the twin ideals of equity and solidarity. For the trends which distinguish the development of law in postliberal society may be seen as aspects of a possible movement toward these ideals.

Formality and equity. The polar opposite to justification by rules is equity, the intuitive sense of justice in the particular case. The formalist views equity as amorphous because it cannot be codified as a system of rules and as tyrannical because all moral judgments are subjective even if they are widely shared. Hence, the most that may be granted to equity is the role of tempering the consequences of formalism that seem intolerably harsh in the light of prevailing moral ideas.

The more equity is sacrificed to the logic of rules, the greater the distance between official law and the lay sentiment of right. As a result, the law loses its intelligibility as well as its legitimacy in the eyes of the layman; he knows it either as a chest of magical tools to be used by the well-placed or as a series of lightning bolts falling randomly on the righteous and the wicked.

To understand why the conflict between formality and equity is unavoidable, we must consider the cognate of equity, which is solidarity.

Formality and solidarity. Legality, which operates through rules established before disputes arise, differs from procedures of justification that resist yielding clear-cut rules. Such might be procedures that were concerned primarily with reconciling the parties or with vindicating, harmonizing, and developing, in the context of dispute settlement, moral ideals cherished by the broader communities to which the judge and the litigants belonged. For this moral sense of the community seems to transcend any system of rules or principles in which one tries to express or to encase it.

What accounts for our seeming inability to devise a set of prescriptions that adequately reflects the subtlety and richness of our moral ideas? Surely the complexity of our ethical commitments is not in and of itself a sufficient explanation; all rules are outcomes of a multitude of conflicting aspirations and interests. The true reason lies in the central role which the idea of solidarity plays in the moral life and in the impossibility of solving the problem of solidarity by any system of rights based upon equality of respect or variations of desert.[45]

The kernel of solidarity is our feeling of responsibility for those whose lives touch in some way upon our own and our greater or lesser willingness to share their fate. Solidarity is the social face of love; it is concern with another as a person rather than just respect for him as a bearer of formally equal rights and duties or admiration for his gifts and achievements.

Respect is owed to men for what they have in common by virtue of their equal dignity; it sets aside each individual's distinctiveness. Admiration recognizes another's skills or accomplishments. Love differs from respect because it prizes the loved one's humanity in the unique form of his individual personality. It differs from admiration because it addresses the total personality rather than some facet of it and because it surpasses the limits of praise and blame. Love is neither an act nor an emotion, but a gift of self, an opening up to another person, which may, for external reasons, fail to eventuate in acts and may also exist in the presence of hostile emotions the lover is unable to overcome. Solidarity does not differ in kind from love; it is merely love struggling to move beyond the circle of intimacy. When we fail to achieve the fuller communion and knowledge required by love, we may nevertheless be able to acknowledge another's unique value as a person to the extent of sharing in some predicament he faces.

There is a simple reason why no set of rules and principles can do justice to the sentiment of solidarity. A legal order confers entitlements and obligations; the more formal it becomes, the more does it treat each entitlement as a power to be exercised in the discretion of the powerholder. An individual's rights and duties, whether assumed by contract or imposed. directly by law, become part of his objective situation. They resemble the forces of nature in the way they set limits to his striving.

But solidarity means that one takes no entitlements for granted. A powerholder who acts out of a sense of solidarity will always have to ask himself whether the exercise of his power in a particular situation would be consistent with the aim of sharing the burden of the people with whom he is dealing. To this question, there can never be a general answer, laid down in advance. Everything will depend on issues like the degree to which the other person has acted wrongly in the particular relationship and his ability to bear the loss that would result from the exercise of the power. These are not factors that can be made the basis of rules;

instead, they are elements of decision that bear on how one uses the rights allocated by existing rules.

Take, for instance, the issue of liability on a contract in the event of changed and unforeseen circumstances. At what point does a shift in the market value of the commodities to be sold by an executory contract become so great that the enforcement of the bargain would violate the duties of solidarity owed by the parties to each other and by the judge to the parties? A contracting party or a judge who acts in the spirit of solidarity will not be satisfied with references to party intent as to the allocation of risks, even if intent seems unequivocal. He will also want to know whether one party is more blameworthy than another for the occurrence of the event that overtook the contractual relation and how any given allocation of losses would affect each party. He will deny that the administration of the rules governing exchange is independent from either conceptions of moral fault or goals of distributive justice.

The opposition of solidarity to formality can be clarified by a discussion of the bearing of the latter on the way one views the interplay of individual and collective interest. The more formal a system of law becomes, the more it is forced to oscillate between radical individualism and an equally unabashed collectivism, one being simply the corollary of the other. As long as the individual takes care to act within the legally defined sphere of his discretion and to clothe his acts in the ceremonies of the law, he may pursue his individual interests ruthlessly, no matter how destructive of others they may be. But as soon as he moves beyond this sphere or fails to act through the required solemnities, he loses all claim to protection regardless of how appealing his case may seem to the moral conscience. The answer one will give him is that it would violate the collective interests in security and freedom to allow him something to which he was not entitled under the preexisting rules.

Neither the individualist nor the collectivist side of formality satisfies the demands of solidarity. For the ideal of solidarity implies that one is never permitted to take advantage of his legal rights so as to pursue his own ends without regard to the effects he may have on others. And this ideal holds that the overriding collective interest is the interest in maintaining a system of social relations in which men are bound to act, if not compassionately, at least as if they had compassion for each other. Thus, one is never entitled to sacrifice an individual to some social interest simply because legality has left him at another's mercy.

Purposes and standards. The legal order as a system of formality encounters two great problems, which dominate modern legal thought. The first is the struggle to escape from the dilemma of blind formalism and arbitrary, tyrannical equity; the second is the effort to make a peace between legality and morality by rejecting the extremes of individualism and collectivism and providing a larger place within the law for the values of solidarity. The various trends described earlier by which the rule of law is eroded in contemporary society must be understood in the context of these aspirations. But now we can make our understanding of such trends more comprehensive.

The characteristic response of modern lawyers to the problem of formality and equity is purposive legal reasoning. One treats the law as a system of intelligible rules whose meaning is controlled by beneficial purposes which the law applier must attribute to the rules, for the intent of the lawmaker is likely to be or ought to be inconclusive. By this means, one hopes to moderate the tension between formality and equity and to avoid unpalatable outcomes in the great majority of cases.

The result, however, is, as I suggested before, a style of legal discourse that eats away at generality and autonomy without necessarily increasing one's assurance that he is doing justice. The attempted compromise between formalism and equity is inherently dissatisfying and unstable; it does not resolve the problem of subjective value that lies at the root of the dilemma of formality and equity, nor need it contribute to transform the circumstances of domination that deprive people of confidence in their own moral judgments. Consequently, the policies by which the modern lawyer wants to justify his elaborations of the law tend either to become abstract to the point of meaninglessness or to appear as expressions of an effort to manipulate all rules so as to further the arbitrary preferences of particular interest groups.

The main reaction to the conflict between legality and solidarity is a greater willingness to regard as part of the law certain moral conceptions that do not seem capable of development and application in ways consistent with the ideals of generality and autonomy. For these conceptions can neither be reduced to rules nor divorced from views about moral obligation.

An example in private law is the idea of good faith and the related notion in continental jurisprudence of the abuse of right.[46] To act in good faith is to exercise one's formal entitlements in the spirit of solidarity. The good faith standard requires one to find in each case a mean between the principle that one party may disregard the interests of the other in the exercise of his own rights and the counterprinciple that he must treat those interests exactly as if they were his own.

It might be said of these approaches to the two basic problems of formality that, far from being peculiar to modern law, they represent continuing traditions throughout the history of legal thought. An age that emphasizes equity and solidarity may follow one more attentive to formality, and where one would see a line of progression there might be only the ebb and flow of currents that recede only to return from a slightly changed direction. Moreover, there may be no necessary connection between either of these tendencies in legal thought and any given political trend.

Equity, solidarity, and domination: the role of substantive justice. To deal with these issues, it is necessary to consider the relationship of equity and solidarity in modern law to the problem of domination. In the welfare-corporate state that emerges under late capitalism, legal doctrines proliferate that attempt to redress some of the most sharply perceived disparities of power. Many of these doctrines represent what I described earlier as an ideal of procedural justice: though they forbear from demanding that private transactions and the governmental distribution of social benefits generate certain preestablished outcomes, they no longer hold to the assumption that the results of private exchange and politics are just by definition. Instead, they seek to strengthen some parties or to weaken others.[47] Alongside tests that focus on equality of bargaining power in private law, there are ideas of interest representation in administrative and corporate law as well as the commitment in labor law to protect the bargaining position of trade unions.

The following four propositions may illuminate the interplay between equity or solidarity, on one side, and domination, on the other.

First, the problems of equity and solidarity are more general than that of domination. Up to a point, one can act out of equity and solidarity whether or not one finds oneself in a position of superiority over others. A legal order that fosters, as formality must, systematic disparities of power may nonetheless be tempered by equitable and communal doctrines. And these doctrines might retain their authority or relevance even if such disparities were eliminated.

Second, it is nevertheless true that attempts to practice equity and solidarity will be confused and even self-defeating insofar as the basic problem of unjustified power is left unsolved. They will be clouded because the same sense of arbitrariness that attaches to moral judgments in liberal and postliberal society also infects conceptions of solidarity and equity. Moreover, to pursue these conceptions without simultaneously dealing with the basic distribution of power and wealth may have the effect of conferring a modicum of legitimacy and hence of stability on the existing order without changing the objective circumstances of domination that make it difficult for equity and solidarity to flourish.

Third, the compromise between formal and substantive justice represented by procedural justice may be peculiarly unsuited either to the vindication of equitable and communitarian ideals or to the lessening of domination. The techniques of procedural justice reproduce formality at another level by adding to the legal order new rules that govern the organization and interaction of bargaining units in the market or in politics. The entitlements conferred on individuals and groups by these norms must themselves be checked by equity and solidarity. More seriously still, experience has bred disillusionment with the capacity of interest representation and of the regulation of bargaining power effectively to transform the structure of society.

My fourth thesis is that the crucial determinant of the progress of equity and solidarity in law is the actual subversion of relationships of dependency and domination. Technical legal doctrines developed and applied through adjudication may have an indispensable though subsidiary role to play in this political struggle. In private law, substantive justice will be preoccupied with the elaboration of criteria for determining the equivalence of performances exchanged through contract and for allocating the losses arising from private disputes on the basis of both comparative fault and relative need. In public law, substantive justice may work through theories of substantive equal protection that define the kinds of differences of treatment that are morally justified or required.

Such doctrines represent interpretations of the idea of solidarity. At the same time, they attack the problem of domination at its core: they refuse to acquiesce in the inevitability of subjective value and they insist on judging the moral quality of social relations and of the powers men exercise over each other.

There is, however, no assurance that theories of substantive justice will continue to develop nor that politics in the welfare-corporate state will in fact change the basic ways in which wealth, power, and knowledge are distributed. In many countries, legal theories of substantive justice may remain isolated in a politically inhospitable atmosphere so that, though sufficiently vital to help legitimate the social order, they may never become strong enough to help transform it.

Cycle or progression? We now have the means with which to answer my question as to whether a heightened interest in equity and solidarity is simply the most recent turn in a cyclical process or whether, on the contrary, it is a stage in a progressive, though halting and sinuous, evolution. If there is something that distinguishes contemporary experiments in solidarity and equity from earlier movements in legal history, it would have to be the intimate association between this modern tendency and the attack on structures of domination in the name of substantive justice. Only to the extent that this attack occurs and succeeds dare one hope that equity and solidarity will become major sources of normative order rather than just residual limitations on formality.

The subversion of personal dependency relationships saves equitable and communitarian ideas from serving as apologies for established power. It also creates the conditions within which people can arrive at judgments about the dictates of equity and solidarity without feeling that these judgments are rendered suspect by the circumstances in which they were made.

Hence, the question as to whether the movement toward

equity and solidarity in contemporary law is simply a cyclical reversion or a genuinely novel breakthrough is more a political question for the future than a historical one about the past. Whether the antinomian tendencies within modern law will or should prevail depends on the degree to which they are connected with the development of doctrines of substantive justice and with the actual disruption of the social mechanisms of personal dependence.

We can now also understand more clearly the sense in which the public and the positive character of law as well as its autonomy and generality are at stake in these developments. The greater the commitment to equity and solidarity as sources and ideals of law, the less it is possible to distinguish state law from ideas of moral obligation or propriety that are entertained in the different social settings within which disputes may arise. And the less importance do positive rules have in the law.

Freedom, transcendence, and hypocrisy. What is the origin of the almost providential force that seems to infuse and to direct every facet of law in postliberal society? If my earlier hypothesis about social change is correct, a decisive factor is people's sense of the conflict between the ideals they hold and the way they experience their everyday lives, a conflict carried to the extreme under liberalism. The ideas of solidarity and equity, on the one hand, and the search for substantive justice, on the other, are efforts to soften or abolish this tension.

Many of the dangers we confront at present in law and society can be understood once we have this ultimate spring of movement in mind. There is the risk that the search for a nonpositive law will lose its dynamism and result in the sanctification of the practices of certain dominant groups, with the repression of other communities or of dissident members of the dominant groups themselves. There is always the chance that moral ideas, however widely shared, may obscure novel forms of dependence and domination and mistake a stage in the development of humanity for the entirety of what human nature can become.

At a still more general level, one must fear a kind of historical entropy: in the measure in which men lose consciousness of a gap between what is and what ought to be, their capacity to rise above themselves and to change is weakened. Thus, the central question of politics becomes how to pursue the goals of equity and solidarity without jeopardizing the power of self-transcendence by which mankind is enlightened and ennobled.

The cost of this power is the pain of hypocrisy. Though the law may be framed to teach men sympathy, all that may be hoped for in the short run is to force them, within wider or narrower bounds, to act as if they were sympathetic. Does it not degrade the moral sentiments thus to treat them as objects of compulsion and display? And is it not the consequence of this policy to create a society that appears to be what it has not yet, and perhaps never can, become? The realities of the heart would forever continue to mock the pretenses of our public selves, and the public realm would at every moment be on the verge of falling victim to the demonic impulses it had tried to submerge.

Hence, one might prefer to commit the propagation of solidarity to persuasion and example rather than to law. But there are two decisive objections to this approach. First, there is the familiar problem of the free rider: the more extensive the duties of solidarity, the more does the cheater stand to gain by receiving help without offering it himself. But there is a second and deeper reason to make these duties legal. In modern society, in which much of religion and morals are seen as prerogatives of individual conscience, law is the preeminently collective order. To embody standards of conduct in the law is to acknowledge their authority over day-to-day life and over society as a whole.

If the ethical precepts accepted in the law are set too far above the modes and motives of ordinary conduct, these precepts become stifling or unworkable. But the precondition of moral growth in community disappears unless a tension between ideal and actuality is maintained as a conflict within the public world itself between what can be and what should be done, rather than just as a rift between private aspiration and public rules. With the blessing of transcendence goes the curse of hypocrisy; society itself becomes the actor playing a role with which its inward nature is still at war.[48]

The retreat from legality: the German story continued

Having tried to make my study of law in postliberal society as abstract and general as possible, I shall now turn in the opposite direction, toward illustration and refinement. For this purpose, I shall extend my outline of trends in German legal history to the period between the end of World War I and the Nazi conquest of power. The Weimar Republic provides the student of these matters with a concentrated setting in which to examine many aspects of the decline of legality. Moreover, some of the best historical writing about the rule of law and its dissolution has addressed these years in German history. Finally, the choice of the German example may help underline the risks inherent in the developments I have described.[49]

Weimar saw the sudden rise to prominence of a number of general clauses. The most extreme instance of this has already been mentioned: the expansive application of the good faith clauses. But many other examples might be found, like the "good morals" concept (articles 138 and 826 of the Civil Code), of which much was to be made under the

National Socialist regime, and the open-ended policy directives contained in economic legislation of the time. The critics of this trend pointed out its subversive effect on the ideals of legal generality and autonomy. They argued that it would weaken the legal order by forcing courts to render highly individualized decisions; that it would make the scope of legal rules uncertain thereby undermining the substance of individual rights; and that it would pave the way for a Byzantine exercise of judicial caprice in the name of equity.[50]

Together with the increasing use of open-ended standards went an ever more pronounced shift to purposive modes of legal reasoning and to concerns with substantive justice, which took the form of equitable discretion exercised on behalf of well-defined social interests. One factor in this process was the acknowledgment by the judiciary of the view and methods of legal reasoning propounded by the theorists of "free law" and of "interest jurisprudence."

Another side of the same tendency was the principle, which originated in the case law of the administrative tax court, that procedural rules should be applied according to their suitability to a particular case. The procedural reforms of 1924 gave the judge a freer hand in shaping procedure and greatly expanded the role of so-called voluntary jurisdiction suits *(freiwillige Gerichtsbarkeit),* in which many constraints on judges' power were removed.[51]

Still another aspect of the growth of adjudicative discretion in the name of policy-oriented legal reasoning and substantive justice was the expansion of judicial review. The courts, as part of their position within the *Rechtsstaat,* had long had the functions of ensuring the conformity of provincial law to federal law and of administrative regulations to laws. The judiciary now collapsed these distinctions and boldly assumed the power to test the validity of all laws. The criteria that defined prohibited legislation were enunciated with extraordinary breadth: laws inadequate to their purpose or arbitrary in the sense of favoring a particular interest over the general interest; laws that violated "good morals"; and laws that confiscated property.

The immediate consequence of these developments was to plunge the courts headlong into the striking of particularistic balances of interests and into the rendering of general policy judgments that wholly escaped the confines of specialized legal doctrine. Judges were now increasingly called upon to establish priorities among opposing equities and to assess the effects of private transactions, administrative ordinances, and even laws on the national economy. Their aims were often in conflict. More seriously, they shook traditional conceptions of the generality and autonomy of law.

The events that produced this assault on the legal order were simply extreme versions of forces at work, with greater or lesser intensity, in all plebiscitarian democracies and welfare states. One trend was the diminution and near paralysis of legislative activity, already modest under the First Reich, in many basic areas of law. It has been remarked that the interest groups represented in the *Reichstag* were too heterogeneous in their internal composition to take coherent positions on many issues of private law. They rallied, when they could, around matters of state organization, but even on these topics the legislature proved unable to formulate and to impose a program of state action.

The space left empty by the retreat of parliament was occupied by the administration and the judiciary, whose old rivalry was rekindled. The administrative bureaucracy worked to create its own regulatory law, shaped and applied by agencies over which the judges had no control.[52] The judiciary gained new importance by virtue of the fact that the leading capitalists no longer had as firm a hold on the republic as they had had on the empire. Like the petty bourgeoisie, they looked to the courts for the "equitable" protection of some of their interests. But like the ministerial bureaucracy, they also tried to increase their own extrastate law, whose execution was supervised by their arbitration tribunals. This attempt carries us to another chapter of the story.

Alongside the welfare state tendencies that undercut the legal order, one can identify in the Weimar Republic corporatist movements that threatened the public and the positive character of law itself. The cartels and professional associations continued to produce their own internal law. The law of the corporate bodies was to be independent in source and application from both the administrative and the judicial bureaucracy. This resulted in what has been called a "destatization" *(Enstaatlichung)* of law.[53]

There was also heavy ideological pressure from all sides to oppose the ultimate ideal of an indwelling, customary law of associations to all made law, whether the regulatory law of the administrators or the legal system of the judges. The left-wing socialists and the communists worked toward the final replacement of positive law and the centralized state by self-regulating community. The conservatives and Nazis put forward a program of the organic corporativist reorganization of society. Many in the Catholic center were committed in principle to the Church's aim of solving the social question through the professional guilds, of medieval inspiration, which were to be described in the encyclical *Quadragesimo Anno.* The jurisprudential equivalent to these political doctrines was the fascination with the "living law" intrinsic to social relations as distinguished from the positive law of lawyers and bureaucrats.

This brief sketch indicates some ways in which the impact of welfare and corporatist politics on German law during the republican interlude exemplified the views about law in postliberal society set out earlier in this essay. The denouement of Weimar must not obscure the fact that fundamentally similar processes continue to operate in other modern industrial societies.

The German case may also serve to point out the enormous dangers to freedom involved in the decline of the legal order and the high risks critical intelligence runs when it attacks the idea of positive law in behalf of an ideal of self-governing community. Many of the trends of Weimar were repeated on a brutal scale under the Nazis. The withdrawal and weakening of the legal order was followed by the expansion of terror. The ideology of corporativist union became a pretext for unchecked bureaucratic dictatorship. And the idea of spontaneous popular sentiments of right was used to impose and express the worship of the established order.[54]

Beyond liberal society

The analysis of the well-known changes I have grouped under the headings of the welfare state and the corporatist tendency has provided a context within which to understand the legal history of postliberal society. The welfare state aspects of that context account for the fading away of generality and autonomy as vital ideals. Consequently, the entire conception of legality peculiarly associated with modern European history is shaken and perhaps mortally wounded.

The corporatist developments have still wider implications. These trends start with institutional and ideological changes that rob the law of much of its distinctively public character. And they bring in their wake a struggle for community that ends up endangering the positive quality of law. Thus, if the welfare state features of postliberal society assault the unique historical phenomenon of the legal order, the corporatist and the communitarian impulse seem to strike at the much more commonplace existence of bureaucratic law.

Do these events suggest a return to the near exclusive primacy of custom? Or do they point the way to a novel kind of normative order? Do they irremediably compromise liberalism's cherished ideals of freedom and of the capacity to distinguish critically between what ought to be and what is? Or do they accommodate these ideals within a broader vision that also embodies the claims of community and of the sense of participation in a natural order permeating society and the entire world? Before we can deal with these issues adequately, we must use what has been learned about the transmutations of law to deepen our insight into the situation of postliberal society.

If the foregoing discussion focused mainly on what changes in social organization and consciousness do to the law, now I can reverse the argument and suggest what these legal events tell us about modifications in the basic patterns of order and belief. The welfare, corporatist, and communitarian tendencies revealed in the evolution of law converge to modify each of the fundamental elements of liberal society.

As society is transformed according to a corporatist pattern and as it accepts the validity of communitarian aspirations, the significant groups in which individual lives are lived may diminish in number and increase in importance. This involves more than the time a person devotes to each of the groups of which he is a member, or the range of the influence each of them in fact exercises over his life. It has to do also with the extent to which the individual is able to accept the legitimacy of collective practices rather than to see them as the tools of dominant groups. In this sense, attacks on hierarchy are part of the same process by which the character of significant groups is transformed.

For similar reasons and in a similar way, the association of interests loses its hold as the primary mechanism of social order. The experience that supports the rule of law is one of antagonism among private wills whose only two basic ways of arranging their relationship to each other are personal subordination and impersonal law. The basis of this alternative is the fact that no standards of right are to be found beyond the arbitrary preferences of individuals or groups; every consensus turns out to mask a personal control of some by others. But the alternative offers more than it can give; the rule of law is in the end incapable of eradicating unjustifiable dependence in everyday life.

Insofar as hierarchy is transformed and the conditions of community are advanced in postliberal society, the chance increases that personal relationships ungoverned by rules might not be subordinative. The association of interests can be at least partially replaced by shared purpose as the generating principle of social order. The disintegration of general, autonomous, public, and positive law accompanies and reveals this metamorphosis.

Perhaps the most inscrutable change, though also the one richest in significance, is the redefinition of the relationship between the ideal and the actual. The high culture of liberal civilization defines itself by opposition to the society of which it is a part: its official law is strongly contrasted with the implicit practices of private associations; its moral ideals are separated from the factual regularities of behavior. And all this antagonism of the *is* and the *ought* rests upon the sense of the radical illegitimacy or arbitrariness of the existing form of social life.

The reapproximation of the ideal and actuality is made possible by the transformation of the social experience chiefly responsible for this contrast in liberal society. The characteristic legal form of the rapprochement is the subversion of positive law, which draws a sharp line between what people in fact do and what they should do. And the ultimate moral tendency of this development is to weaken, or even to deny, the tension between private moral aspirations on the one hand, and the objective structure of the public world, on the other.

THE VARIETIES OF MODERNITY

Comparing modern societies

One needs a comparative vantage point from which to gain perspective on the evolution of postliberal society. Only comparison can allow us to grasp the unity of this form of social life by distinguishing what is peculiar to it from what it shares with other societies. The comparative method is likely to be especially fruitful when the types of societies compared can be understood as variations on a small number of common themes. For it may be that the analogous predicaments these societies confront reveal their generic similarities while making their specific differences intelligible. To apply this strategy to the study of liberal and postliberal society, I must carry my criticism of the perspective of modernization a step further.

It was suggested earlier that the contrast of tradition and modernity and the identification of the latter with liberal society can be, and has been, dismantled in three main ways. First, one may attack the contrast on its own ground by rejecting it as an ideological delusion that mistakes changing visions for changing realities. Second, one can argue that the society with which the classic social theorists were either explicitly or implicitly concerned when they developed the perspective of modernization does not correspond to contemporary society. Third, there is the thesis that the proliferation of types of modern society has made the conception of modernism useless, for either it is a blanket category employed to juxtapose countries with little in common, or it is a parochial and politically loaded identification of modernity with liberal capitalism.

Each of these criticisms of the perspective of modernization seems to contain an important element of truth. Yet,
carried to the extreme, each of them leads to serious mistakes. Thus, the task is to separate the sense in which they are
acceptable from the sense in which they must be rejected. In
this way, one can advance the program of revising the tradition of classic social theory while retaining its still useful
insights.

Up to now, my argument has addressed the first two
problems. It has sought to elucidate the relationship between
consciousness and order in modern liberal society. It has also
suggested how that society and its law change into a form of
social life profoundly different from the one the classic social
theorists tried to understand and yet comprehensible only
through an interpretation of the society that preceded it.
There remains the third issue: What is one to make of the
diversity of modern societies, which threatens to shatter the
conception of modernity itself?

My proposal is to expand at this point the conception of
modernity to include two nonliberal types of society, which
will be called the traditionalistic and the revolutionary socialist. Each of them differs from the postliberal as well as from
the liberal society in its characteristic type of consciousness, in
its favored mode of organization, and in its law. Yet each
confronts a set of crucial dilemmas and tensions similar to
those faced by postliberal society. The comparative excursus
promises to help answer the questions left open in my discussion of the welfare-corporate state.

Traditionalistic society

Traditionalistic society is perhaps best exemplified by
Japan in the period from the Meiji Restoration to the present.
But many elements of the type can be found in other recently

modernizing societies in Asia, Africa, and Latin America. Indeed, even some European societies like nineteenth-century Germany had traditionalistic traits.

A rough, preliminary mark of traditionalistic society is its partial and perhaps transitory reconciliation of Western industrialism with outlooks and institutions foreign to liberal or postliberal society. Sometimes this reconciliation has been a more or less deliberate policy on the part of an indigenous elite that wanted to increase national power through drastic economic and technological change while maintaining the social order and the attitudes on which its hegemony depended. At other times, traditionalism has been promoted by a colonial power that chose to transform only those aspects of native civilization that seemed most important to the attainment of its imperialist objectives.

The concept of a traditionalistic society should not be confused with the spurious idea of "traditional" societies, which throws into one bag everything that differs from the European nation-state. It designates, instead, a unique way of dealing with industrialism, bureaucratization, and national rivalry.

All traditionalistic societies have a dual structure, often sharply divided between the modern and the nonmodern sector. And in all of them "traditional" institutions serve more or less effectively as instruments of "modernization," with effects that ultimately overflow the economic and the technological sphere and contribute to the transformation of the culture and the social structure. Thus, the Japanese *batsu* and the *oyabun-kobun* (patron-client) relationship strengthen organizational unity and loyalty, helping make them consistent with a high degree of competitiveness within and among organizations;[55] the Indian caste associations[56] and the African urban associations[57] may perpetuate in hostile conditions something of the cohesion of peasant societies, with their closed and inclusive hierarchies; the Latin American closely held family corporation can act as an agent of advanced capitalism in a commercially backward setting.

There is a dominant consciousness in traditionalistic society, an image of nature, society, and the individual that persists alongside economic or technological change despite countless variations from individual to individual, from group to group, and from country to country.[58] It is an outlook fostered by the elite and widespread among the populace.

One element of this consciousness is the sense that society is graced by a natural order that ought to be learned and preserved. The naturalness of social arrangements generally, and of hierarchic distinctions in particular, is associated with the perception that social life occupies a predetermined place within nature. The import of these views is that the structure of society and even the phenomena of nature have a sanctity that puts them beyond the arbitrary human will.

Another aspect of culture in traditionalistic society is the perception of the primacy of the group over the individual. The number of significant groups for the individual is comparatively small and the importance to him of each of these groups is correspondingly great. This collectivist orientation may coexist with ruthless hostility toward strangers and even with a high measure of aggression within the group.

A third feature of the dominant mentality is that the individual's idea of self is almost completely defined by the place and the job he holds in the social order. There is little sense of individuality as a manifestation of a universal humanity that transcends every particular role or status.

In the history of traditionalistic societies, it is characteristic for the mode of consciousness I have described to be increasingly met with ambivalence by both the ruling groups and the populace. The elite is caught between acceptance of the traditionalistic outlook and attraction to the dominant culture of the liberal capitalist societies whose success it seeks to emulate. To the extent the elite tends toward the latter, it views traditionalistic conceptions as weapons in the power struggle, but it does not believe in them. The working classes, for their part, are exposed to an experience of manipulation of natural or social arrangements, shattering of established status differences through meritocratic promotion, and intense role specialization. These trends endanger the very basis of the traditionalistic consciousness. Thus, both ruling groups and populace find themselves in a situation of divided loyalties, torn between two conceptions of the world.[59]

This cultural schizophrenia is matched by a marked duality in social structure and political organization. At first, there is a relatively closed and inclusive rank order in which each person occupies a fixed status. But, increasingly, the imperatives of industrialization and bureaucratization call for criteria of advancement that cut across conventional rank lines. In Japan, for example, though lip service was paid to the promotion of "men of talent" from the earliest days of the Restoration, it was only much later that meritocracy seems to have become a powerful force.[60] Thus, the hierarchy of inherited statuses coexists uneasily with the hierarchy of meritocratic roles, for though they somewhat overlap, they also partly contradict each other. Educational and family background supplant estate position as the major determinants of the individual's social place.[61]

This conflict in the social structure is mirrored by an oscillation in the character of the state. The state begins as simply the highest corporate organization. Governmental paternalism and corporativist power complement each other so that no clear distinction can be drawn between public and private institutions.[62] But as the closure and the inclusiveness of the rank system are weakened, the governmental apparatus is more easily distinguishable from other entities, and it becomes the privileged weapon of factional fighting.

In law, the dualism of traditionalistic society takes the

form of a juxtaposition of two very different kinds of legal life. On one side, there is the central legal order, formulated by the indigenous elite or imposed by the colonial authorities in imitation of foreign models. This official legal system may be introduced as an expression of elite ideology, as a device for the solution of a limited range of conflicts within the elite, or as a way to appease foreign powers. (In Japan, for example, the importation of codes was closely connected with the effort to abolish consular jurisdiction.) But whatever its origins, the rule of law appears to have an even smaller hold over life in traditionalistic society than it does in liberal society.[63]

Alongside the central legal order, there is an informal system of customary law that embodies the dominant consciousness of traditionalistic society and buttresses its rank order. Just as "traditional" institutions are turned to account by developments that might seem inconsistent with them, so there often emerges a symbiotic relationship between the central legal order and informal custom. To return to the Japanese example, one finds the official legal system referring disputes to nonofficial means of conciliation or relying, through its own general clauses and open-ended standards, on customary understandings. Conversely, customary law is influenced by the central legal order, and its informal procedures are often increasingly legalized.[64]

Even more important than the interpenetration of custom and legal order in the history of traditionalistic societies is the growth of a sprawling body of bureaucratic law that mainly regulates the economy. This law is often designed to circumvent the central legal system, which is perceived as remote and rigid or as committed to procedures, interests, and ideals opposed by the dominant elite. The new regulations are formulated and administered largely beyond the reach of the courts and with little concern for established methods of legal reasoning. Hence, the conflict between the law of the lawyers and the law of the bureaucrats may become even more acute in traditionalistic societies than in postliberal ones.[65]

Thus, a similar dualistic pattern reappears in the culture, the organization, and the law of traditionalistic society. There are times when the two elements seem to reinforce each other, and times when they appear antagonistic. But what is the general significance of the dualism and what prospects does it hold open for the society it characterizes?

In a sense, the unifying dialectic is the conflict between economy and technology, on the one hand, and social structure and culture, on the other. A more precise formulation would be that there is a tension between the ideal of hierarchic community, embodied in the dominant consciousness and in the institutions associated with it, and the experience of social disintegration, bred by life in the modernizing sector.

This suggests still another way of looking at the predicament of traditionalistic society. To the extent modernization means the breakup or erosion of established communities, it may encourage the individual to acquire a greater sense of his moral autonomy from the groups to which he belongs and a deeper perception of the unjustified domination that permeates the ideals and practices of those groups. As a result, however, the person is deprived of a stable communal setting for his existence. From this derives his ambivalence toward both aspects of the society: he fears the existing communities as well as the processes that may destroy them. His distress could be relieved only through a transformation of community that purged communal life of the hierarchic relations of personal dependence that heretofore determined its structure. With this view of the central influence on traditionalistic society in mind, one can identify the two main mistakes to avoid in the understanding of that society.

One error is to take the traditionalistic ideology at its word and to suppose that this society is indeed totally different from its Western liberal counterpart because it succeeds in combining Western industrialism and technology with indigenous institutions and beliefs. This would be comparable to identifying liberalism with its idealized self-image. In fact, however, my account suggests that, despite the frequent collaboration of modernity and tradition, the forces at work in the society's economy cannot be contained in the economic sphere. They spill over, eroding the basis of established forms of consciousness and organization.

The other mistaken approach to traditionalistic society would discount its ideological pretensions altogether. Such a view would claim that traditionalistic society is simply a way station to a liberal or postliberal order. Whatever the intentions of its ruling groups, its economic and technological experience must eventually remake society and culture in the Western image. What this hypothesis fails to recognize is that the ideal of hierarchic community and its attendant styles of organization constitute an essential element in the basic dialectic of the society. Even if this element cannot survive intact, the outcome of its interaction with modern Western influences is likely to bear its mark.

The substantive error of this view rests upon a methodological fallacy. If the first interpretation of traditionalism confuses ideology with reality, the second one treats reality as something that could be understood apart from ideology. In both cases, the most important features of the society—those that have to do with the tension between belief and experience—go unnoticed.

If traditionalistic society is neither just a step toward liberal capitalism nor a stable alternative to it, where then does it stand in relation to the Western welfare-corporate state? Before suggesting an answer to this question, I must complete my comparison through the study of another type of modern society.

Revolutionary socialist society

The foremost distinguishing attribute of revolutionary socialist society is its attempt to reconcile industrialism, bureaucratization, and national power with the achievement of an ideal of fraternal or egalitarian community. The expropriation of the "means of production" is only one of the signs and devices, though perhaps the most basic, of the communitarian program. My characterization of this type of modern society is chiefly inspired by the People's Republic of China, though once again many of the type's elements appear in a number of other countries.

Let us begin with the dominant mode of consciousness, the one instilled by the ruling groups and implicit in the ideals people articulate and in their fundamental perceptions about different aspects of social life.

The first aspect of this outlook is the willingness to subject society and nature to ruthless and radical manipulation. But this willingness is coupled with the belief that thoroughgoing instrumentalism will hasten the advent of a situation in which the conflict among individual will, social order, and nature will have disappeared because whatever oppresses man in society or nature will have been wiped out.

The second side of the culture is its assertion of the primacy of collective bonds over individual interests. This collectivism, however, is meant to help bring about a situation in which individual autonomy will be able to flourish all the more securely since unjustified hierarchy will no longer transform every act of participation in social relationships into a sacrifice of individuality.

Finally, the dominant mentality prescribes complete

devotion to one's role in the present society. But it imagines that this discipline will contribute to the eventual overcoming of the division of labor.

Thus, the revolutionary socialist consciousness suffers from a schizophrenia that differs from, but is connected with, the one that characterizes the traditionalistic state of mind. But the dualism of its culture speaks the language of time, emphasizing the contrast between the present and the future.[66] To be sure, the present is justified as both a means to the achievement of the future and as a process of liberation whose characteristics already foreshadow those of the coming order. Yet the idea of treating the present as a means in fact often conflicts with the aim of approaching it as an anticipation. Radical departures from the ideal in the name of expediency may threaten to disfigure the objective pursued, but they may also be a necessary condition of effective action. The suppressed awareness of this dilemma is the major obsession of the revolutionary socialist outlook and may account for much of its characteristic hesitation between Machiavellianism and utopianism, between the demand for silent obedience and the provocation of insurrectionary tumult.

Revolutionary socialism runs into similar problems in its forms of organization. The achievement of its political and economic objectives seems to require a steep hierarchy of roles. But this hierarchy endangers the society's fidelity to its ideological program.

The ruling party destroys the institutions of the presocialist society that stood between the central government and the individual, and it creates other institutions in their place. These new organizations are state instruments for the control and transformation of society. Yet they are set up on behalf of a system in which the state is to be dominated and eventually destroyed by society. How can they be at the same time vehicles of self-education or self-management and instruments of governmental guidance or control? The revolutionary socialist order fluctuates between participation and centralism.[67]

The society has two kinds of law. There is a law of bureaucratic commands and a law of autonomous self-regulation.[68] Each one represents one of the two faces of consciousness and organization under revolutionary socialism. In the area of the law of bureaucratic commands, concerns with legal generality and autonomy are decisively subordinated to the achievement of the desired political or economic result in each particular situation. The use of open-ended standards, the turn to instrumental rationality, and the emphasis on substantive justice assume more uncompromising forms in revolutionary socialist society than in postliberal society. Side by side with this bureaucratic law, there is an emergent quasi-customary law of communal organizations. The chief task of the popular tribunals, councils, or committees is to reconcile these two aspects of law: to educate the people in the law of the bureaucracy while allowing them to begin regulating themselves.[69]

The fundamental dialectic of revolutionary socialist society can be viewed as the conflict between the imperatives of industrial organization and political centralization, on one side, and the promise of self-regulating community, on the other. An alternative way to put it is that the society is pulled between the trials of its present and the image of its future. For the purposes of my argument, however, the most useful statement of the dialectic would emphasize the contest between the persistent experience of personal dependence in everyday life and the ideal of egalitarian community. Insofar as the society must accept a present in contradiction with its desired future and sacrifice some of its communitarian purposes to its other aims, it continues to be marked by hierarchic relationships of personal subordination. But these relationships have no justification other than their alleged service to an ideal they seem to belie.

To the extent the previous argument is correct, there are two main ways to go wrong in understanding a revolutionary socialist society; they parallel the two erroneous interpretations of the liberal and the traditionalistic society. One mistaken view confuses the actuality of revolutionary socialism with its future-oriented ideal of egalitarian community. The other misconception denies that there is a significant difference between revolutionary socialism and the state capitalism of postliberal or traditionalistic society. The first approach reduces reality to ideology; the second is blind to their interplay.

The unity of modernism

The major types of modern society are the traditionalistic, the revolutionary socialist, and the postliberal, which is the contemporary form of liberalism. In what sense are they connected? And what light does their unity shed on each of them?

In traditionalistic society, there is a recurring experience of personal subjection in the workplace. This subjection loses its accustomed supports as labor comes to be set up in ways partially incompatible with earlier forms of social organization. Other aspects of life, however, continue to lend vitality to the ideal of hierarchic community, which assigns to each person a fixed place in a self-justifying system of ranks. The tension between this ideal and the disintegrated, shifting, and seemingly arbitrary dependence relationships that mark so much of everyday life is perhaps the single most powerful force in traditionalistic society.

An analogous tension exists in revolutionary socialist societies. Insofar as revolutionary socialism tends toward political centralization, a sharp division of labor, and a hierarchy of roles, it too encourages the proliferation of new relationships of personal dependence and domination. Such relationships come into conflict with its professed ideal of egalitarian community. The antagonism of these two factors runs through every level of belief and organization.

We can now reexamine with fresh insight the situation of liberal and postliberal society. As the rank order becomes more partial and open, the remaining disparities of social advantage also become less acceptable. Thus, there arises the paradox of equality and authority discussed earlier. The ideal of personal autonomy is asserted in opposition to liberalism's class system as well as in contrast to the more inclusive and closed hierarchy of the aristocratic society from which liberalism emerges.

As this conflict is worked out, its terms are modified. The aim of governmental impersonality in the service of individual freedom, an aim represented by the rule of law, is sufficiently powerful to deprive existing forms of hierarchy by class or role of their felt legitimacy. But it is not strong enough to destroy them. At the same time, the welfare and the corporatist tendency encourage a new concern with community through their influence on group life and on perceptions of the link between the ideal and actuality. The consequence of these trends is that the focus of tension and change in postliberal society becomes the conflict between the persistence of illegitimate dependency relationships and the quest for community.

In understanding this postliberal phenomenon, one must bear in mind that it could arise only through the previous undermining of a more closed and inclusive hierarchy. In this sense, the search for community is the child, rather than the opponent, of the demand for personal autonomy.

We can now identify how the different kinds of modern

society resemble each other and differ. They are all caught in the dialectic of the experience of personal dependence and the ideal of community. All come to this dialectic through a disruption of earlier forms of more closed and inclusive hierarchy. All find that the logic of state or private capitalism is to create new kinds of dependency relationships by class or role, relationships that are robbed of legitimacy by the very same process that creates them. And for all these societies, the ultimate political issue is the sense in which and the extent to which individual freedom can be reconciled with community cohesiveness.

The three types of modern society diverge in their relationship to their predecessors, in the way they respond to the problem of personal dependence and domination, and in their characteristic approaches to the ideal of community.

In traditionalistic society, the breakup of earlier established hierarchies is halting, partial, and largely unintended. Under revolutionary socialism, it is sudden, comprehensive, and deliberate. Liberal societies have followed either of these two patterns. Thus, some grew slowly out of an aristocratic order, whereas others were born in a revolutionary act, though one prepared by a long period of social change and ideological ferment.

For traditionalistic society, the problem of unjustified subjection and dominance appears in a realm of social life, the ordinary world of work, that is increasingly shorn of the attributes and therefore the legitimacy of traditional organizations. In revolutionary socialist society, the issue arises as a result of the impossibility of fully realizing the communitarian program in everyday life without harm to the other political and economic ambitions of the state. For liberal society and for its postliberal successor, the cutting edge of the difficulty is the failure of the rule of law to solve the problem of power.

Finally, the three sorts of modern society contrast in the

way their ruling ideologies tend to define the meaning of community itself. For the traditionalistic type, the communitarian ideal is a hierarchic one. For the revolutionary socialist type, it is egalitarian. For postliberal society, it can be either: thus, the protracted rivalry between rightist and leftist views of community in Western thought.

There seems no reason to suppose that this pattern of similarities and differences among types of modern society will lead to an ultimate convergence any more than that it will produce a growing separation. Either result would be compatible with the existence of a common problem. Thus, the dialectic of modernity has no foreordained result; one can imagine it either continuing indefinitely or going through a sea change.

It may nevertheless be possible to specify the conditions under which the conflict between ideal and experience in modernity would be resolved because the competing demands that brought it into being would have been satisfied. The first condition is the reconciliation of the commitment to industrialism, and thus also to industrialism's apparent need for centralization and specialization, with the longing for community. The second requirement is that the communitarian ideal be defined and realized so as to strengthen, rather than weaken, the sense of individual autonomy and to make autonomy compatible with authority. Otherwise, the ordeal of illegitimate dependency relationships, and the more general perception of the arbitrariness of the social world, will continue to plague us in a different disguise.

This essay does not try to establish how these conditions might be fulfilled, nor even whether their fulfillment is possible, for these questions would carry us to larger issues of human nature and the human good. In keeping with the narrower focus of my inquiry, I shall suggest how some of the opportunities and risks inherent in the modern situation bear upon the law and are illuminated by it.

LAW BEYOND MODERN SOCIETY: TWO POSSIBILITIES

There are two main ways in which one can interpret the significance for law of the tendencies at work in modern, and particularly in postliberal, society. Neither interpretation can be proved true or false at the present time, for both represent possibilities intrinsic to modernism.

The first hypothesis might be summarized by the metaphor of the closed circle. It would present the entire history of law as one of movement toward a certain point, followed by a return to the origin. We have seen how, in Western legal history, bureaucratic law, with its public and positive rules, builds upon customary practices, and how this bureaucratic law is in turn partly superseded by the rule of law, with its commitment to the generality and the autonomy of legal norms. The welfare trend in postliberal society moves the rule of law ideal back in the direction of bureaucratic law by undermining the social and ideological bases of that ideal. The corporatist tendency and the communitarian aspirations that follow it begin to subvert bureaucratic law itself. Thus, they prepare the way for the return to the custom of each group as the fundamental and almost exclusive instrument of social order.

This hypothetical development would have a profound impact on morals and politics. The rule of law is intimately associated with individual freedom, even though it fails to resolve the problem of illegitimate personal dependency in social life. Bureaucratic law is premised on the conception that social arrangements can be grasped by the mind and transformed by the will; it refuses to treat them as an unchanging part of nature.

Thus, the decline of the rule of law might endanger, or even destroy, individual freedom. The abandonment of bureaucratic law could mean a relapse into the logic of tribalism, which sanctifies the existing order of the group as an irrevocable decree of nature. If these were to be the outcomes of the transformation of modern society, the negative utopias of our day would have been vindicated. We would have lost the treasures of freedom and of transcendence and would have condemned ourselves to a society of unreflective adaptation, in which the power of criticism and the spirit of revolt would have been smothered.

An alternative approach to the prospects of modern society and to their legal implications might be represented by the metaphor of a spiral that reverses direction without returning to its starting point. This would mean that individual freedom could be rescued from the demise of the rule of law and brought into harmony with the reassertion of communitarian concerns. It would also signify that the capacity to see and to treat each form of social life as a creation rather than as a fate could survive the disintegration of public and positive law and be reconciled with the sense of an immanent order in society. Let us examine briefly each of these possibilities.

The rule of law is the liberal state's most emphatic response to the problems of power and freedom. But we have seen that, whatever its efficacy in preventing immediate government oppression of the individual, the strategy of legalism fails to deal with these issues in the basic relationships of work and everyday life. Whether "public" persecution can still be prevented and "private" domination at last be tamed once the rule of law is given up depends in part on the possibility of refining ancient methods for the dispersal of power. The chief of these methods is the plurality of groups itself: the liberty of the individual to pass from one to another and to participate in the decisions that shape life in each of the associations to which he belongs.

But this by itself is not enough. One also needs criteria by which to choose among different ways of ranking, among legitimate and illegitimate uses of power, among permissible and prohibited inequalities. In the absence of such principles, the predicament of liberal society will simply be repeated: men will be condemned to search for a justice they cannot find, and all social arrangements will be rendered suspect by their lack of a moral foundation.

The problem of power carries us to the other aspect of the spirallike process I envisage. Unless people regain the sense that the practices of society represent some sort of natural order instead of a set of arbitrary choices, they cannot hope to escape from the dilemma of unjustified power. But how can this perception of immanent order be achieved in the circumstances of modern society?

The mere existence of moral agreement within a particular association would not bring about this end. First, it would be necessary for the subversion of inequality to proceed to such a point that people would be entitled to place greater confidence in collective choices as expressions of a shared human nature or of the intrinsic demands of social order rather than as a product of the interests of dominant groups. Second, it would be indispensable that this experience of increasing equality also make possible an ever more universal consensus about the immanent order of social life and thus help refine further the understanding of what equality means. The first condition without the second is empty. The second without the first is dangerous because it threatens to consecrate the outlook of the most powerful and articulate elements in the society.

Even if one assumes that the vision of an indwelling pattern of right be created and justified, one may still wonder whether this vision could be kept from stifling criticism and change. To preserve the possibility of transcending the present, it is important to remain aware of the inherent imperfection of any one system of community practices as a source of insight into the requirements of social life. For if one takes seriously the notion that men make themselves in history, these requirements develop over time rather than remain static. Openness toward the future means that one must value the conflictual process by which communities are created over time and satisfactory relations are established among them as much as the internal cohesion of any communal group.

Such a reconciliation of immanent order and transcendent criticism would imply a greater replacement than we could now comprehend of bureaucratic law or the rule of law by what in a sense could be called custom. This customary law would have many of the marks we associate with custom: its lack of a positive and a public character and its largely emergent and implicit quality. Yet it would differ from custom in making room for a distinction between what is and what ought to be. It would become less the stable normative order of a particular group than the developing moral language of mankind.

Whether one accepts the hypothesis of the circle or that of the spiral, it is important to remember that the three kinds of law present themselves historically as overlapping and interpenetrating realms, rather than as neatly separated worlds. The legal profession and legal education in postliberal society show the juxtaposition of concerns with all these forms of law and legal thought. This universe has an outer sphere of blackletter law: the area wherein the rule of law ideal and the specialized methods of legal analysis flourish. Then there is an inner sphere of bureaucratic law and bureaucratic rhetoric. At this level, law is approached instrumentally; one talks of costs and benefits, and one searches for a science of policy that can help the administrative and the professional elite exercise its power in the name of impersonal technique and social welfare. But, beyond legalistic formality and bureaucratic instrumentalism, lie the inchoate senses of equity and solidarity.

I have argued that these ideas of solidarity and equity can

be seen in two different lights, which correspond respectively to the two senses of custom. On the one hand, they can be devices with which to defend the established beliefs and values of a particular community, as articulated by those who have governed it in the past or control it in the present. But, in conjunction with a program of substantive justice, they may also serve as the primitive form taken by the struggle to discover a universal given order in social life.

The search for this latent and living law—not the law of prescriptive rules or of bureaucratic policies, but the elementary code of human interaction—has been the staple of the lawyer's art wherever this art was practiced with most depth and skill. What united the great Islamic *'ulama'*, the Roman jurisconsults, and the English common lawyers was the sense they shared that the law, rather than being made chiefly by judges and princes, was already present in society itself.[70] Throughout history there has been a bond between the legal profession and the search for an order inherent in social life. The existence of this bond suggests that the lawyer's insight, which preceded the advent of the legal order, can survive its decline.

The same processes that promise to reconcile freedom and transcendence with community and immanent order also threaten to sacrifice the former to the latter. In a brief passage of his *Republic,* Plato evokes a society in which men, reduced to animal contentment, have lost the capacity of self-criticism together with the sense of incompleteness. He calls this society the City of Pigs.[71] The significance of the historical tendencies discussed in this chapter lies in this: with a single gesture they frighten us with the image of the City of Pigs and entice us with the prospect of the Heavenly City. By offering us the extremes of good and evil, they speak at once to what is bestial and to what is sublime in our humanity.

4

THE PREDICAMENT OF
SOCIAL THEORY REVISITED

Revisiting social theory

It is now time to reconsider, in light of what has been
learned from the social study of law, the issues set out
at the beginning of this essay. The preceding chapters have
suggested, and this chapter will confirm, that the problems of
method, order, and modernity are closely connected. A complete solution to any of them presupposes a solution to the
others. An advance in our understanding of any of them
immediately improves our ability to deal with the remaining
problems.

Nevertheless, the topics come to our attention in different ways. Questions about method are the easiest to pursue
independently of a particular historical context and to answer
with general propositions. Even if one concludes that a cate-

gory or procedure of explanation suits some circumstances better than others, there must still be universal criteria to determine when a method is preferable.

The problem of modernity lies at the opposite end of the spectrum. It has to do with particular events. Hence, a response to it makes sense only in the context of a concrete historical argument. To be sure, unless historical claims had some level of generality, unless they went beyond the elucidation of unique events, they would not be part of social theory at all. But this hardly says much: even the most focused historical statement must refer implicitly to general categories of thought and rely on general conceptions of social order and human action. There is no way to avoid the puzzle of the relationship between the understanding of historical particulars and the reference to general truths.

Midway between the problems of method and of modernity stands the question of social order. Conceptions of the social bond participate in both the universality of beliefs about explanation and in the particularity of historical study. We may have views about what holds each society or each form of social order together. But these more concrete visions of coexistence rest upon assumptions about what makes any kind of order possible.

The reason for this intermediate position of ideas on social order is that they resist classification into the categories of subject matter and method. They refer to the types of organization and consciousness that underlie human associations. But they also serve as the fund of concepts from which we draw, overtly or not, in our efforts to describe and to explain historical events. They occupy the mysterious point at which the line between the procedures and the productions of thought fades away.

The continuum of diminishing generality along which the problems of method, order, and modernity are situated accounts for the emphasis of discussion in this chapter. The largest amount of space is devoted to method, for the methodological implications of my historical argument are the least evident in the argument itself. A shorter treatment of the issue of social order follows. The briefest section addresses the question of modernity, not because this question is less important than the others, but because it is the topic on which my earlier discussion speaks best for itself.

THE PROBLEM OF METHOD

The problem of method, as laid out in the first part of this essay, includes four main issues: the possibility of an alternative to logic and causation, capable of overcoming the inadequacies of both rationalism and historicism; the link between this third method and causality; the connection between the meaning of an act for its agent and its meaning for an observer; and the relationship of systematic theory to historical understanding.

The social study of law turns out to have a special significance for a view of the methodological situation of modern social thought. The same gap between the ideal and the actual that plays so large a role in modern society and modern culture sets the stage for both our methodological difficulties and our characteristic forms of law. We are puzzled by the connection between acts and beliefs, especially when the latter have an overt normative aspect. Our law appears as a set of rules that prescribe how people ought to behave rather than describing how they do behave.

The weaker the ties of agreement about what things are as well as about what they ought to be, the greater the likelihood that in any one group an act will have different meanings for its agent and for the people who are affected by it or who observe it. Thus, it will become all the more important to have impersonal rules that fix the limits of individual entitlement and duty.

So it is not surprising that the attempt to understand the relationship between law and other aspects of social life helps us pick up the thread of methodological controversy in classic social theory. Let us, then, reexamine each of the four matters involved in the dispute about method.

The alternative to rationalism and historicism is a method of common meaning or of interpretive explanation. Its chief concerns are the embeddedness of action in belief and the clustering of units of action-belief into totalities whose inner unity is neither logical nor causal. Action refers to externally observable behavior; belief to what one thinks and feels about facts or values.

Many of the riddles of social theory have resulted from the insistence on contrasting belief and conduct and the subsequent attempt to determine their relationship to each other. Sometimes, the preeminence of "material" factors is asserted. At other times, "spiritual" forces are held to be paramount. With increasing frequency, the spiritual and the material in history are described as equally powerful and independent influences on conduct, but little progress has been made in showing just how they interact.

The method of common meaning redefines the terms of the debate by viewing the smallest unit of social study as a certain correspondence between belief and conduct rather than as either one alone. This correspondence is called meaning. The intelligibility of human conduct presupposes that action can be understood by reference to ideas about the ends an individual pursues and about the conditions that serve or impede the attainment of those ends. A person's conduct is comprehensible in specifically human or social terms only when we are able to see why he acted in a certain way at a certain moment, given his beliefs about the purposes he wished to achieve and about the circumstances in which he had to act.[1] To understand the effects and the development of his action, we must then compare his judgments about the world with our own knowledge of reality, and we must ascertain what he himself learns from his mistakes. This emphasis on the inseparability of action from belief raises a number of difficult and familiar questions.

It should be clear that what I have called human or social understanding is not the only possible way to account for conduct. Conduct might also be described and explained in purely physical terms if we wished to, but at the cost of ruling out an aspect of our experience. A more precise way to put this would be that, because human action is embedded in belief, social phenomena contain in themselves a self-interpretation. To treat them merely as objects of thought rather than also as forms of knowledge is to disregard an aspect of their being. No degree of completeness in purely physical explanation could ever compensate for such a distortion.

Another problem with the thesis of the embeddedness of action in belief has to do with its implications for the possibilities of insincerity, false consciousness, and unconscious behavior. There is the danger that an insistence on the inseparability of conduct from consciousness will be taken to mean that whatever people think or say they are doing is what they are in fact doing. If this were the outcome of the argument, we would have escaped from behaviorism only to fall into idealism.

Thus, the interpretive method does not identify stated beliefs with actual beliefs or actual beliefs with the reality of the believer's conduct. Instead, it uses each of these as a context for comprehending the others. Such a procedure is consistent with recognizing discrepancies between what the agent professes and what he actually intends. Indeed, it is compatible with a conviction that purposes are likely to be in conflict with each other and to coexist at many different levels of articulation and awareness.

So, also, we assign meaning to conduct on the assumption that the actor may have a mistaken understanding of the circumstances and of the effects of his acts. Thus, one of the indispensable steps of this method is the contrast of what the agent thinks the world is like with what, to the best of our information, we know it to be like.

Finally, it remains true that some actions may be wholly, and all actions may be partly, unintended or unreflective. To the extent that they remain below the threshold of consciousness, they may be causally explained, but they cannot be meaningfully interpreted.

One may ask whether the attribution of meaning necessarily breaks with traditional notions of causality. The purposes of choice might be taken as primary causes and the circumstances of choice as background causes or conditions. There would still, however, be an important qualification to this use of causality. To speak in the language of means and ends rather than in that of causes and effects makes sense only if the ends of an individual are treated as more than immediate, determined effects of other causes, and if the purposes of each individual or group are in some sense uniquely his or its own.

To view action through the prism of meaning is to regard it as an event in history. There is a superficial sense in which historical knowledge is retrospective. But in fact all understanding is based upon what has been learned from the past even when it is concerned with the prediction of the future. What distinguishes historical knowledge is its effort to grasp, and to assume, the position of the actor. The actor may know some of the consequences of his actions, but he cannot know all of them, nor can he avoid the experience of choosing among different possible purposes and courses of conduct.

The inappropriateness of identifying the method of common meaning with causal explanation becomes all the more clear when one turns from the first to the second dimension of the interpretive method, from the embeddedness of conduct in belief to the way social phenomena cluster together into meaningful totalities. No conduct has meaning independent of its social context. A statement, a gesture, or an act can display purpose precisely because it draws on a background of social rules, practices, and understandings.

Like language itself, this broader code of social interaction is a collective patrimony. But, again like language, it includes many dialects or subsystems, with varying degrees of cohesion and concreteness. Phenomena capable of being decoded by the same criteria have a unity that is neither logical nor causal. Theirs is a unique semantic wholeness.

Social phenomena cluster into wholes according to the code of meaning by which they are, as it were, programmed. The more two cases of conduct are set against the background of the same rules, practices, and understandings, the more are we entitled to view them as members of the same whole. Thus, two doctrines in a system of legal thought, two ritual acts within a certain religious community at a given time, or two contemporaneous paintings expressive of the same style, may be seen as messages within a single language, as units of action-belief within a single totality. But this totality would likely be harder or even impossible to identify if we drew the legal doctrines from different legal systems, the rituals from different religions, or the paintings from different styles. A form of social life also represents a meaningful whole. It provides a universal language of interaction that penetrates many areas of existence.

More is required for two social phenomena to belong to the same cluster than that they be capable of being interpreted within the same code. It is also necessary that they convey a similar message, a message from which people can infer guidance about what they ought to do and what others may be expected to do. This similarity involves something more than logical consistency and something less than logical entailment or identity.

Its two main forms are functional differentiation and resemblance. There is functional differentiation when phenomena with special implications for different areas of social life combine, like pieces of a jigsaw puzzle, into a more comprehensive view of some aspect of reality. There is resemblance when several social facts, observed in context and in the richness of their detail, turn out to have analogous implications for belief and conduct. Often resemblance and differentiation operate simultaneously. Thus, the doctrines of a legal system may start as a set of functionally differentiated concepts. Yet each member of the set may develop over time so as to address the problems and to echo the policies of other members.

The two criteria of clustering—the capacity to be decoded in the same way and the ability to convey a similar message—are not as different as they might at first seem. There may be strict limits on the kinds of message any one set of shared understandings, practices, and rules can transmit. And it may be even more difficult to convey similar messages on different codes. This is precisely the chief obstacle to comparative social study.

The wholes into which social phenomena cluster may range from the characteristic orientation of an individual to an entire form of social life. For the dominant culture of a society stands in the same relationship to the society's modes of organization as does the simplest belief to the context of behavior in which it is embedded. A society's law constitutes the chief bond between its culture and its organization; it is the external manifestation of the embeddedness of the former in the latter.

Nowhere is this more evident than in the most basic and universal type of normative order—custom. Custom consists of tacit standards of right that are actual patterns of conduct. Yet they also stamp a meaning upon every act committed in obedience to them or in violation of them; they give a determinate significance to conduct that would otherwise be meaningless because it would be open to an indefinite number of possible interpretations. In this way, a vassal's gesture of defiance of his lord can acquire its identity only within the context of the norms that govern interaction between lords and vassals.

This is the same phenomenon that allows the poet to express meaning by using the conventions of a particular literary tradition. At a still more basic level, it is the principle that makes natural languages vehicles of communication: one can say an indefinite number of things in any one language precisely because its rules are definite and its fund of sounds, words, and syntax is limited. Indeed, the normative order of society represents in a very real sense the language of its social relations.

What kind of a meaningful whole do a society's organization, its culture, and its normative order amount to? Surely, such a whole cannot refer to a particular aspect of life, like the vassal's relation to his lord, or it would fail to confer a meaning on the variety of possible experiences within the society. A meaningful whole of this kind must therefore present a complete picture of man's place in the world, a vision of life in which the view of the individual's relationship to society occupies an especially important place. The analogy of language may once again be helpful.

Linguistics has accustomed us to recognize that each language classifies the world completely. In the same sense, each system of social relations, seen as a totality, contains a picture of the whole of human existence. We infer the total scheme of meaning from its constituent parts at the same time that we assign meanings to the parts by placing them within the whole. Analogously, we grasp the meaning of a distinction made within a language by understanding the relationship of that distinction to other distinctions and ultimately to the total categorization of reality the language embodies. At the same time, however, one's insight into this total classification must always be exemplified in, and tested against, one's comprehension of particular ways of speaking the language. What prevents the circle that leads from the meaning of the parts to that of the whole and then back again from being a vicious circle?

Take another look at my linguistic example. Once the speaker has gained a primitive and inarticulate sense of the universe of meaning with which his language provides him and which is expressed in the rules that govern its use, he can also begin to assign meanings to particular trains of thought he has never before heard expressed. A similar procedure enables the social theorist or the active participant in social life to ascribe significance to new acts and beliefs by giving them a tentative place within a dimly apprehended framework. With each new interpretation of a specific social relation or belief, the larger picture becomes more precise. Hence, the understanding of society can break out of the closed circle in which it would otherwise be trapped.

Each of the forms of social life discussed in this book—tribal, aristocratic, and liberal society, or the postliberal, the traditionalistic, and the revolutionary socialist variant of modernity—is a meaningful whole of the most comprehensive kind. Each embodies an entire mode of human existence. And for each the law plays a crucial role in revealing and determining the relationship of belief to organization.

This relationship may be one of conflict as well as reinforcement. In a liberal society, inclined to contrast the ideal with actuality, one may still speak of the embeddedness of belief in organization, for interpersonal relationships in such a society continually generate their own negations. A particular set of oppositions between men's consciously held values and their real experiences is constantly repeated.

Consider now some possible objections to interpretive explanation in general, and to the idea of clustering in particular. Both might seem fatally lacking in the precision of causal judgments. This advantage of the causal method becomes less credible, however, once the paradox of causality has been acknowledged: the tension between the need to impute particular effects to particular causes and the need to show how everything causes everything else. The more complete the causal account, the more circular and vague it becomes.

Another difficulty is that any given social phenomenon is likely to belong to a variety of clusters. Forms of social life will differ in the degree to which they provide a unified code of interpretation or include a variety of partially conflicting codes. There is one aspect of this duality that deserves special attention: Who is to determine the relevant background code for the interpretation of conduct? The thesis of embeddedness of action in belief seems to commit us to saying that it must be the individual agent or the group to which he belongs. But this conclusion makes generalization and comparison impossible. Here we have, once again, the issue of subjective and objective meaning. I shall return to it later.

The outline of the method of interpretive explanation, of its two stages, and of its principal difficulties is now complete. No important feature of the theory or practice of this method is novel. It has always in fact been the favored tool of the great European historians. The genius of these historians often lay precisely in their ability to place conduct in the setting of belief and to evoke the elements of unity and conflict in a whole tradition, period, or society. The classical social theorists brought this method to theoretical consciousness.' And contemporary authors have discussed and developed it.[2] What remains missing is a grasp of the precise character of the method, an understanding that can be perfected only when the methodological question is seen in its integrity and related to the other problems of social theory.

This essay has illustrated each of the two main aspects of interpretive explanation, though at a level of considerable abstraction and generality, because it has been concerned more with entire societies than with particular groups or individuals. Thus, it has insisted on the inseparability of organization and consciousness, the collective counterparts to individual behavior and belief. Each historical condition of the different kinds of law was viewed both as a manner of arranging society and as a way to understand the world; each form of social life was studied as a totality in which institutions and ideas make up an indissoluble whole. The effort was to define the basic code of meaning at work in a variety of historical situations and to show how these codes can change. The same procedures might perhaps be used with much greater success in illuminating more concrete historical events.

Though I have sketched the method of common meaning, I have not yet clarified its relationship to causal explanation. Surely the method does not absolve us of the need to show how and why one event or meaningful whole follows another. A superficial answer to this question would be that the method of common meaning is concerned with description, whereas causality is a tool for explanation.[3] If, however, my previous argument is correct, there are two senses in which a social phenomenon may be explained. To explain may be to state how, given certain facts, other facts will succeed them in time, with greater or lesser probability. But to explain may also be to show the sense an act makes against the background of a social code of rules, practices, and beliefs.

This latter kind of explanation is sometimes also called interpretation. It uses the language of purpose. And it is concerned with the "logic of situations": the extent to which similar messages are conveyed by different acts. The "logic of the situation" may make some acts in any given circumstance more probable than others, not because they result from specific causes, but because of the tendency of social phenomena to join into meaningful wholes. Thus, if we encounter certain features of an artistic style in a painting, we also expect to find other traits of the style in it, though the stylistic attributes cannot be said either to cause or logically to imply each other.

To the extent that interpretive explanation is concerned with sequence, it focuses on the way men deal with incoherence within or among meaningful wholes. It is dialectical in the sense that it identifies conflict and its resolution as the substance of change. Among these conflicts the most important are those that oppose people's ideas or ideals to their experience, for these dissolve the fundamental units of action-belief that constitute the texture of social life.

Though causal and interpretive explanation are distinct, they also overlap. On the one hand, purposive activity expresses itself through the manipulation of causal chains: the means chosen by the agent to realize his ends are intended to cause the achievement of those objectives. On the other hand, in making causal judgments about historical events, we characteristically have to distinguish between primary and secondary causes or between causes and background conditions. To do this, one must have a sense of what is normal or trivial as opposed to novel or significant in a given historical situation. This sense requires us to have at least an inarticulate grasp of the meaningful framework of a form of social life.

With respect to their subject matters, the causal and the interpretive method are best conceived as two concentric circles, the former larger than the latter. Whatever can be interpreted meaningfully can also be explained causally. A form of consciousness, such as a system of legal doctrine or an artistic work, may be approached as a set of symbols that convey a similar message, capable of being decoded. But it can also be treated genetically, as the outcome of past events, perhaps unknown to the persons who make and manipulate the symbols.

Not everything, however, in society that one can explain causally can be interpreted meaningfully. Whatever is unintended, whatever lies beyond the reach of consciousness, whatever is impelled by forces over which men have no mastery or of which they have no awareness, escapes the interpretive method. This residuum may in fact be an enormously important part of social life. The conclusion is that much that human beings do in society is not open to a specifically human or social understanding.

The root of the relatively limited range of the interpretive method lies in the dualism of human nature. Man is consciousness capable of intentionality. But he is also a member of the physical world. Though his intentions permeate some of the aspects of his situation, they never reach all of them.

Whenever we set aside the fact of consciousness, we fall into behaviorism. Whenever we disregard the limitations of consciousness, we slide into idealism.[4] Behaviorism and idealism are the two great sins a method of social study can commit, for both distort crucial traits of human existence.

In my study of law, I have emphasized both the opportunities of interpretive explanation and the restraints on it. Thus, a major part of the discussion of conditions of law was concerned with the unintended and largely unperceived effects of types of organization or ideological commitment.

Now that the method of common meaning has been

defined and its relationship to causality described, we can take a new look at the issue of subjectivity and objectivity in social understanding. Interpretive explanation requires the interpreter to take the agent's purposes seriously, to grasp his conduct, as has often been said, from the actor's own point of view. But for the observer, the social theorist, or historian to understand a subject's behavior meaningfully, he must be able to decipher what the subject is saying and then to recode that message into the language of the observer's own culture. In other words, the greater the distance between the observer and the observed, the more important and the more difficult it becomes to translate from one symbol system into another. This is the first aspect of the problem of objectivity.

The second aspect appears when we wish not merely to help a member of one society comprehend a member of another but to formulate a general comparative theory of society. For we then need a general language into which all the more particular codes, including the observer's, can be translated. In fact, the two sides to the issue of objectivity are inseparable. Translation among cultures presupposes the existence of universal, though perhaps inarticulate, criteria of comparison.[5]

The theoretical postulate of comparison among cultures is the unity of the human spirit. One must be careful to define just what entitles us to make this assumption and how far it can carry us. The problem of translation among cultures is simply a dramatic form of the more general issue of communication among individuals.

Though social codes are a collective property, each person understands and employs them in a unique way. His comprehension and use of them is inseparable from the situation of his own existence. Hence the separateness of persons imposes limits on the transparency of one mind to another. These limits may be faint in a tribal society or in one to which the doctrine of consensus applies with special force, but they are always present.

Communication among persons presupposes two things. The first presupposition is that the communicants, as members of the same species, have the same kind of being or mind. The second is that this potential or latent similarity be actualized in a set of shared experiences, understandings, and values. Experiences are inseparable from understandings: the embeddedness of conduct in belief implies as much. Understandings are inseparable from values: our vision of the world conditions the ends we hold, and our most general forms of consciousness combine ideas and ideals into a single system of belief.

The conclusion of the preceding argument is that the demands of objectivity and subjectivity in social study can be reconciled only to the extent that an actual universal community of experience, understanding, and value comes into existence. All moves toward such a community may be compromised by the separateness of persons. But it is only in this political sense that the methodological problem might be solved, if it can be solved at all. The more fragile our own ties of shared experience, understanding, and value to the society we study, the less able are we to gain a subjective knowledge of that society, to apply interpretive explanation to it. The fewer the communal links among the societies we study, the more are we forced to abandon the method of common meaning when we formulate comprehensive or comparative social theories.

This is why when I compared widely diverse societies as settings for different kinds of law in Chapter Two, I was obliged to deal with them largely in causal terms. When, however, my focus shifted to the varieties of modern society in Chapter Three, their similarity made it possible to approach them more freely as meaningful wholes and to compare the inner dialectic of consciousness and experience in each of them. But today these societies include most of the world; modernism creates a basis for the universalization of the human understanding of human affairs.

A grasp of the method of interpretive explanation, of its relationship to causality, and of the sense in which it can reconcile the demands of objectivity and subjectivity may deepen our insight into the remaining methodological problem—the tie between systematic theory and historiography.

The crucial device for the reconciliation of systematic and historical understanding is the type. The type is a meaningful whole and the unity of its elements is a unity of sense rather than of logic or causation. The basis or justification of the typological method is therefore the tendency of social phenomena to cluster into meaningful wholes. These totalities are just as real as the units of action-belief out of which they are made. The clustering tendency does not, however, suffice to explain how we can formulate theories that compare many forms of social life, nor does it provide any self-evident guidance about the level of abstraction at which theoretical statements should be cast. To deal with these issues, one must return to the metaphysical idea of the unity of human nature, and develop it.

We have seen how types of organization, of law, and of consciousness come together into more comprehensive wholes, the forms of social life. These forms of social life, exemplified in my essay by tribal, liberal, and aristocratic society and then again by the varieties of modernity, are the most general types available to social theory. Each of them represents a unique interpretation of what it means to be human. Each confronts its individual members with the recurring demands of human existence, but each presents these in a special way and limits the resources of matter and of thought that can be used to meet them. Perhaps the most pervasive of these continuing problems have to do with the antagonism between the requirements of human individuality and of human sociability, and with the attempt either to subordinate one to the other or to reconcile the two.

As it interprets human nature, each form of social life changes what humanity is and what it can become. Thus, the opportunities and obstacles faced by postliberal, traditionalistic, and revolutionary socialist societies differ from those with which earlier societies had to deal. For not only do the former present the contest between individuality and sociability, of freedom and community, in an ever more acute and conscious manner, but they also provide an unprecedented wealth of spiritual and material means for its resolution.

The view I have just sketched of the relationship between the most general types—the forms of social life—and human nature is based upon two key ideas that might appear contradictory. The first notion holds that there exists a limited fund of problems and possibilities of human association. Each form of social life is defined by the way it responds to the problems and pursues the possibilities. The fact that the fund is limited makes comprehensive theory and universal comparison possible. This principle, however, seems incompatible with the other half of my thesis: that the forms of social life are constituents and re-creators, rather than just examples, of human nature.

The way to reconcile these two equally important ideas is to conceive of human nature as an entity embodied in particular forms of social life, though never exhausted by them. Consequently, humanity can always transcend any one of the kinds of society that develop it in a certain direction. Nonetheless, human nature is known, indeed it exists, only through the historical types of social life.

Yet as human nature is affected by the rich diversity of social forms, it keeps its own identity. The source of this unity is the permanent problem of man's relationship to nature, to others, and to his own work. The transformation of society may change the emphasis given to different parts of this predicament, the depth of our insight into it, or the extent to which its internal conflicts are resolved. But it cannot modify the structure of the situation. The aspect of that situation singled out for closer study in this essay has been the tension between the requirements of personal autonomy and of community, a tension exemplified by the interplay of principles of social order and by the antagonistic forces at work within each mode of social life.

Such a conception of the relationship between human nature and history could be fully worked out only with the help of a metaphysics we do not yet possess. It was suggested earlier that our entire conception of reason continues to rest on the idea of universals as abstract generalizations from particulars. For my present purposes, the universal is human nature or the structural constraints on a person's relationship to nature, to others, and to himself; the particulars are the forms of social life and the individual personalities by which that humanity is represented and through which it is built. Here the universal is viewed as an actual being that can neither exist apart from a particular manifestation nor be reduced to any one embodiment. Its unity lies in the constantly developing set of its incarnations.

This doctrine of universals and particulars indicates the lines along which the problem of abstractness of the types, and thus ultimately of systematic theory and historiography, would have to be resolved. Each type, as a theoretical construct or as a social reality, would be seen as the representation of a coherent set of possibilities and problems. The ultimate type is human nature itself. The social theorist can make a typological scheme indefinitely more concrete without destroying its uniqueness. Similarly, a society or a personality can assume different concrete forms without disappearing. The identity of the type is destroyed only when its underlying framework of possibilities and constraints is overstepped.

Viewed in this manner, the problem of abstraction and concreteness in social study takes on a new aspect. It becomes like the process by which one adds coats of paint to an object, or by which an organism grows successive layers of skin, rather than like the procedure for determining the possible values of an algebraic equation. Instead of seeking examples of a preestablished formula, one adds a new level of determinateness to something that might have other determinations as well.

So we see that just as the dilemma of subjectivity and objectivity requires a political resolution, the alliance of generalizing thought and historiography presupposes a change in our philosophical ideas. To redress its own failings, social theory must reach out beyond itself to politics and metaphysics.

THE PROBLEM OF SOCIAL ORDER

The social study of law suggests a response to our puzzlement over the basis of order in society. It puts the controversy between the doctrines of private interest and of consensus, and hence between the instrumental and the noninstrumental view of rules, in perspective.

In the present state of social thought, there are two apparent ways to approach the issue of what holds society together. One can look for a general conception of the social bond that somehow synthesizes the doctrines of legitimacy and instrumentalism so as to avoid the defects of each. Or one can abandon the search for a comprehensive thesis as futile and try to ascertain the circumstances to which each account of social order most suitably applies.

The view that emerges from this essay, however, lies somewhere in between these two solutions. It recognizes that one of the theories of social order may come closer to expressing the truth of a given relationship, group, or society than its rival. But it also insists that, in a deeper sense, no society has resolved its own problem of order until it has succeeded in meeting the human demands represented by both doctrines. And, strangely enough, the further away a society moves from this ideal, the more difficult will it be to arrive at a coherent understanding of order in the society.

The doctrine of legitimacy applies with particular force to the form of social life I called tribal, and, more generally, to all sorts of hierarchic community. It is most at home in the social setting of customary law. The theoretical deficiencies of the doctrine turn out to be the actual political problems of the societies it describes.

The consensus theory makes it difficult to account for conflict and change. The consensus society has difficulty in allowing for change and conflict and then in dealing with them when, nevertheless, they occur. Its whole existence is based upon the attempt to make custom do for human association what instinct does for animal association. But custom, unlike instinct, is always in danger of disintegrating thanks to the subjectivity of consciousness, which no agreement can ever entirely override.

The doctrine of private interest is most applicable to liberal society, and more generally, to all those aspects of modernity characterized by the antagonism of individual ends and the felt illegitimacy of consensus. The social situations it portrays are those that serve as the settings for an imposed bureaucratic law or for an allegedly impartial legal order.

Once again, we have found that the theoretical objections to this view correspond to tribulations actually undergone by the societies to which the view refers. The doctrine has trouble accounting for social stability and cohesion. So, too, in liberal society every collective agreement and every allocation of power are ultimately experienced as fragile and illegitimate. Liberalism is the form of social life that most depends on impersonal rules, yet it is also the one least able to shape and to apply them.

The crisis of social order becomes a conscious subject of human concern whenever consensus breaks down or loses its ability to command allegiance. For it then becomes evident that custom cannot indeed become a surrogate for instinct. Neither bureaucratic law nor a legal order can undo this crisis.

Each of the two main variants of social life, together with the doctrine of order that describes it, draws its vitality from a basic aspect of human nature: in one case the individuality, in the other the sociability, of persons. The ultimate reason why no society can resolve its problem of order by leaning exclusively on one of these two features of personality is that neither of these two attributes of humanity allows itself to be completely suppressed.

A society resolves the crisis of order insofar as it manages to reconcile individual freedom with community cohesion, and the sense of an immanent order with the possibility of transcendent criticism. The more perfect this reconciliation becomes, the more does the society's emergent interactional law reveal the requirements of human nature and social coexistence. Thus, people can find criteria with which to evaluate agreement and to define equality. The availability of these standards to everyone makes cohesion and stability possible. At the same time, such a society acknowledges that the requirements of association change as human nature itself is transformed. Thus, it provides for dissidence and change.

In this imaginary situation, the controversy between the doctrines of private interest and of consensus would have lost its significance in theory, but only because it would have been overcome in practice. In fact, because of the inherent limitations on our ability to universalize the experience of community, we cannot show that this synthesis will, or even can, be fully achieved. Hence, we have no assurance of ever answering completely the theoretical question of social order.

There are two implications of this line of analysis that should be especially emphasized. The first is that there exists a relationship between a society's intelligibility and its perfection. A society that has sacrificed a side of the dilemma of social order to the other falls mainly under one of the partial doctrines of social order. But these doctrines are themselves paradoxical in their conclusions. The weaknesses of the theories of order, far from being mere intellectual failures, correspond to deficiencies in the actual existence of the societies to which they refer. The further a society is from the ideal, the less one can frame a coherent view of its order, because the less of a coherent order does it possess. The other implication of the argument is that the theoretical problem of order, like that of method, is also a problem of politics. The limits to its solution are the limits of politics itself.

THE PROBLEM OF MODERNITY

The same framework of ideas used to answer the questions of method and social order also sheds light on the issue of modernism. When we study the dialectic of consciousness and experience in modern society with the method of interpretive explanation and when we examine the implications for that society of the failure to resolve the problem of order, we are able to grasp the inmost nature of modernity.

This approach has forced us to reject the two most popular interpretations of modern society. One of these sees that society, in the fashion of liberal political thought, as an association of individuals who have conflicting ends and whose security and freedom are guaranteed by the rule of law. The other account conceives of the society as a structure of group, and specifically of class, domination whose true character is hidden, rather than revealed, by the prevailing ideology. The first interpretation reifies consciousness; the second disregards it. By contrast, the core of the approach to modern liberal society in this essay is a conception of the interplay between belief and experience, between consciousness and organization.

When liberalism passes into postliberalism, and when traditionalistic and revolutionary socialist society emerge as deviant types of modernity, this interplay takes on new forms. Liberal society is involved in the paradoxes of a mode of association that denies both community and immanent order and is therefore best described by the doctrine of private interest. But postliberal, traditionalistic, and revolutionary socialist society are all obsessed, in different ways, with the reconciliation of freedom and community. This alliance is part of a broader responsibility; the sense of a latent or natural order in social life must be harmonized with the capacity to let the will remake social arrangements. To achieve this reconciliation, and thereby to work toward the ideal of a universal community, is the great political task of modern societies. But it is also the precondition to our ability, as theorists, to bridge the gap between subjectivity and objectivity in social understanding and to perfect our vision of social order.

SOCIAL THEORY, METAPHYSICS, AND POLITICS

Much of social science has been built as a citadel against metaphysics and politics. Faithful to the outlook produced by the modern revolt against ancient philosophy, the classic social theorists were anxious to free themselves first from the illusions of metaphysics, then from the seeming arbitrariness of political judgments. They wanted to create a body of objective knowledge of society that would not be at the mercy of metaphysical speculation or political controversy, and, up to a point, they succeeded.

But now we see that to resolve its own dilemmas, social theory must once again become, in a sense, both metaphysical and political. It must take a stand on issues of human nature and human knowledge for which no "scientific" elucidation is, or may ever be, available. And it must acknowledge that its own future is inseparable from the fate of society. The progress of theory depends upon political events. The doctrines theory embraces are ideals as well as descriptions: the choices theory must make are choices among conceptions of what society ought to be as well as among views of what it is. These choices are neither arbitrary nor capable of logical or empirical proof. They build upon speculative conceptions of the requirements of social order and of the demands of human nature, conceptions that are informed by historical knowledge but which cannot pretend to follow necessarily from it.

Thus, the path of return to metaphysics and politics in social theory is made dangerous by the chance that slowly acquired learning will be exchanged cheaply for fancy and passion. Any evaluation of this risk should, however, bear two points in mind. First, there is no real escape. It is the internal program of social theory itself, its burden of unanswered questions, unresolved paradoxes, and unjustified assumptions, which forces us to take this course. Moreover, there is extraordinary promise as well as danger in the reunion of social study with metaphysics and politics. For surely it is as true of social theory as of other branches of knowledge that the deepest insight is likely to be gained when one is in passage from a more general to a more particular perception, or from the particular to the general. Either way, the richness of immediate concerns combines with the longing for universality in thought to give the mind an enthusiasm that prompts it to boldness, opens it up to the unusual and to the commonplace, and awakens it to the unity of things.

The great social theorists had this experience when they went from the speculative generalities of their predecessors to the narrower conjectures of a social science. Now it is for us to imitate our teachers by traveling in the opposite direction, back along the road by which they came.

NOTES

See page 1.   1. See W. Jackson Bate, *The Burden of the Past and the English Poet* (New York, Norton, 1972), pp. 3–11.

See page 2.   2. See João Mangabeira, *Rui. O Estadista da República* (Rio de Janeiro, Olympio, 1943), p. 15.

See page 4.   3. See Louis Althusser, *Montesquieu. La Politique et l'Histoire* (Paris, Presses Universitaires, 1959), pp. 20–21.

See page 5.   4. See Émile Durkheim, *Montesquieu et Rousseau. Précurseurs de la Sociologie* (Paris, Rivière, 1953), p. 47.

See page 5.   5. See Robert Cumming, *Human Nature and History. A Study of the Development of Liberal Political Thought* (Chicago, Chicago, 1969), vol. I, pp. 66–75.

See page 6.   6. For two versions of this thesis, see Talcott Parsons, *The Structure of Social Action. A Study in Social Theory with Special Reference to a Group of Recent European Writers* (New York, Free Press, 1968); and Robert A. Nisbet, *The Sociological Tradition* (New York, Basic Books, 1966). For overviews of the tradition of social theory, see

270 / LAW IN MODERN SOCIETY

Carlo Antoni, *Dallo Storicismo alla Sociologia* (Florence, Sansoni, 1940); Anthony Giddens, *Capitalism and Modern Social Theory. An Analysis of the Writings of Marx, Durkheim, and Max Weber* (Cambridge, Cambridge, 1971); and Gianfranco Poggi, *Images of Society. Essays on the Sociological Theories of Tocqueville, Marx, and Durkheim* (Stanford, Stanford, 1972).

See page 6.   7. See Alvin Gouldner, *The Coming Crisis of Western Sociology* (New York, Basic Books, 1970).

See page 10.   8. See Bertrand Russell, *A Critical Exposition of the Philosophy of Leibniz* (London, Allen, 1971), pp. 98–99.

See page 11.   9. See Lionel Robbins, *An Essay on the Nature and Significance of Economic Science* (London, Macmillan, 1948), especially pp. 104–135, 151–158.

See page 12.   10. See Friedrich Meinecke, *Die Entstehung des Historismus,* ed. Carl Hinrichs, *Werke,* ed. Hans Herzfeld et al. (Munich, Oldenbourg, 1959); Pietro Rossi, *Lo Storicismo Tedesco Contemporaneo* (Einaudi, 1956); and Carlo Antoni, *Lo Storicismo* (Radio Italiana, 1957).

See page 13.   11. Weber misunderstands the artistic form as a mere expository device. See Max Weber, *Objektive Möglichkeit und adäquate Verursachung in der historischen Kausalbetrachtung* in *Gesammelte Aufsätze zur Wissenschaftslehre,* ed. Johannes Winckelmann (Tübingen, Mohr, 1968), p. 278.

See page 15.   12. For an example of how the dilemma of subjectivity and objectivity comes up in a particular field of social theory, see Max Gluckman, *Concepts in the Comparative Study of Tribal Law* in *Law in Culture and Society,* ed. Laura Nader (Chicago, Aldine, 1969), pp. 349–373; and Paul Bohannan, *Ethnography and Comparison in Legal Anthropology* in *Law in Culture and Society,* pp. 401–418.

See page 17.   13. But for qualifications see Alexander von Schelting, *Max Webers Wissenschaftslehre* (Tübingen,

Mohr, 1934), pp. 329–335; and Dieter Henrich, *Die Einheit der Wissenschaftslehre Max Webers* (Tübingen, Mohr, 1952), pp. 83–103.

See page 17.   14. See Karl Marx, *Das Kapital,* ed. H.-J. Lieber and B. Kautsky (Stuttgart, Cotta, 1962), vol. I, pp. 47–48.

See page 17.   15. See Noam Chomsky, *Language and Mind* (New York, Harcourt, 1972), pp. 62–63; Claude Lévi-Strauss, *Anthropologie Structurale* (Paris, Plon, 1958), pp. 308–310; and Kurt Koffka, *Principles of Gestalt Psychology* (New York, Harcourt, 1935), p. 175.

See page 21.   16. See Eugene Wigner, "The Unreasonable Effectiveness of Mathematics in the Natural Sciences," *Communications on Pure and Applied Mathematics* (1960), vol. XIII, pp. 11–14.

See page 24.   17. See Jeremy Bentham, *An Introduction to the Principles of Morals and Legislation,* ed. J. H. Burns and H. L. A. Hart (London, Athlone, 1970), pp. 11–12.

See page 26.   18. See John Rawls, "Two Concepts of Rules," *The Philosophical Review* (1956), vol. LXIV, pp. 18–29; and Georg von Wright, *Norm and Action. A Logical Enquiry* (London, Routledge, 1963), pp. 9–11.

See page 30.   19. Among the classic social theorists, Durkheim is less a proponent of the reunion of the doctrines of instrumentalism and legitimacy than a defender of the latter view. See Émile Durkheim, *Les Formes Élémentaires de la Vie Religieuse. Le système totémique en Australie* (Paris, Presses Universitaires, 1968), pp. 603–605.

See page 31.   20. See Émile Durkheim, *Le Suicide. Étude de Sociologie* (Paris, Presses Universitaires, 1967), p. 279. But see Émile Durkheim, *Sociologie et Philosophie* (Paris, Presses Universitaires, 1967), pp. 82–85.

See page 34.   21. See Talcott Parsons, *The Structure of Social Action,* vol. II, pp. 698–719.

See page 36.   22. See Max Weber, *Wirtschaft und Gesellschaft,* ed. Johannes Winckelmann (Tübingen, Mohr, 1972), pp. 12–13.

See page 36.   23. See Vilfredo Pareto, *Trattato di Sociologia Generale* (Milan, Communità, 1964), vol. II, pp. 237–540.

See page 36.   24. See my *Knowledge and Politics* (New York, Free Press, 1975), pp. 88–103.

See page 38.   25. See Reinhard Bendix, *Tradition and Modernity Reconsidered* in *Embattled Reason. Essays on Social Knowledge* (New York, Oxford, 1970), pp. 250–314.

See page 38.   26. See J. W. Gough, *The Social Contract. A Critical Study of its Development* (Oxford, Oxford, 1967), especially pp. 105–125.

See page 43.   27. See my *Knowledge and Politics,* pp. 191–235.

See page 44.   28. See William Shakespeare, *Hamlet,* act 2, sc. 1, line 66: "By indirections find directions out."

See page 44.   29. See Émile Durkheim, *De la Division du Travail Social* (Paris, Alcan, 1922), p. 32: "Because law reproduces the main forms of social solidarity, we have but to classify the different kinds of law to find the different kinds of social solidarity that correspond to them."

CHAPTER 2   *Law and the Forms of Society*

See page 49.   1. See Bronislaw Malinowski, *Crime and Custom in Savage Society* (London, Routledge, 1947), pp. 68–69.

See page 49.   2. See A. R. Radcliffe-Brown, *Primitive Law* in *Encyclopedia of the Social Sciences* (New York, Macmillan, 1933), vol. IX, p. 202; and E. E. Evans-Pritchard, *The Nuer* (Oxford, Oxford, 1947), pp. 68–69. But see E. E. Evans-Pritchard, *The Nuer of the Southern Sudan* in *African Political Systems,* ed. Meyer Fortes and E. E. Evans-Pritchard (Oxford, Oxford, 1940), p. 278.

See page 49. 3. There is a broader sense in which all law is "interactional." See Lon Fuller, "Human Interaction and the Law," *The American Journal of Jurisprudence* (1969), vol. XIV, pp. 1–36.

See page 49. 4. See Ulpianus, *Regulae,* 1.4.

See page 50. 5. See Lloyd Fallers, *Law Without Precedent. Legal Ideas in Action in the Courts of Colonial Busoga* (Chicago, Chicago, 1969), pp. 310–314. See also Ferdinand Tönnies, *Die Sitte* (Frankfurt, Ruetten, 1909); and F. A. Hayek, *Law, Legislation and Liberty* (Chicago, Chicago, 1973), pp. 38–39.

See page 51. 6. See Henry Maine, *Lectures on the Early History of Institutions* (London, Murray, 1897), pp. 373–386; and Max Weber, *Wirtschaft und Gesellschaft,* ed. Johannes Winckelmann (Tübingen, Mohr, 1972), p. 563.

See page 52. 7. See note 59.

See page 52. 8. See note 56.

See page 52. 9. See Max Kaser, *Das Römische Privatrecht* (Munich, Beck, 1959), vol. II, p. 12.

See page 53. 10. Institutional, methodological, and occupational autonomy are all closely related to the concept of role differentiation. See Richard Abel, "A Comparative Theory of Dispute Institutions in Society," *Law and Society Review* (1974), vol. VIII, pp. 217–347.

See page 54. 11. See A. V. Dicey, *Introduction to the Study of the Law of the Constitution* (London, Macmillan, 1968), pp. 188–196. My definition of the rule of law includes Dicey's first two senses of the term: "no man is punishable or can be lawfully made to suffer in body or goods except for a distinct breach of law established in the ordinary legal manner before the ordinary courts of the land" (p. 188); and "every man, whatever be his rank or condition is subject to the ordinary law of the realm and amenable to the jurisdiction of the ordinary tribunals" (p. 193). But it does not encompass his third sense—"the general principles of the constitution . . . are with us the result of judicial decisions determining the rights of private persons in particular cases brought before the courts" (p. 195)—which is the child of English political history and of the modern doctrine of natural right.

See page 55.   12. See Lon Fuller, "Mediation—Its Forms and Functions," *Southern California Law Review* (1971), vol. XLIV, p. 331.

See page 55.   13. See Marc Galanter, "Why the 'Haves' Come out Ahead: Speculations on the Limits of Legal Change," *Law and Society Review* (1974), vol. IX, pp. 95–160.

See page 57.   14. See Talcott Parsons, *The Social System* (New York, Free Press, 1968), pp. 11–12.

See page 57.   15. What Kant takes as metaphysical attributes of all law, I view as useful though imprecise criteria of classification. See Immanuel Kant, *Die Metaphysik der Sitten, Kants Werke,* ed. Prussian Academy of Sciences (Berlin, Gruyter, 1968), vol. VI, pp. 218–221.

See page 58.   16. See Franz Oppenheimer, *Der Staat* (Stuttgart, Fischer, 1954), pp. 5–8.

See page 60.   17. See Lucy Mair, *Primitive Government* (Penguin, 1962), p. 13; and Morton Fried, *The Evolution of Political Society* (New York, Random, 1969), pp. 235–240. But see Georges Balandier, *Anthropologie Politique* (Paris, Presses Universitaires, 1967), pp. 92–93.

See page 62.   18. See Max Weber, *Wirtschaft and Gesellschaft,* p. 198.

See page 63.   19. On the tendency of the division of labor to take the form of a system of personal domination, see Johann Karl Rodbertus, third letter to von Kirchmann, *Gesammelte Werke und Briefe,* ed. Th. Raum (Osnabrück, Zeller, 1972), pt. 1, vol. I, pp. 124–125. On the division of labor and "efficiency," see Adam Smith, *The Wealth of Nations,* bk. 1, ch. 2 (London, Strahan, 1784), vol. I, pp. 19–25; and Talcott Parsons, *Evolu-*

tionary *Universals in Society* in *Sociological Theory and Modern Society* (New York, Free Press, 1967), pp. 496–500.

See page 63.　20. See Émile Durkheim, *De la Division du Travail Social* (Paris, Alcan, 1922), pp. 267–276.

See page 67.　21. See S. N. Eisenstadt, *The Political Systems of Empires* (New York, Free Press, 1963), pp. 137–140.

See page 72.　22. See Hans-Joachim Torke, *Das russische Beamtentum in der ersten Hälfte des 19. Jahrhunderts* in *Forschungen zur Osteuropäischen Geschichte,* ed. Mathias Bernath et al. (Berlin, Harrasowitz, 1967), pp. 285–309; Marc Raeff, *Michael Speransky. Statesman of Imperial Russia 1772–1839* (The Hague, Nijhoff, 1969), p. 45; Richard Wortman, "Judicial Personnel and the Court Reform of 1864," *Canadian Slavic Studies* (1969), vol. III, pp. 224–234; and Friedhelm Kaiser, *Die russische Justizreform von 1864. Zur Geschichte der russischen Justiz von Katharina II bis 1917* (Leiden, Brill, 1972).

See page 73.　23. See Max Weber, *Wirtschaft und Gesellschaft,* pp. 487–488.

See page 73.　24. See John Noonan, *The Scholastic Analysis of Usury* (Cambridge, Harvard, 1957), pp. 365–376.

See page 74.　25. See Levin Goldschmidt, *Universalgeschichte des Handelsrechts* (Stuttgart, Enke, 1891), pp. 124–131.

See page 76.　26. See René Descartes, letter to Mersenne of April 15, 1630, *Oeuvres de Descartes,* ed. Charles Adam and Paul Tannery (Paris, Vrin, 1969), vol. I, p. 145; and Edgar Zilsel, "The Genesis of the Concept of Physical Law," *The Philosophical Review* (1942), vol. LI, pp. 245–279.

See page 77.　27. See Harry Wolfson, *Philo* (Cambridge, Harvard, 1968), vol. II, pp. 439–460.

See page 78.　28. See Max Weber, *Wirtschaft und Gesellschaft,* pp. 319–321.

See page 79.　29. See Hans Kelsen, *Vergeltung und Kausalität.*

Eine soziologische Untersuchung (The Hague, Stockum, 1941), pp. 280–281.

See page 80.   30. Two caveats are in order. First, the general idea of natural law should not be confused with the particular modern European doctrine of natural right, which I discuss later. Second, despite its revolutionary potential, a natural law view may be, and often has been, a device for the legitimation of established power. On the latter point, see Franz Neumann, *Types of Natural Law* in *The Democratic and the Authoritarian State. Essays in Political and Legal Theory,* ed. Herbert Marcuse (Glencoe, Free Press, 1957), pp. 69–91.

See page 82.   31. See Max Weber, *Das antike Judentum* in *Gesammelte Aufsätze zur Religionssoziologie* (Tübingen, Mohr, 1971), vol. III, pp. 397–400. The priestly supervision of prophecy may be institutionalized. For an example, see Adolphe Lods, *Les Prophètes d'Israël et les Débuts du Judaïsme* (Paris, Renaissance, 1935), pp. 65, 186–7.

See page 85.   32. See Leo Strauss, *Natural Right and History* (Chicago, Chicago, 1953), pp. 165–251.

See page 89.   33. I have relied mainly on Otto Franke, *Geschichte des chinesischen Reiches* (Berlin, Gruyter, 1930), vol. I, pp. 133–178; Henri Maspero, *Le régime féodal et la propriété foncière dans la Chine Antique* in *Mélanges Posthumes sur les Religions et l'Histoire de la Chine* (Paris, Musée Guimet, 1950), vol. III, pp. 111–146; Marcel Granet, *La Féodalité Chinoise* (Oslo, Aschehoug, 1952); Derk Bodde, *Feudalism in China* in *Feudalism in History,* ed. Rushton Coulbourn (Hamden, Archen, 1965), pp. 49–92; Wolfram Eberhard, *Conquerors and Rulers. Social Forces in Medieval China* (Leiden, Brill, 1965); and Herlee Creel, *The Origins of Statecraft in China,* vol. I, *The Western Chou Empire* (Chicago, Chicago, 1970).

See page 90.   34. But see Herlee Creel, *The Origins of Statecraft in China,* vol. I, pp. 331–335.

See page 91. 35. See C. K. Yang, *Religion in Chinese Society* (Berkeley, California, 1970), p. 106.

See page 91. 36. See Alfred Forke, *Geschichte der alten chinesischen Philosophie* (Hamburg, Friederichsen, 1927), pp. 39–46; and Joseph Needham, *Science and Civilisation in China* (Cambridge, Cambridge, 1969), vol. III, pp. 580–581.

See page 92. 37. See Joseph Needham, *Science and Civilisation in China,* vol. II, p. 576.

See page 93. 38. See Benjamin Schwartz, *On Attitudes Toward Law in China* in Milton Katz et al., *Government under Law and the Individual* (Washington, American Council of Learned Societies, 1957), pp. 28–33.

See page 97. 39. See Otto Franke, *Geschichte des chinesischen Reiches,* vol. I, pp. 178–222; Henri Maspero, *De la Seigneurie à la Principauté et à l'Empire* in Henri Maspero and Étienne Balazs, *Histoire et Institutions de la Chine Ancienne des Origines au XIIe Siècle après J.-C.* (Paris, Presses Universitaires, 1967), pp. 20–39; and, above all, Cho-yun Hsu, *Ancient China in Transition. An Analysis of Social Mobility, 722–222 B.C.* (Stanford, Stanford, 1965).

See page 97. 40. See Eduard Kroker, *Der Gedanke der Macht im Shang-kün-shu. Betrachtungen eines alten chinesischen Philosophen* (Vienna, St.-Gabriel, undated), pp. 9–20.

See page 98. 41. See Cho-yun Hsu, *Ancient China in Transition,* pp. 34–37.

See page 99. 42. See Wolfram Eberhard, *Chinas Geschichte* (Bern, Francke, 1948), p. 67.

See page 102. 43. See Karl Bünger, "Die Rechtsidee in der chinesischen Geschichte," *Saeculum,* vol. III (1952), pp. 193–201; and Derk Bodde and Clarence Morris, *Law in Imperial China* (Cambridge, Harvard, 1967), pp. 15–17.

See page 102. 44. See Benjamin Schwartz, *On Attitudes Toward Law in China* in Milton Katz et al., *Government under Law and the Individual,* pp. 32–35.

See page 106. 45. See *The Complete Works of Han Fei Tzŭ. A Classic of Chinese Legalism,* trans. W. K. Liao (London, Probsthain, 1939), two volumes; *The Book of Lord Shang. A Classic of the Chinese School of Law,* trans. J. J. L. Duyvendak (Chicago, Chicago, 1963); *The Analects of Confucius,* trans. Arthur Waley (London, Allen, 1938); and *Mencius,* trans. W. A. C. H. Dobson (Toronto, Toronto, 1963). For my discussion of the dispute between Confucianists and Legalists, I have used, together with these translated sources, the following secondary works: Otto Franke, *Geschichte des chinesischen Reiches,* vol. I, pp. 199–222; Alfred Forke, *Geschichte der alten chinesischen Philosophie,* pp. 99–241, 441–482; Fung Yu-lan, *A History of Chinese Philosophy,* trans. Derk Bodde (Princeton, Princeton, 1952), vol. I, pp. 43–75, 312–336; Lliang Chi-Chao, *History of Political Thought during the early Tsin Period,* trans. L. T. Chen (London, Routledge, 1930), pp. 38–52, 113–138; Otto Franke, *Studien zur Geschichte des konfuzianischen Dogmas und der chinesischen Staatsreligion* (Hamburg, Friederichsen, 1920); Erich Haenisch, *Politische Systeme und Kämpfe im alten China* (Berlin, Gruyter, 1951); Eduard Kroker, *Der Gedanke der Macht im Shang-kün-shu;* P. Jos. Thiel, "Die Staatsauffassung des Han-Fei-tzû, dargestellt in einigen beudeutsamen Kapiteln," *Sinologica* (1961), vol. VI, pp. 171–192, 225–270; Peter Weber-Schäfer, *Oikumene und Imperium. Studien zur Ziviltheologie des chinesischen Kaiserreichs* (Munich, List, 1968); and Herlee Creel, *The Fa-chia: "Legalists" or "Administrators"?* in *What Is Taoism? and Other Studies in Chinese Cultural History* (Chicago, Chicago, 1970), pp. 92–120.

See page 106. 46. See T'ung-Tsu Ch'ü, *Law and Society in Traditional China* (Paris, Mouton, 1965), pp. 267–297. But see Herlee Creel, *The Fa-Chia:*

"Legalists" or "Administrators"? in *What is Taoism? and Other Studies in Chinese Cultural History,* pp. 119–120.

See page 107. 47. See Donald Munro, *The Concept of Man in Early China* (Stanford, Stanford, 1969), pp. 49–83. For a somewhat different interpretation of Confucianist doctrine, see Herbert Fingarette, *Confucius—the Secular as Sacred* (New York, Harper, 1972).

See page 109. 48. See Friedrich Meinecke, *Die Idee der Staatsräson in der neueren Geschichte,* ed. W. Hofer (Munich, Oldenbourg, 1957).

See page 110. 49. See Robert Lingat, *Les Sources du Droit dans le Système Traditionnel de l'Inde* (Paris, Mouton, 1967), pp. 19–20. I have drawn extensively from this work in my discussion of classical Hindu law.

See page 111. 50. See Ignaz Goldziher, *Vorlesungen über den Islam* (Heidelberg, Winter, 1963), pp. 30–70; Joseph Schacht, *An Introduction to Islamic Law* (Oxford, Oxford, 1966), p. 60; and Fazlur Rahman, *Functional Interdependence of Law and Theology* in *Theology and Law in Islam,* ed. Gustave von Grunebaum (Wiesbaden, Harassowitz, 1971), pp. 89–97.

See page 111. 51. See Benjamin De-Vries, *Dogmatics of the Halakhah* in *Encyclopedia Judaica* (New York, Macmillan, 1971), vol. VII, pp. 1158–1161.

See page 111. 52. See Ze'ev Falk, *Hebrew Law in Biblical Times. An Introduction* (Jerusalem, Wahrmann, 1964), p. 27.

See page 111. 53. See John A. Wilson, "Authority and Law in Ancient Egypt," *Journal of the American Oriental Society* (1954), *Supplement: Authority and Law in the Ancient Orient,* pp. 1–7; and E. Seidl, *Altägyptisches Recht* in *Orientalisches Recht, Handbuch der Orientalistik,* ed. B. Spuler (Leiden, Brill, 1964), pt. I, supplementary vol. III, pp. 13–14.

See page 112. 54. See C. J. Gadd, *Ideas of Divine Rule in the Ancient East* (London, British Academy, 1948;

Godfrey Driver and John Miles, *The Babylonian Laws* (Oxford, Oxford, 1952), pp. 17–23; Thorkild Jacobsen, *An Ancient Mesopotamian Trial for Homicide* in *Toward the Image of Tammuz and Other Essays in Mesopotamian History and Culture* (Cambridge, Harvard, 1970), pp. 193–195; and Barry Eichler, *Indenture at Nuzi: The Personal Tidennūtu. Contract and its Mesopotamian Analogues* (New Haven, Yale, 1973), pp. 80–83. On the early limitation of monarchic power, see Thorkild Jacobsen, "Early Political Development in Mesopotamia," *Zeitschrift für Assyriologie and vorderasiatische Archäologie,* New Series (1957), vol. XVIII, pp. 100–112.

See page 113. 55. See *The Kautilīya Arthaśāstra,* pt. 2, a translation, and pt. 3, a study, by R. P. Kangle (Bombay, Bombay, 1963 and 1965).

See page 113. 56. See Robert Lingat, *Les Sources du Droit dans le Système Traditionnel de l'Inde,* pp. 231–240, 249–257; J. Duncan Derrett, *Law and the Social Order before the Muhammadan Conquests* in *Religion, Law and the State in India* (New York, Free Press, 1968), pp. 194–195; J. Duncan Derrett, *History of Indian Law (Dharmaśāstra)* in *Handbuch der Orientalistik,* ed. B. Spuler (Leiden, Brill, 1973), pt. 2, vol. III, sec. 1, pp. 21–22; and Louis Dumont, "The Conception of Kingship," *Contributions to Indian Sociology* (1962), vol. VI, pp. 48–77.

See page 113. 57. See Shiro Ishii, *Pre-modern Law and the Tokugawa Political Structure,* trans. Arthur Mitchell (on file in the Harvard Law School, 1973), p. 13.

See page 113. 58. See Robert Lingat, *Les Sources du Droit dans le Système Traditionnel de l'Inde,* pp. 218–229; and J. Duncan Derrett, *Custom and Law in Ancient India* in *Religion, Law and the State in India,* pp. 148–170.

See page 113. 59. See Joseph Schacht, *An Introduction to Islamic Law,* p. 54.

See page 113. 60. See Ignaz Goldziher, *Die Zâhiriten. Ihr Lehrsystem und ihre Geschichte* (Hildesheim, Olms, 1967), pp. 204–206; and Joseph Schacht, "Zur soziologischen Betrachtung des islamischen Rechts," *Der Islam* (1935), vol. XXII, pp. 211–212.

See page 114. 61. See Noel Coulson, *Conflicts and Tensions in Islamic Jurisprudence* (Chicago, Chicago, 1969), pp. 7, 17.

See page 114. 62. I am acutely aware that my generalizations about classical Islamic law would have to be broken down to take account of differences among the major schools. Indeed, the warning that "he who ignores the disputes of the schools has not smelt the scent of the *fiḳh*" applies with redoubled force to the problem of the interpenetration of the *sharī ʿa* and local custom. See Robert Brunschwig, "Considérations Sociologiques sur le Droit Musulman Ancien," *Studia Islamica* (1955), vol. III, pp. 61–73.

See page 114. 63. But see George Mendenhall, "Ancient Oriental and Biblical Law," *The Biblical Archaeologist* (1954), vol. XVII, pp. 40–44.

See page 115. 64. See Menachem Elom, *Minhag* in *Encyclopedia Judaica,* vol. XII, pp. 13–14.

See page 115. 65. See Max Weber, *Wirtschaft und Gesellschaft,* pp. 459–460.

See page 116. 66. See Robert Lingat, *Les Sources du Droit dans le Système Traditionnel de l'Inde,* pp. 168–178; and D. Rothermund, "Die historische Analyse des Bodenrechts Indiens," *Jahrbuch des Südasien-Instituts, Heidelberg* (1966), p. 161.

See page 116. 67. See M. Mielziner, *Introduction to the Talmud* (New York, Funk, 1903), pp. 142–155.

See page 116. 68. See Malcolm Kerr, *Islamic Reform. The Political and Legal Theories of Muhammad ʿAbduh and Rashūd Ridā* (Berkeley, California, 1966), pp. 66–79.

See page 117. 69. See Moshe Silberg, *Talmudic Law and the Modern State,* trans. Ben Zion Bokser, ed. Marvin

Wiener (New York, Burning Bush, 1973), pp. 22–41.

See page 117. 70. See Ignaz Goldziher, *Vorlesungen über den Islam,* pp. 68–69; Abū Bakr Ahmad ibn 'Umar ibn Muhair aš Šaibānī-al-Hassāf, *Kitāb al-hiial ualmahārig,* ed. and partly trans. Joseph Schacht in *Beiträge zur semitischen Philologie und Literatur,* ed. G. Bergsträsser (Hannover, Lafaire, 1923), number 4; and Abū Hātun Mahmūd ibn al Hasan al-Qazuīnī, *Kitāb al-hiial fil-fiqh,* ed. and trans. Joseph Schacht in *Beiträge zur semitischen Philologie und Linguistik,* number 5.

See page 117. 71. See Ze'ev Falk, *Introduction to Jewish Law of the Second Commonwealth* (Leiden, Brill, 1972), pp. 32–33.

See page 117. 72. See Sublú Mahmassani, *Falsafat Al-Tashū Fi Al-Islām. The Philosophy of Jurisprudence in Islam,* trans. Farhat Ziadeh (Leiden, Brill, 1961), pp. 87–89.

See page 117. 73. See Joseph Schacht, *The Origins of Muhammadan Jurisprudence* (Oxford, Oxford, 1950), pp. 82–132; and Joseph Schacht, *An Introduction to Islamic Law,* pp. 69–75.

See page 117. 74. See Hermann Strack, *Einleitung in Talmud und Midrasch* (Munich, Beck, 1961), pp. 70–71.

See page 117. 75. See Walter Ruben, *Die Gesellschaftliche Entwicklung im alten Indien,* vol. III, *Die Entwicklung der Religion* (Berlin, Akademie, 1971), pp. 38–47. For the doctrinal foundations of the control of royal power, see Ananda Coomaraswamy, *Spiritual Authority and Temporal Power in the Indian Theory of Government* (New Haven, American Oriental Society, 1942).

See page 118. 76. See Max Weber, *Hinduismus und Buddhismus* in *Gesammelte Aufsätze zur Religionssoziologie,* vol. III, p. 142.

See page 118. 77. See R. C. Zaehner, *Hinduism* (London, Oxford, 1972), pp. 125–146.

See page 118. 78. See Franz Rosenthal, *The Muslim Concept of Freedom prior to the Nineteenth Century* (Leiden, Brill, 1960), p. 122; Gustave von Grunebaum, *Medieval Islam. A Study in Cultural Orientation* (Chicago, Chicago, 1966), pp. 170–177; and Reuben Levy, *The Social Structure of Islam* (Cambridge, Cambridge, 1969), pp. 53–90.

See page 118. 79. See S. D. Goitein, *The Rise of the Middle-Eastern Bourgeoisie in Early Islamic Times* in *Studies in Islamic History and Institutions* (Leiden, Brill, 1966), pp. 217–241.

See page 118. 80. On the law merchant in the context of Hanafi jurisprudence, see Abraham Udovitch, *Partnership and Profit in Medieval Islam* (Princeton, Princeton, 1970), pp. 249–261.

See page 119. 81. See Ze'ev Falk, *Introduction to Jewish Law of the Second Commonwealth,* pp. 48–58; and Hugo Mantel, *Studies in the History of the Sanhedrin* (Cambridge, Harvard, 1965), pp. 70–75.

See page 120. 82. But the theocratic ideal may be peculiar to the days of the Second Temple. See Yehezkel Kaufmann, *The Religion of Israel from its Beginnings to the Babylonian Exile,* trans. and abridged Moshe Greenberg (New York, Schocken, 1972), pp. 184–187. On the increase of social stratification during this era of Jewish history, see Salo Baron, *A Social and Religious History of the Jews* (New York, Columbia, 1952), vol. I, pp. 271–276.

See page 121. 83. See Georg Busolt, *Griechische Staatskunde* (Munich, Beck, 1920), vol. I, pp. 177, 212.

See page 122. 84. See J. Gernet and J.-P. Vernant, "L'Évolution des idées en Chine et en Grèce, du VIe au IIe siècle avant notre ère," *Bulletin de l'Association Guillaume Budé* (1964), fourth series, number 3, pp. 308–325.

See page 122. 85. But see A. Andrews, *The Greek Tyrants* (London, Hutchison, 1956), pp. 102–107.

See page 122. 86. See A. French, *The Growth of the Athenian*

Economy (London, Routledge, 1964), pp. 10–17.

See page 123. 87. See P. A. Brunt, Social Conflicts in the Roman Republic (New York, Norton, 1971), pp. 42–59.

See page 123. 88. See Claude Nicolet, L'Ordre Équestre à l' Époque Républicaine (312–43 av. J.–C.) (Paris, Boccard, 1966), vol. I; and M. I. Henderson, "The Establishment of the Equester Ordo," The Journal of Roman Studies (1963), vol. LIII, pp. 61–72.

See page 123. 89. See Ronald Syme, The Roman Revolution (Oxford, Oxford, 1960), pp. 10–27.

See page 123. 90. See Martin Ostwald, Nomos and the Beginnings of the Athenian Democracy (Oxford, Oxford, 1969), pp. 55–56. See also Victor Ehrenburg, Die Rechtsidee in frühen Griechentum. Untersuchungen zur Geschichte der werdenden Polis (Leipzig, Hinzel, 1921), pp. 113–116.

See page 123. 91. See Georg Busolt, Griechische Staatskunde, vol. II, pp. 939–954; and Victor Ehrenberg, The Greek State (New York, Norton, 1964), pp. 39–43.

See page 124. 92. See, with respect to "precapitalist periods," Georg Lukács, Klassenbewusstsein in Geschichte und Klassenbewusstsein (Neuwied, Luchterhand, 1968), p. 137, discussed in M. I. Finley, The Ancient Economy (Berkeley, California, 1973), pp. 49–51. See also J.-P. Vernant, "Remarques sur la lutte de classes dans la Grèce ancienne," Eirene (1965), vol. IV, pp. 5–19.

See page 124. 93. See Felix Heinimann, Nomos und Physis. Herkunft und Bedeutung einer Antithese im griechischen Denken des 5. Jahrhunderts (Basel, Reinhardt, 1965).

See page 124. 94. See Jacqueline de Romilly, La loi dans la Pensée Greque des Origines à Aristote (Paris, Belles Lettres, 1971), pp. 25–49.

See page 125. 95. See Werner Jaeger, Die Theologie der frühen *griechischen Denker* (Stuttgart, Kohlhammer, 1953), p. 55.

See page 125. 96. See Walter Otto, *Die Götter Griechenlands. Das Bild des Göttlichen im Spiegel des griechischen Geistes* (Frankfurt, Schulte-Bulmke, 1947), p. 233.

See page 125. 97. See Harry Wolfson, *The Philosophy of the Church Fathers,* vol. I, *Faith, Trinity, Incarnation* (Cambridge, Harvard, 1970), pp. 288–294.

See page 125. 98. See Kurt Latte, *Römische Religionsgeschichte* (Munich, Beck, 1960), pp. 331–338.

See page 125. 99. See Martin Nilsson, *Geschichte der griechischen Religion* (Munich, Beck, 1967), vol. I, p. 708.

See page 125. 100. See Lily Taylor, *Party Politics in the Age of Caesar* (Berkeley, California, 1961), pp. 76–97.

See page 126. 101. But there remained a great deal of overlap: many legislative, administrative, and judicial tasks were concentrated in the same agencies. See generally A. R. W. Harrison, *The Law of Athens* (Oxford, Oxford, 1971), vol. II; and P. J. Rhodes, *The Athenian Boule* (Oxford, Oxford, 1972).

See page 126. 102. See Rudolf Hirzel, *Themis, Dike und Verwandtes. Ein Beitrag zur Geschichte der Rechtsidee bei den Griechen* (Leipzig, Hirzel, 1907), pp. 240–250; and J. Walter Jones, *The Law and Legal Theory of the Greeks* (Oxford, Oxford, 1956), pp. 84–87.

See page 126. 103. See Peter Garnsey, *Social Status and Legal Privilege in the Roman Empire* (Oxford, Oxford, 1970), pp. 260–280; and A. H. M. Jones, "The Caste System in the Later Roman Empire," *Eirene* (1970), vol. VIII, pp. 79–96.

See page 133. 104. See Claude Lévi-Strauss, *Les Structures Élémentaires de la Parenté* (Paris, Presses Universitaires, 1949), p. 8. For a more recent suggestion along similar lines, see Adriaan Kortland, "Chimpanzees in the Wild," *Scientific American* (1962), vol. CCVI, number 5, p. 138.

CHAPTER 3   *Law and Modernity*

See page 138.   1. See Georg Simmel, *Soziologie* (Liepzig, Duncker, 1908), pp. 685–708.

See page 140.   2. I use the term tribal society only in the special sense given to it by my comparison of forms of social life, thereby hoping to avoid the confusions discussed in Morton Fried, "On the Concepts of 'Tribe' and 'Tribal Society,'" *Transactions of the New York Academy of Sciences* (1966), series II, vol. XXVIII, pp. 527–540.

See page 142.   3. See Henry Maine, *Village-Communities in the East and West* (New York, Holt, 1876), pp. 225–227; and Max Weber, *Wirtschaft und Gesellschaft,* ed. J. Winckelmann (Tübingen, Mohr, 1972), p. 383.

See page 142.   4. See Benjamin Nelson, *The Idea of Usury. From Tribal Brotherhood to Universal Otherhood* (Chicago, Chicago, 1969).

See page 143.   5. The contrast of tribal and liberal society resembles, though it is not identical with, Tönnies' opposition of "community" and "society." See Ferdinand Tönnies, *Gemeinschaft and Gesellschaft. Abhandlung des Communismus und des Socialismus als Empirischer Culturformen* (Leipzig, Fues, 1887), pp. 60–63.

See page 147.   6. My conception of the aristocratic society owes more to Montesquieu's view of monarchy than to his analysis of aristocracy. See Montesquieu, *De l'Esprit des Lois,* bk. 2, ch. 4, *Oeuvres Complètes,* ed. R. Caillois (Paris, Pléiade, 1966), vol. II, pp. 247–249. See also Gianfranco Poggi, *Images of Society* (Stanford, Stanford, 1974), pp. 3–28.

See page 150.   7. See Montesquieu, *De l'Esprit des Lois,* bk. 3, ch. 7, *Oeuvres Complètes,* vol. II, pp. 257–258; Alexis de Tocqueville, *De la Démocratie en Amérique,* vol. II, pt. 3, ch. 18, *Oeuvres Complètes,* ed. J.-P. Mayer (Paris, Gallimard, 1951), vol. I-II, pp. 238–249; and Paul Bénichou, *Morales du Grand Siècle* (Paris, Gallimard, 1970), pp. 19–79.

See page 153. 8. See Marc Bloch, *La Société Féodale,* vol. II, *Les Classes et le Gouvernement des Hommes* (Paris, Michel, 1949), pp. 53–57.

See page 156. 9. See the distinction made between *seigneurie* and *féodalité* with respect to European feudalism in Robert Boutruche, *Seigneurie et Féodalité* (Paris, Aubier, 1959), vol. I, p. 8.

See page 156. 10. See H. G. Koenigsberger, *The Powers of Deputies in Sixteenth-Century Assemblies* in *Estates and Revolutions. Essays in Early Modern European History* (Ithaca, Cornell, 1971), pp. 176–210.

See page 157. 11. See Alexis de Tocqueville, *L'Ancien Régime et la Révolution,* bk. 2, ch. XI, *Oeuvres Complètes,* vol. II, pt. 1, pp. 168–177.

See page 157. 12. See Otto Hintze, "Typologie der ständischen Verfassungen des Abendlandes," *Historische Zeitschrift* (1930), vol. CXLI, pp. 229–248.

See page 160. 13. See Fritz Kern, *Gottesgnadentum und Widerstandsrecht im früheren Mittelalter. Zur Entwicklungsgeschichte der Monarchie* (Cologne, Böhlau, 1954), pp. 121–137; Fritz Kern, *Recht und Verfassung im Mittelalter* (Basel, Schwade, undated), pp. 67–75; and Otto von Brunner, *Vom Gottesgnade zum monarchischen Prinzip* in *Das Königtum. Seine geistigen und rechtlichen Grundlagen* (Lindau, Thorbecke, 1956), pp. 279–305. See also Walter Ullmann, *Law and Politics in the Middle Ages. An Introduction to the Sources of Medieval Political Ideas* (Ithaca, Cornell, 1975), pp. 30–32.

See page 162. 14. See Heinrich Mitteis, *Der Staat des Hohen Mittelalters. Grundlinien einer vergleichenden Verfassungsgeschichte des Lehnzeitalters* (Weimar, Böhlaus, 1953), p. 433.

See page 164. 15. See Charles McIlwain, *The High Court of Parliament and its Supremacy* (New Haven, Yale,

1910), pp. 42–100; and J. W. Gough, *Fundamental Law in English Constitutional History* (Oxford, Oxford, 1961), pp. 50–51.

See page 164. 16. But for a criticism of this distinction with respect to seventeenth-century England, see F. Hartung and R. Mousnier, *Quelques Problèmes concernant la Monarchie Absolue* in *Relazioni dei X Congresso Internazionale di Scienze Storiche* (Florence, Sansoni, 1955), vol. IV, pp. 3–55. Some European countries hesitated between parliamentary constitutionalism and bureaucratic absolutism. In Spain, for example, the constitutionalist impulse proved abortive with the suppression of the Communero Revolt of Castille in 1521. See José Antonio Maravall, *Las Comunidades de Castilla. Una primera revolución moderna* (Madrid, Revista de Occidente, 1970), pp. 181–218; and Antonio Domínguez Ortíz, *El Antiguo Régimen: los Reyes Católicos y los Austrias* (Alfaguara, Alianza, 1973), pp. 245–246.

See page 165. 17. See Günther Stökl, "Gab es im Moskauer Staat 'Stände'?" *Jahrbücher für Geschichte Osteuropas* (1963), new series, vol. XI, pp. 321–342.

See page 168. 18. See my *Knowledge and Politics* (New York, Free Press, 1975), pp. 184, 220–222, 259–262.

See page 173. 19. See Alexis de Tocqueville, *De la Démocratie en Amérique,* vol. II, pt. 2, ch. 13, *Oeuvres Complètes,* vol. I-I, p. 144.

See page 174. 20. See Karl Marx, *Manifest der Kommunistischen Partei, Marx-Engels Werke* (Berlin, Dietz, 1959), vol. IV, p. 462.

See page 182. 21. See Joseph Strayer, *On the Medieval Origins of the Modern State* (Princeton, Princeton, 1970), pp. 17–18.

See page 182. 22. See Erich Caspar, *Roger II (1101–1154) und die Gründung der Normannisch-Sicilischen Monarchie* (Innsbruck, Wagner, 1904), pp. 297–319; and Francesco Giunta, *Bizantini e Bizantinismo nella Sicilia Normanna* (Palermo, Priulla, 1950), pp. 122–126.

See page 183. 23. See Martin Göhring, *Die Ämterkäuflichkeit im Ancien régime* (Berlin, Ebering, 1938); and Roland Mousnier, *La Vénalité des Offices sous Henri IV et Louis XIII* (Paris, Presses Universitaires, 1971). For later developments, see Franklin Ford, *Robe and Sword. The Regrouping of the French Aristocracy after Louis XIV* (New York, Harper, 1965), pp. 105–123.

See page 183. 24. On the other hand, the *commissaires,* though prohibited from treating their offices as private patrimony, lacked established legal authority. See Otto Hintze, *Der Commissarius und seine Bedeutung in der allgemeinen Verwaltungsgeschichte* in *Staat und Verfassung. Gesammelte Abhandlungen zur Allgemeinen Verfassungsgeschichte,* ed. G. Oestreich (Göttingen, Vandenhoek, 1970), pp. 254–255.

See page 184. 25. For a discussion of this development in an Austrian setting, see Henry Strakosch, *State Absolutism and the Rule of Law* (Sidney, Sidney, 1967), pp. 29–49.

See page 184. 26. See Franz Wieacker, *Privatrechtsgeschichte der Neuzeit* (Göttingen, Vandenhoek, 1967), pp. 331–335.

See page 184. 27. I am greatly indebted here to Hans Rosenberg, *Bureaucracy, Aristocracy, and Autocracy. The Prussian Experience 1660–1815* (Boston, Beacon, 1966), pp. 1–25. See also Otto Hintze, *Der Beamtenstand* in *Soziologie und Geschichte* (Göttingen, Vandenhoek, 1964), pp. 66–125; Eckart Kehr, *Zur Genesis der preussischen Bürokratie und des Rechtsstaates* in *Moderne deutsche Sozialgeschichte,* ed. Hans-Ulrich Wehler (Cologne, Kiepenheuer, 1973), pp. 37–54; and Henry Jacoby, *Die Bürokratisierung der Welt* (Neuwied, Luchterhand, 1969), pp. 37–86.

See page 186. 28. See Reimund Asanger, *Beiträge zur Lehre vom*

Rechtsstaat im 19. Jahrhundert (Bochum, Pöppinghaus, 1938); and Leonard Krieger, *The German Idea of Freedom* (Chicago, Chicago, 1972), pp. 252–261.

See page 186. 29. For a classic statement of the Prussian theory of the *Rechtsstaat,* see Rudolf von Gneist, *Der Rechtsstaat und die Verwaltungsgerichte in Deutschland* (Darmstadt, Gentner, 1958). See also Guido de Ruggiero, *Storia del Liberalismo Europeo* (Bari, Laterza, 1925), pp. 273–288.

See page 186. 30. See Eckart Kehr, *Zur Genesis der preussischen Bürokratie und des Rechtsstaates* in *Moderne deutsche Sozialgeschichte,* p. 46; Herbert Marcuse, *Reason and Revolution* (Boston, Beacon, 1960), p. 15; Hajo Holborn, "Der deutsche Idealismus in sozialgeschichtlicher Beleuchtung," *Historische Zeitschrift* (1952), vol. 174, pp. 359–384; and Theodore Hamerow, *Restoration, Revolution, Reaction. Economics and Politics in Germany 1815–1871* (Princeton, Princeton, 1972), pp. 173–195.

See page 187. 31. See Otto Pflanze, *Juridical and Political Responsibility in Nineteenth-Century Germany* in *The Responsibility of Power,* ed. L. Krieger and F. Stern (Garden City, Doubleday, 1967), pp. 162–182.

See page 188. 32. See Eckart Kehr, *Zur Genesis der preussischen Bürokratie und des Rechtsstaates* in *Moderne deutsche Sozialgeschichte,* pp. 49–50.

See page 188. 33. See Eckart Kehr, *Zur Genesis der preussischen Bürokratie und des Rechtsstaates* in *Moderne deutsche Sozialgeschichte,* p. 53; and Max Horkheimer, "Bemerkungen zur Philosophischen Anthropologie," *Zeitschrift für Sozialforschung* (1935), vol. IV, p. 14.

See page 189. 34. See John Dawson, *The Oracles of the Law* (Ann Arbor, Michigan Law School, 1968), pp. 461–479.

See page 190. 35. See Ernst Fraenkel, *Zur Soziologie der Klassenjustiz* (Berlin, Laub, 1927), pp. 39–45.

See page 191.   36. Alexis de Tocqueville, *Democracy in America,* trans. P. Bradley (New York, Vintage, 1961), vol. I, p. 285.

See page 197.   37. See Fritz Schulz, *History of Roman Legal Science* (Oxford, Oxford, 1946), pp. 285–289.

See page 197.   38. See S. F. C. Milsom, *Historical Foundations of the Common Law* (London, Butterworths, 1969), pp. 85–87.

See page 198.   39. See J. Duncan Derrett, *The British as Patrons of the Śāstra* in *Religion, Law and the State in India* (New York, Free Press, 1968), p. 250; Marc Galanter, "The Displacement of Traditional Law in Modern India," *Journal of Social Issues* (1968), vol. XXIV, p. 72; and J. S. Furnivall, *Colonial Policy and Practice. A Comparative Study of Burma and Netherlands India* (New York, New York, 1956), p. 133.

See page 198.   40. See Friedrich Hayek, *The Road to Serfdom* (Chicago, Chicago, 1967), pp. 72–87.

See page 199.   41. See Grant Gilmore, *The Death of Contract* (Ohio, Ohio, 1974), p. 14.

See page 201.   42. See Georges Gurvitch, *L'Idée du Droit Social* (Paris, Sirey, 1932), pp. 15–46; and Philip Selznick, *Law, Society, and Industrial Justice* (New York, Russell Sage, 1969), pp. 244–250.

See page 203.   43. See Eugen Ehrlich, *Grundlegung der Soziologie des Rechts* (Munich, Duncker, 1913), p. 399.

See page 203.   44. See Duncan Kennedy, "Legal Formality," *Journal of Legal Studies* (1973), vol. II, pp. 351–398. Many of the ideas in this section originated in conversations with Duncan Kennedy.

See page 206.   45. See Émile Durkheim, *Leçons de Sociologie. Physique des Moeurs et du Droit* (Paris, Presses Universitaires, 1950), pp. 257–259.

See page 210.   46. See Raymond Saleilles, *De la Déclaration de la Volonté. Contribution à l'Étude de l'Acte Juridique dans le Code Civil Allemand (Art. 116 à 144)* (Paris, Libraire Générale, 1929), pp. 299–301; and Georges Ripert, *La Règle Morale dans les*

Obligations Civiles (Paris, Libraire Générale, 1927), pp. 162–188.

See page 211. 47. See Robert Hale, "Bargaining, Duress, and Economic Liberty," *Columbia Law Review* (1943), vol. XLIII, pp. 626–628.

See page 216. 48. A consequence of my argument is that no stable or sharp distinction ought to be drawn between a morality of duty and a morality of aspiration. See Henri Bergson, *Les Deux Sources de la Morale et de la Religion, Oeuvres,* ed. A. Robinet (Paris, Presses Universitaires, 1970), pp. 1024–1029; and Lon Fuller, *The Morality of Law* (New Haven, Yale, 1971), pp. 3–32.

See page 216. 49. I have relied heavily on Friedrich Dessauer, *Recht, Richtertum und Ministerialbürokratie. Eine Studie über den Einfluss von Machtverschiebungen auf die Gestaltung des Privatrechts* (Mannheim, Bensheimer, 1928).

See page 217. 50. See Justus Hedemann, *Die Flucht in die Generalklauseln. Eine Gefahr für Recht und Staat* (Tübingen, Mohr, 1933). Under the Nazi regime, reliance on general clauses increased greatly. Thus, the prohibition, in article 138, paragraph 1, of acts offensive to "good morals" was used to strike down contracts when the performances appeared to be of unequal value and one of the parties had acted inconsistently with community standards of proper conduct. See, for example, the decision of the *Reichsgericht* of March 31, 1936, RGZ, 150,1. By an amendment of July 28, 1935, to the Criminal Code, acts contrary to the basic aim of a penal statute and to the "sound sentiment of the people" were made punishable as crimes. See Roland Freisler, *Willenstrafrecht. Versuch und Vollendung* in *Das kommende deutsche Strafrecht. Allgemeiner Teil,* ed. Franz Gürtner (Berlin, Vahlen, 1934), pp. 3–36; and *Reichs-Strafgesetzbuch nach dem neuesten Stand der Gesetzgebung (Leipziger Kommentar),* ed. Johannes Nagler et al. (Berlin, Gruyter,

1944), vol. I, p. 99. On the decline of legal generality and autonomy, see Rudolf Echterhölter, *Das öffentliche Recht im nationalsozialistischen Staat* (Stuttgart, Deutsche, 1970), pp. 227–239.

See page 217. 51. See Friedrich Dessauer, *Recht, Richtertum und Ministerialbürokratie,* pp. 38–40.

See page 218. 52. See Adolph Lobe, "Der Untergang des Rechtstaates," *Deutsche Juristen-Zeitung* (1925), vol. XXX, pp. 15–22.

See page 219. 53. See Friedrich Dessauer, *Recht, Richtertum und Ministerialbürokratie,* p. 92.

See page 220. 54. See Franz Neumann, "Der Funktionswandel des Gesetzes im Recht der bürgerlichen Gesellschaft," *Zeitschrift für Sozialforschung* (1937), vol. VI, pp. 585–587.

See page 225. 55. See Ezra Vogel, *Japan's New Middle Class* (Berkeley, California, 1971), p. 105.

See page 225. 56. See Lloyd Rudolph and Susanne Rudolph, *The Modernity of Tradition. Political Development in India* (Chicago, Chicago, 1967), pp. 63–64.

See page 225. 57. See P. C. Lloyd, *Africa in Social Change* (Penguin, 1974), pp. 193–213.

See page 226. 58. See Ezra Vogel, *Japan's New Middle Class,* pp. 142–162; Takeo Ishida, *Japanese Society* (New York, Random, 1971), pp. 37–48; and Chie Nakane, *Japanese Society* (Berkeley, California, 1972), pp. 120–130.

See page 227. 59. See Ezra Vogel, *Japan's New Middle Class,* pp. 263–268.

See page 227. 60. See Thomas Smith, *"Merit" as Ideology in the Tokugawa Period* in *Aspects of Social Change in Modern Japan,* ed. R. P. Dore (Princeton, Princeton, 1971), pp. 71–90; and W. G. Beasley, *The Meiji Restoration* (Stanford, Stanford, 1972), pp. 62, 348–349. Another example of the conflict between principles of stratification in traditionalistic society is the relationship of complementarity and tension between caste and class in contemporary India. See G. S. Ghurye,

Caste and Class in India (Bombay, Popular Book, 1950); and Louis Dumont, Homo hierarchicus. Essai sur le système des castes (Paris, Gallimard, 1966), pp. 122–128, 305–323.

See page 227. 61. See R. P. Dore, Mobility, Equality, and Individuation in Modern Japan in Aspects of Social Change in Modern Japan, pp. 113–150.

See page 227. 62. See M. Y. Yoshino, Japan's Managerial System. Tradition and Innovation (Cambridge, MIT, 1971), pp. 65–84.

See page 228. 63. See Takeoyshi Kawashima, Dispute Resolution in Contemporary Japan in Law in Japan. The Legal Order in a Changing Society, ed. Arthur von Mehren (Harvard, Cambridge, 1963), pp. 40–59; and Dan Henderson, Conciliation and Japanese Law (Tokyo, Tokyo, 1965), especially vol. II, pp. 207–234.

See page 228. 64. See Dan Henderson, Law and Political Modernization in Japan in Political Development in Modern Japan (Princeton, Princeton, 1968), p. 399.

See page 229. 65. For a Brazilian example, see David Trubek, "Toward a Social Theory of Law: An Essay on the Study of Law and Development," The Yale Law Journal (1972), vol. LXXXII, pp. 40–42.

See page 232. 66. But there is also an ambiguous attitude toward the dominant consciousness of the past, as something to be both used and overcome. See Richard Solomon, Mao's Revolution and the Chinese Political Culture (California, California, 1972), especially pp. 2–6, 251–255. See also Lucian Pye, The Spirit of Chinese Politics. A Psychocultural Study of the Authority Crisis in Political Development (Cambridge, MIT, 1970), especially pp. 164–196.

See page 233. 67. See Franz Schurmann, Ideology and Organization in Communist China (Berkeley, California, 1968), pp. 85–90; Robert Scalapino, The Transition in Chinese Party Leadership: A Comparison of the Eighth and Ninth Central Committees in Elites in the People's Republic of China, ed. R.

Scalapino (Seattle, Washington, 1972), especially p. 148; and Stuart Schram, *Introduction: the Cultural Revolution in Historical Perspective* in *Authority, Participation and Cultural Change,* ed. S. Schram (Cambridge, Cambridge, 1973), pp. 29–32.

See page 233. 68. See Jerome Cohen, *The Criminal Process in the People's Republic of China 1949–1963* (Cambridge, Harvard, 1968), pp. 46–53.

See page 233. 69. See Stanley Lubman, "Mao and Mediation: Politics and Dispute Resolution in Communist China," *California Law Review* (1967), vol. LV, pp. 1284–1359; Jerome Cohen, *Drafting People's Mediation Rules for China's Cities* in *Legal Thought in the United States of America under Contemporary Pressures,* ed. J. N. Hazard and W. J. Wagner (Brussels, Bruylant, 1970), pp. 295–328; Harold Berman and James Spindler, "Soviet Comrades' Courts," *Washington Law Review* (1963), vol. XXXVIII, pp. 842–910; P. T. Georges, *The Court in the Tanzania One-Party State* in *East African Law and Social Change,* ed. G. F. A. Sawyerr (Nairobi, East African, 1967), pp. 26–47; Jesse Berman, "The Cuban Popular Tribunals," *Columbia Law Review* (1969), vol LXIX, pp. 1317–1354; and Neelakandan Tiruchelvam, "The Popular Tribunals of Sri Lanka: A Socio-Legal Inquiry" (on file in the Harvard Law School, 1973).

See page 242. 70. See Francois Gcny, *Science et Technique en Droit Privé Positif* (Paris, Sirey, 1915), vol. I, pp. 96–97.

See page 242. 71. See Plato *Republic* 372D.

CHAPTER 4 *The Predicament of Social Theory Revisited*

See page 247. 1. See Alasdair MacIntyre, *A Mistake about Causality in Social Science* in *Philosophy, Politics and Society,* second series, ed. Peter Laslett and W.

G. Runciman (Oxford, Blackwell, 1969), pp. 48–51.

See page 254. 2. For two approaches see Hans-Georg Gadamer, *Wahrheit und Methode* (Tübingen, Mohr, 1965); and Clifford Geertz, *Thick Description: Toward an Interpretive Theory of Culture* in *The Interpretation of Cultures* (New York, Basic Books, 1973), pp. 3–30.

See page 254. 3. See W. G. Runciman, *A Critique of Max Weber's Philosophy of Social Science* (Cambridge, Cambridge, 1972), pp. 85–86.

See page 256. 4. See Ernest Gellner, *The New Idealism—Cause and Meaning in the Social Sciences* in Ernest Gellner, *Cause and Meaning in the Social Sciences,* ed. I. C. Jarvie and Joseph Agassi (London, Routledge, 1973), pp. 50–77.

See page 257. 5. Otherwise, the problem of translation might be insoluble. See W. V. Quine, *Epistemology Naturalized* in *Ontological Relativity and Other Essays* (New York, Columbia, 1969), pp. 80–82.

INDEX

INDEX

The letter *n.*, following a number, designates a note.

Abuse of right, 210
Ācārā, 112–113
'Āda. 113–114
Adequacy, relationship of, 14
Allah, 111
Almoravids, 114
Aristocracies:
  and legal order, 72–73
  and the law of corporate prerogatives, 158–164
Aristocratic society:
  as one of the forms of social life, 147–153
  and the European *Ständestaat,* 155–158
  and law in Europe, 158–166
Aristotelian tradition, 7, 20, 38, 44
Artha, 110
Arthaśāstra, 112–113
Atomists, 124
Authority, the need for:
  in liberal society, 132–133, 146, 153–154
  and the struggle for equality in liberal society, 170–176, 235–237
Autonomy (freedom):
  and the instrumentalist view of social order, 24–26
  and the consensus view of social order, 32–33
  and the emergence of bureaucratic law, 61–62
Autonomy (freedom):
  and interest group pluralism, 68–70, 84–85
  and natural law, 82–85
  and the decline of custom, 127–133
  and consensus in liberal society, 166–170
  and hierarchy in liberal society, 170–176
  and the effort to render power impersonal through law in liberal society, 176–181
  in postliberal society, 221–222
  in traditionalistic society, 226–227, 229
  in revolutionary socialist society, 231, 233
  and the prospects of modern society, 234–237
Autonomy (of the legal order):
  as an ideal and as a fact, 44, 52–57
  and group pluralism, 66–76
  and belief in higher law, 76–86
  and the structure of liberal society, 176–181
  disintegration of, in the welfare state, 193–200
  in traditionalistic society, 227–229
  in revolutionary socialist society, 233

Bakufu, 113
Batsu, 225–226
Bet din, 111
Bhakti, 116, 118
Brahmins, 115, 117–118

Bureaucracy:
 and bureaucratic law, 51
 and princely interest, 71–72, 75–76
 and law in liberal society, 177–178, 180
 and law in Imperial Germany, 182–190
 and law in the welfare state, 199–200
 and law in the Weimar Republic, 218–
  219
 and law in traditionalistic society, 227–
  229
 and law in revolutionary socialist society,
  232–233
Bureaucratic law:
 characteristics of, 50–52
 in ancient India, 52, 65, 112–113
 in Islam, 52, 65, 113–114
 in the Roman empire, 52, 126
 and the separation of state from society,
  58–61
 and the disintegration of community,
  61–63
 and the division of labor and social
  hierarchy, 63–64
 internal tension of, 64–66
 in ancient China, 65–66, 96–105
 and liberal society, 71–72, 75, 164–166
 in ancient Israel, 114
 and the decline of custom, 127–133
 in Imperial Germany, 183–191
 in the Weimar Republic, 216–217
 in traditionalistic society, 228–229
 in revolutionary socialist society, 233
 and the prospects of modern society,
  238–242
 see also Bureaucracy

Carolingian empire and feudalism, 158
Caste associations (Indian), 225–226
Causality:
 as a basic scheme of thought, 9
 paradox of, 10, 12
 and historicism, 12–13
 and the dialectic, 16–19
 and the ideal-type, 16–19, 23
 and structuralism, 16–19
 and the interpretive method, 248–249,
  254–256
 see also Logic
Chancery, the English, 182
Ch'in unification, 87, 96–97, 101

China:
 Ancient, and law, 86–109
 People's Republic of, and law, 231–234
Chomsky, Noam, 17
Chün tzu, 90, 93
Classes:
 and bureaucratic law, 60–64
 and the development of the legal order,
  68–75
 and the nature of hierarchy in liberal
  society, 151–152, 170–181
 in postliberal society, 193–235
Cleisthenes and his reforms, 123, 126
Cognitio extraordinaria, 52, 126
Commissaires, 289 *n.*24
Commonwealth (of ancient Israel):
 First, and its law, 111, 114–115, 120
 Second, and its law, 111, 116–117, 119–
  120
Community:
 and the instrumentalist view of social
  order, 29
 and the nature of modern society, 39–
  40, 174
 and customary law and bureaucratic law,
  61–63
 and the idea of immanent order, 127–
  133
 in tribal society, 141–143
 in liberal society, 144–146
 in aristocratic society, 148–150
 and consensus in liberal society, 166–
  170
 in postliberal society, 202–203, 221–
  222, 236–237
 and traditionalistic society, 229, 236–
  237
 and revolutionary socialist society, 233–
  234, 236–237
 and the unity of modernism, 234–237
 and the prospects of modern society,
  238–242
 and the method of social study, 258, 265
 and the reconciliation of the modes of
  social order, 262–265
 see also Autonomy, Solidarity
Confucianism:
 and the *li,* 93–96
 and the religiosity of immanence, 99–100
 and Legalism, 104–109

Consensus:
  its attributes, 30
  and the need for rules, 30–32
  disintegration of, and the decline of
      custom, 61–63, 127–133
  disintegration of, and the division of
      labor and social hierarchy, 63–64
  and the legal order, 68–69, 176, 203–
      205
  in liberal society, 166–170
  and hierarchy in liberal society, 170–174
Consensus (doctrine of social order):
  meaning of, 29–30
  and rules, 30–31, 32
  defects of, 31–33
  reconciliation of, with the
      instrumentalist view of order, 33–
      37, 44, 127–133, 262–265
  see also Instrumentalism (doctrine of
      social order)
Constitutionalism, 163–166
  see also Higher law, Law of corporate
      prerogatives
Corporate state:
  in postliberal society, 193
  and the attack on public and positive law,
      200–202
  in traditionalistic society, 227–228
  see also Postliberal society, Welfare state
Cortes, 156
Council of Elders, 119
Cour des comptes, 182
Custom:
  attributes of, 49–50
  and legal order, 54–55
  weakening of conditions of, 58–66, 127–
      133
  in traditionalistic society, 228
  in revolutionary socialist society, 233
  and the universal moral order, 238–244,
      264–265

Dependency, *see* Domination
Determinism, 13–14, 18
Dharma, 110
Dharmaśāstra, 52, 65, 82, 110, 112–113,
    117–118
Dialectic, 16–17
Division of labor:
  and bureaucratic law, 63–64

Division of labor:
  and hierarchy in liberal society, 171–172
  and hierarchy in postliberal society, 221–
      222
  and hierarchy in traditionalistic society,
      226, 227, 229
  and hierarchy in revolutionary socialist
      society, 231–232, 233
Domination:
  and the appearance of bureaucratic law,
      60, 62, 63–64
  and the division of labor, 63–64
  in liberal society, 68–70, 151–152, 170–
      176
  and the effort to render power
      impersonal through law in liberal
      society, 68–70, 176–181
  and the decline of custom, 127–133
  in postliberal society, 221–222
  in traditionalistic society, 229–230
  in revolutionary socialist society, 232–
      233
  and the future of modern society, 234–
      237
  see also Hierarchy
Durkheim, Émile, 3, 6

Efficiency, the division of labor, and class
    stratification:
  in the emergence of bureaucratic law,
      63–64
  in revolutionary socialist society, 231,
      233
Equality:
  diminution of, and the decline of custom,
      63–64
  in liberal society, 68–70, 170–172
  and the need for authority in liberal
      society, 170–176
  in traditionalistic society, 227, 229, 236
  in revolutionary socialist society, 232,
      233, 236
  in postliberal society, 235–237
  see also Authority, Hierarchy
Equity in modern law, 205–206, 213–214
Equity (English) and the common law, 197
England, 72, 157, 164–165, 190, 197
Enlightenment, 12, 149
États, 156
Entstaatlichung, 219

Equites (equester ordo), 98, 123
Etruscans, 122
Eupatrids, 122
Evolution:
    and the idea of modernity, 37, 134–135
    and the emergence of bureaucratic law,
        64
    and the comparison of societies, 137
    and the basis of social change, 155
    and the intelligibility of societies, 264–
        265
Exchequer, Court of the, 182

Fa, 102–104, 108
Fa chia, 106–109
Family corporations (Latin American), 226
Fas, 52, 82
Feudalism:
    and aristocratic society, 147
    and the *Ständestaat,* 155–158
Fikh, 111
Formal justice:
    defined, 194–195
    erosion of, in the welfare state, 195–196,
        198–199
    see also Formalistic legal reasoning,
        Formality in law, Procedural
        justice, Substantive justice
Formalistic legal reasoning:
    role and assumptions of, in liberal
        society, 177–181
    in Imperial Germany, 187–190
    defined, 194
    the tendency to abandon it in postliberal
        society, 199–200
    in the Weimar Republic, 216–220
    see also Equity, Formality in law,
        Purposive legal reasoning
Formality in law, 203–216
France, 72, 98, 158, 182, 183
Freedom, see *Autonomy*
Freiwillige Gerichtsbarkeit, 217
Freud, Sigmund, 173
Fulanis, 114
Fundamental law, *see* Constitutionalism,
    Higher law, Law of corporate
    prerogatives

Generality (of the legal order):
    as an ideal and as a fact, 52, 55–57
    and group pluralism, 67–76, 83–86

Generality (of the legal order):
    and belief in higher law, 76–86
    and the law of princely edicts in the
        European *Ständestaat,* 162–163
    and the structure of liberal society, 176–
        181
    weakening of, in the welfare state, 193–
        200
    decline of, in the Weimar Republic, 216–
        217
    in traditionalistic society, 228–229
    in revolutionary socialist society, 233
    see also Formality in law, Legal order
German Civil Code (B.G.B.), 189, 216
Germany:
    and the *Ständestaat,* 72, 164–165
    Imperial Germany and law, 181–192
    Weimar Republic and law, 216–220
    and traditionalistic society, 224–225
Gestalt psychology, 17
Gezera shava, 116
Gezerot, 111
God, the conception of:
    and the fact-value distinction, 4
    and belief in higher law, 76–86
    and the absence of legal order in ancient
        China, 99–101, 105
    and the relation between ideals and
        actuality in tribal society, 143
    and the relation between ideals and
        actuality in liberal society, 146–147
    and the relation between ideals and
        actuality in aristocratic society,
        152–153
    and the relation between ideals and
        actuality in postliberal society, 222–
        223
    and the prospects of modern society,
        238–244, 266
Good faith, 189, 210
Great Synagogue, 119
Greece:
    and the idea of higher law, 76–77, 124–
        125
    and the failure fully to develop a legal
        order, 120–126

Ha'aramah, 116–117
Halakhah, 82, 111, 114–115, 119–120
Hap, 112
Hanbali school of Islam, 113

Hekkesh, 116
Hercules, 2
Hierarchy:
  and the emergence of bureaucratic law,
      60–61, 62, 63–64
  and the development of legal order, 68–
      70, 83–85
  and the decline of custom, 127–133
  in aristocratic society, 148–152, 156–157
  in liberal society, 151–152, 170–176
  and the rule of law, 170–181
  in postliberal society, 221–222, 235
  in traditionalistic society, 227, 229–230,
      236
  in revolutionary socialist society, 232,
      233, 236
  and the prospects of modern society,
      234–237
  see also Authority, Domination, Equality
Higher law:
  and the legal order, 76–83
  and the conception of God, 76–78
  in Graeco-Roman antiquity, 76–77,
      124–125
  and liberal society, 83–86
  in ancient China, 91–92, 99–101
  in ancient India, 110–111, 118
  in Islam, 111, 118
  in ancient Israel, 111, 119
Hintze, Otto, 157
Hippocratic tradition, 124
Historicism (as a method of social study),
      12–14
  see also Rationalism
Historiography and social theory, 19–23,
      45–46, 259–262
  see also Method
Ḥiyal, 117
Hohenzollerns, 185
Hsiao jen, 90, 93
Hu, 111
Ḥudūd, 113
Human nature:
  and history, 4–6, 8, 40–43, 64, 132–
      133, 155, 259–262
  and the types of social order, 24–25, 30,
      264–265
Hypocrisy and transcendence, 215–216

I, 105
Ibn Taymiyya, 116

Ijmā', 111
Ideals and actuality, the conception of the
      relation between:
  and customary law, 49
  and bureaucratic law, 51
  and the idea of higher law, 79
  and the effort to reconcile the ideas of
      immanent order and transcendence,
      133, 240–244
  as a criterion for the comparison of forms
      of social life, 139–140
  in tribal society, 143
  in liberal society, 146–147
  in aristocratic society, 152–153
  in postliberal society, 222–223
Immanence:
  as a mode of religious consciousness, 77–
      79
  in ancient China, 91–92, 99–101
  and the decline of custom, 127–133
  and postliberal society, 222–223
  and the reconciliation of autonomy and
      community, 133, 240–242, 264–
      265
  see also Ideals and actuality,
      Transcendence
India:
  Ancient, and legal order, 52, 65, 110–
      111, 112–113, 115–116, 117–118,
      120
  Modern, and traditionalistic society, 225,
      293–294 *n*.60
Instrumentalism (doctrine of social order):
  meaning of, 24–25
  and individualism, 25–26
  and rules, 26–27, 27–28
  defects of, 27–29
  reconciliation of, with the consensus
      view of order, 33–37, 44, 127–133,
      262–265
  see also Consensus (doctrine of social
      order)
Interactional law, *see* Custom
Interest association in liberal society, 68–
      69, 84, 144–146, 221–222
Islam, 51–52, 65, 78, 82, 111, 113–114,
      116–117, 118–119, 120
Israel, 78, 82, 111, 114–115, 116–117,
      119–120, 276 *n*.31
Istiḥsān, 114
Istiṣlāḥ, 117

Ius civile, 52
Ius gentium, 77

Japan:
    mercantile law in, 74
    feudalism in, 93
    as an example of traditionalistic society,
        224–231
Jen, 105
Justizsache, 159–160

Kabbalah, 78
Ḳāḍīs, 52
Kāma, 110
Ḳānūn, 113
Kittum, 112
Ḳiyās, 111
Kobun, 225
Koran, 111
Kṣatra, 52, 112–113

Land and the territoriality of law, 183–184
Landesordnungen, 160
Law:
    study of, and the predicament of social
        theory, 43–44
    varieties of, 48–57
    and normative order, 57
    and the prospects of modern society,
        238–244
    see also Bureaucratic law, Custom,
        Formality in law, Higher law, Law
        of edicts, Law of corporate
        prerogatives, Legal order, Sacred
        law
Law of corporate prerogatives or privileges,
    72–73, 158–166
    see also Law of edicts
Law of edicts, 51–52, 64–66, 158–166
    see also Bureaucratic law, Law of
        corporate prerogatives
Legal order:
    and the conception of modernity, 39–40,
        44
    attributes of, 52–54
    relation of, to custom and bureaucratic
        law, 54–56
    as ideal and as reality, 55–57, 176–181
    historical conditions of emergence of,
        66–86
    and group pluralism, 66–76, 83–86

Legal order:
    and belief in higher law, 76–86
    in ancient China, 104–105
    in ancient India, 117–118, 120
    in Islam, 118–119, 120
    in ancient Israel, 119–120
    in Graeco-Roman antiquity, 125–126
    development of, out of the *Ständestaat,*
        158–166
    and consensus and hierarchy in liberal
        society, 176–181
    in Imperial Germany, 181–192
    in the welfare state, 193–200
    and equity and solidarity, 203–216
    in the Weimar Republic, 216–220
    in traditionalistic society, 227–229
    in revolutionary socialist society, 233
    and the prospects of modern society,
        238–244
Legalism (ancient Chinese school of
        thought), 106–109, 131–132
Legal profession:
    and the legal order, 53
    social origins of, in the West, 71–72, 98
    absence of, in ancient China, 97–99,
        104–105
    absence of, in Islam, 116, 118–119
    absence of, in ancient Israel, 116, 119–
        120
    in Graeco-Roman antiquity, 126
    in the welfare state, 200, 241
    in traditionalistic society, 228–229
    in revolutionary socialist society, 233
    the essence of art of, 242–243
Legitimacy:
    and the conception of modernity, 39
    and the rule of law, 56–57, 176–181
    and the decline of custom, 131–132
    and consensus in liberal society, 166–
        170
    and hierarchy in liberal society, 170–176
Legitimacy (doctrine of social order), *see*
        Consensus (doctrine of social
        order)
Lévi-Strauss, Claude, 17, 19, 132
Li, 93–96, 108
Liberal society:
    and the conception of modernity, 37–40
    and the ideal of autonomy, 38–40, 68–
        69, 128–129, 176, 204–205, 238–
        244, 262–265

Liberal society:
  as group pluralism, 66–76, 83–86
  and the ideal of community, 68–69,
      128–129, 167–169, 202–203,
      206–211, 214–216, 238–244,
      262–265
  and belief in higher law, 76–86
  as a basic form of social life, 143–147
  emergence of, out of European
      aristocratic society, 164–166
  and consensus, 166–170
  and hierarchy, 170–176
  and law and the state, 176–181
  transformation of, 192–193, 220–223
  relation of, to other kinds of modern
      society, 223–224, 234–237
Liberalism, *see* Liberal society
Linguistics, 17, 251–252
Logic:
  as a basic scheme of thought, 9
  applicability of, to the world, 10
  and rationalism, 11–12
  and the dialectic, 16
  and the ideal-type, 16
  and structuralism, 16
  and the interpretive method, 245–246,
      249
  see also Causality
Love, 206–207

Ma'at, 111
Machiavelli, 109
Maliki school of Islam, 114
Marsūm, 113
Marx, Karl, 3, 6, 16, 17, 39, 173, 174–175
Maṣlaḥa, 117
Meaning:
  and the problem of method, 14–15,
      245–246
  the method of common meaning, 15–19,
      246–254
  and causal explanation, 18–19, 254–256
Meiji Restoration, 224
Mercantile law, 73–74
  see also Merchants
Merchants:
  independence of, and group pluralism in
      Europe, 72–76
  and the rule of law, 73–76, 189
  and law in medieval Islam, 74
  and law in Japan, 74

Merchants:
  and law in Graeco-Roman antiquity, 74
  and law in Imperial Germany, 188–189
  see also Mercantile law
Meritocracy, 172
Mēšarum, 112
Metaphysics and social theory, 3–6, 40–43,
      153–155, 266–268
Method, the problem of, 7–23, 245–265
  see also Causality, Dialectic, Historicism,
      Ideal type, Logic, Objectivity,
      Rationalism, Structuralism,
      Subjectivity
Metikoi, 122
Miasma, 77
Mi-divrei, 111
Mīmāṃsā, 116
Minhag, 111
Modernity:
  the problem of modernity in social
      theory, 37–43, 134–137, 265–266
  the conception of modernity, 38
  as ideal and as fact, 39–40
  the relation among types of modern
      society, 234–237
  the prospects of modern society, 238–
      244, 265–266
Montesquieu, 3, 4, 157

Naples, Kingdom of, 158
Napoleon, 186
Natural law, *see* Higher law
Nazi regime, 220, 292 *n.* 50
Nieztsche, Friedrich, 173
Niẓām, 113
Noblesse de la robe, 98
Nomos, 123–124
Normative order, 57
Novi homines, 98

Objectivity (of meaning):
  and the problem of method, 17–19,
      256–258
  and subjectivity, 17–19, 256
  and the ideal-type, 17–18
  and the dialectic, 17–18
  and structuralism, 17–18
  and universal community, 257–258,
      262, 265
  see also Method, Subjectivity
Officiers, 183

Oral law (Jewish), 116
Order, *see* Social order
Ordonnances, 160
Oyabun, 225–226

Pa, 89
Pantheism, 77, 91–92, 99–100
   see also God, Immanence, Transcendence
Pareto, Vilfredo, 36
Parlamenti, 156
Parlements, 182
Parsons, Talcott, 34
Peisistratus, 122
Peloponnesian War, 121
Pharisees, 116
Physis, 124
Plato, 77
Pluralism of groups:
   as a condition of legal order, 66–76
   and higher law, 83–86
   and the breakdown of the distinction
      between strangers and insiders in
      liberal society, 143–144
   and the association of interests in liberal
      society, 144–146
   and the relation of ideals to actuality in
      liberal society, 146–147
   and consensus in liberal society, 166–
      170
   and hierarchy in liberal society, 170–176
   and freedom, 240–241
Political economy:
   and the rationalist method, 11
   and the instrumentalist conception of
      social order, 24
   and the view of the relation between
      human nature and history, 38–39
Political philosophy:
   ancient, and modern social theory, 6–8
   the mainstream of, in the West, 109
   and the revision of social theory, 266–
      268
Polizeisache, 159–160
Polytheism, 91–92
Popular tribunals, 233
Positive character of law:
   absence of, in custom, 50
   as an attribute of bureaucratic law, 50
   as an attribute of legal orders, 52
   and the disintegration of community,
      61–63

Positive character of law:
   and the division of labor and social
      hierarchy, 63–64
   absence of, in the Chinese *li,* 94–95
   and the Chinese *fa,* 102–103
   and the decline of custom, 127–133
   and the distinction between ideals and
      actuality, 139–140
   the attack on positive law in the
      corporate state, 200–203
   and custom in traditionalistic society,
      228–229
   and communal self-regulation in
      revolutionary socialist society, 233
   and the prospects of modern society,
      238–244
   see also Bureaucratic law, Legal order,
      Public character of law
Post-Hasmonean period, 116
Postliberal society:
   the conception of, 192–193
   and law, 193–203
   tendencies of development of, 220–223
   relation of, to other kinds of modern
      society, 234–237
   central dilemmas of, 238–242
   see also Corporate state, Modernity,
      Welfare state
Praetorian law, 197
Pre-Socratics, 124
Preussische Allgemeine Landrecht, 184
Priesthood:
   as a custodian of sacred law, 49, 82–83
   and prophecy, 81–82
   absence or weakness of, in ancient
      China, 100–101
Procedural justice, 194–196, 212
Prophecy:
   and the containment of state power, 81–
      82
   and priesthood, 82
   absence of, in ancient China, 100–101
Protestant Ethic, 16–17
Prussia, *see* Germany
Public character of law:
   absence of, in custom, 50
   as an attribute of bureaucratic law, 50–
      51
   as an attribute of legal orders, 52
   and the separation of state from society,
      58–61

Public character of law:
  and the division of labor and social
      hierarchy, 63–64
  and princely interest, 71
  absence of, in the Chinese *li,* 95–96
  and the Chinese *fa,* 103–104
  and the decline of custom, 127
  and the distinction between ideals and
      actuality, 139–140
  the attack on the public character of law
      in the corporate state, 200–202
  and custom in traditionalistic society,
      228–229
  and communal self-regulation in
      revolutionary socialist society, 233
  and the prospects of modern society,
      238–244
  see also Bureaucratic law, Legal order,
      Positive character of law
Public interest, 194
Purposive legal reasoning:
  in Imperial Germany, 188–190
  defined, 194
  reasons for appearance of, 196–197
  consequences of, for legal generality, 198
  consequences of, for legal autonomy,
      199–200
  in the Weimar Republic, 217
  and bureaucratic law in traditionalistic
      society, 228–229
  and bureaucratic law in revolutionary
      socialist society, 233
  see also Formalistic legal reasoning

Quadragesimo Anno, 219

Raison d'état, 109
Rationalism (as a method of social study),
      11–12
  see also Historicism
Rechtsstaat:
  as the rule of law, *see* Legal order
  in Imperial Germany, 185–187
Regulatory law, *see* Bureaucratic law
Reich (German) and law, *see* Germany
Reichstag, 218
Religion:
  and normative order, 57
  and anticommercial prohibitions, 73
  and the conditions of legal order, 76–86
  and law in ancient China, 91–92, 99–101

Religion:
  and the sacred laws of ancient India,
      Islam, and Israel, 110–120
  and law in Graeco-Roman antiquity,
      124–125
  and the reconciliation of immanence and
      transcendence, 127–133, 238–244
  in aristocratic societies, 148–149
  see also Immanence, Transcendence
Roger II of Naples, 182
Romanticism, 12, 74
Rome and Roman law, 52, 77, 98, 120–126
Rule application:
  and the attempt to render power
      impersonal in liberal society, 68–
      76, 176–181
  and the administrator, 177
  and the judge, 177
  methods of, 194
  and standards, 197–198
  and formality, 203–205
  and equity and solidarity, 205–216
  and instrumentalism in revolutionary
      socialist society, 233
  see also Formalistic legal reasoning, Legal
      order, Purposive legal reasoning,
      Rulemaking, Rules
Rule of law:
  conception of, 52–54, 273–274 *n.*11
  see also Legal order
Rulemaking:
  and custom, 50
  and bureaucratic law, 50–51
  and the attempt to render power
      impersonal in liberal society, 68–
      70, 176–181
  and the attack on positive law in
      postliberal society, 202–203
  and formality, 203–205
  and equity and solidarity, 205–216
  in revolutionary socialist society, 231
  see also Legal order, Positive character of
      law, Rule application, Rules
Rules:
  and the instrumentalist view of social
      order, 26–27, 27–29, 44
  and the consensus view of social order,
      30–31, 32, 44
  and the conception of modernity, 39–44
  and the problem of method, 44
  and custom, 49–50

Rules:
   and bureaucratic law, 50–52
   and legal order, 52–54
   and the attempt to render power
      impersonal in liberal society, 68–
      70, 176–181
   and Confucianism, 108
   and the Chinese Legalists, 108–109
   and the evolving moral language of
      mankind, 238–242
   see also Formality in law, Rule
      application, Rulemaking
Russia (Tsarist), the absence of a
      Ständestaat, and the failure to
      institutionalize the rule of law, 72,
      164–165

Sadducees, 116
Salvation religions, 77–78, 80–81
Samurai, 90
Sanhedrin, 119
Śāstras, 114
Sedeq, 111
Shang Ti, 91, 99
Shared values, *see* Community, Consensus
Sharī'a, 52, 82, 97–99, 113–114, 116–117
Shih, 90, 94
Shih Ching, 94
Sia, 111
Significant groups:
   defined, 137
   in tribal society, 140–141
   in liberal society, 143–144
   in aristocratic society, 147–149
   in postliberal society, 220–221
Siyāsa, 52, 65, 113–114
Smrtis, 114
Social change:
   and the method of social study, 18–19,
      254–262
   in tribal, liberal, and aristocratic society,
      153–155
Social consciousness, 5
Social hierarchy, *see* Hierarchy
Social order, the problem of, 7, 23–37,
      127–133, 174–175, 262–265
   see also Consensus (doctrine of social
      order), Instrumentalism (doctrine
      of social order)
Social theory:
   and the "burden of the past," 1–2

Social theory:
   as a classical tradition, 3–8
   and ancient political philosophy, 3–6
   and the distinction between facts and
      values, 3–4, 8, 267
   and the relation between human nature
      and history, 4–6, 8, 40–43, 64,
      132–133, 155, 259–262
   problem of method in, 8–21, 44, 245–
      262
   problem of order in, 23–37, 44, 127–
      133, 262–265
   problem of modernity in, 37–40, 44,
      134–137, 234–244, 265–266
   and the social contract tradition, 38–39
   and metaphysics and politics, 266–268
Soferim, 111
Solidarity, 206–216
   see also Community
Sophists, 124
Spain, 288 *n.*16
Speransky, Michael, 72
Spring and Autumn (period of Chinese
      history), 88–89, 96
Standards:
   defined, 193–194
   and the erosion of legal generality, 197–
      198
   and the erosion of legal autonomy, 199
   and formality, 210
   in the Weimar Republic, 216–217
   under the Nazi regime, 220, 292 *n.*50
Stände, 156
Ständestaat:
   characteristics of, 88, 156–158
   and law, 158–164
   and the emergence of liberal society,
      164–166
State:
   separation of, from society and the
      public character of law, 50–51, 58–
      61
   and the division of labor and class
      stratification, 63–64
   and the reconciliation of immanence and
      transcendence, 127–133, 238–242
   and law in liberal society, 176–181
   in postliberal society, 200–202
   in traditionalistic society, 227–228
   in revolutionary socialist society, 230–231
   see also Bureaucratic law

Stein-Hardenberg reforms, 184
Strangers and insiders in the comparison of
    societies, 137–138
  see also Significant groups
Structuralism, 16, 17, 19
Subjectivity (of meaning):
  and the problem of method, 16–18,
    256–262
  and the ideal-type, 16–17
  and the dialectic, 17
  and structuralism, 17
  and universal community, 257–258, 266
  see also Method, Objectivity
Substantive justice:
  defined, 194–195
  reasons for the quest for, in the welfare
    state, 196–197
  implications of, for legal generality, 198
  implications of, for legal autonomy, 199–
    200
  and the problem of domination, 211–213
  and the unique character of
    contemporary legal experience,
    213–214
  in revolutionary socialist society, 233
  see also Authority, Domination, Equality,
    Formal justice, Hierarchy,
    Procedural justice
Sufism, 78
Sunna, 111
Sunyata, 77

Takkanah of the sages, 111, 115
Tao, 77
Taoism, 99–100
Ta'zīr, 113
Themis, 123
Third estate:
  implications of independence of, in the
    modern West, 72
  and the conditions of legal order, 73, 75
  significance of weakness of, in ancient
    China, 99, 105
  and the European *Ständestaat,* 157, 164–
    165
  see also Merchants
T'ien, 99
Tocqueville, Alexis de, 6, 157, 173
Torah, 119
Transcendence:
  as a mode of religious consciousness, 76–77

Transcendence:
  and liberal society and legal order, 76–
    84, 148–149
  weakness of, in ancient China, 91–92,
    99–100
  and postliberal society, 222–223
  and the prospects of modern society,
    238–242, 266
  see also Ideals and actuality, Immanence
Tribal society:
  and custom, 50
  as one of the forms of social life, 140–
    143
Types, the method of:
  and the problem of rationalism and
    historicism, 16
  and the problem of objective and
    subjective meaning, 16–17
  and the problem of social theory and
    historiography, 45–46, 249–262
  see also Method, the problem of

'Ulamā', 116, 242
Umayyad Caliphate, 117
Urban associations (African), 225–226
'Urf. 113–114

Values and facts:
  in ancient political philosophy, 3–4
  in modern social theory, 4, 8, 29, 32–33,
    264–265, 267
  see also Community, Consensus, Ideals
    and actuality
Varna, 110

Wahhabis, 114
Warring States (period of Chinese history),
    88–89, 96
Weber, Max, 3, 6, 16, 17, 18, 22, 82
Weimar Republic, law in the, 216–220
Welfare-corporate state, *see* Corporate
    state, Postliberal society, Welfare
    state
Welfare state:
  in postliberal society, 192–193
  and the erosion of legal generality and
    autonomy, 193–200
  see also Corporate state, Postliberal
    society
Western Chou (period of Chinese history),
    88